Delivering
BPM
Excellence

Delivering
BPM Excellence
Business Process Management in Practice

Edited by
LAYNA FISCHER

Excellence in Practice Series

Future Strategies Inc.
Lighthouse Point, Florida, USA

Delivering BPM Excellence: Business Process Management in Practice

Copyright © 2012 by Future Strategies Inc.

ISBN13: 978-0-9819870-9-5

Published by Future Strategies Inc., Book Division
3640-B3 North Federal Highway, #421, Lighthouse Point FL 33064 USA
954.782.3376 / 954.719.3746 fax
www.FutStrat.com email: books@FutStrat.com

Publisher's Cataloging-in-Publication Data
ISBN13: 978-0-9819870-9-5
Library of Congress Control Number: 2011940979

Delivering BPM Excellence
/Layna Fischer (Editor)

p. cm.

Includes bibliographical references and appendices.

1. Business Process Management. 2. Organizational Change. 3. Technological Innovation. 4. Information Technology. 5. Total Quality Management. 6. Management Information Systems. 7. Office Practice-Automation. 8. Knowledge Management. 9. Workflow. 10. Process Analysis

Fischer, Layna. (ed)

Delivering BPM Excellence
Table of Contents

Section 4: Pacific Rim

Section 5: South and Central America

Section 6 Appendix

Delivering BPM Excellence

Business Process Management in Practice
Layna Fischer, Global Awards Executive Director

The companies whose award-winning case studies are featured in this book have proven excellence in their creative and successful deployment of advanced and business process management concepts. The positive impact to their corporations includes increased revenues, more productive and satisfied employees, product enhancements, better customer service and quality improvements.

The prestigious annual **Global Excellence Awards for BPM and Workflow** are highly coveted by organizations that seek recognition for their achievements. Now evolved into their 19th year, originally starting with, and moving through, imaging, documentation, knowledge management and more, as our industry moved forward, these awards not only provide a spotlight for companies that truly deserve recognition, but provide tremendous insights for organizations wishing to emulate the winners' successes.

These winners are companies that successfully used BPM in gaining competitive advantage within their industries.

CRITERIA

The criteria for submitting an entry are fairly simple: the project should have been operational for six months prior to nomination, and have been installed within the past two years. The submission guidelines, however, are more detailed. To be recognized as winners, companies must address three critical areas: excellence in *innovation*, excellence in *implementation* and excellence in strategic *impact* to the organization. Details are at www.bpmf.org.

Innovation

Innovation encompasses the innovative use of technology for strategic business objectives; the complexity of the underlying business process and IT architecture; the creative and successful deployment of advanced workflow and imaging concepts; and process innovations through business process reengineering and/or continuous improvements.

- Innovative use of BPM technology to solve unique problems
- Creative and successful implementation of advanced BPM concepts
- Level of integration with other technologies and legacy systems
- Degree of complexity in the business process and underlying IT architecture

Implementation

Hallmarks of a successful *implementation* include extensive user and line management involvement in the project while successfully managing change during the implementation process. Factors impacting the level of difficulty in achieving a successful implementation include the system complexity; integration with other advanced technologies; and the scope and scale of the implementation (e.g. size, geography, inter-company processes).

- Successful BPM and/or workflow implementation methodology
- Size, scope and quality of change management process

- Scope and scale of the implementation (e.g. size, geography, inter- and intra-company processes)

Impact

Impact is the bottom line, answering the question, "What benefit does BPM deliver to my business? Why should I care?"

- Extent and quantifiable impact of productivity improvements
- Significance of cost savings
- Level of increased revenues, product enhancements, customer service or quality improvements
- Impact of the system on competitive positioning in the marketplace
- Proven strategic importance to the organization's mission
- Degree to which the system enabled a culture change within the organization and methodology for achieving that change

Using BPM for Competitive Advantage

Examples of potential benefits include: productivity improvements; cost savings; increased revenues; product enhancements; improved customer service; improved quality; strategic impact to the organization's mission; enabling culture change; and—most importantly—changing the company's competitive position in the market. The visionary focus is now toward strategic benefits, in contrast to marginal cost savings and productivity enhancements.

While successes in these categories are prerequisites for winning a Global Excellence Award, it would reward all companies to focus on excelling in *innovation*, *implementation* and *impact* when installing BPM and workflow technologies. Companies must recognize that implementing innovative technology is useless unless the organization has a successful approach that delivers—and even surpasses—the anticipated benefits.

SUBMIT AN ENTRY

Submissions for the annual **Global Excellence Awards for BPM and Workflow** open in the September timeframe. The Awards program is managed by Future Strategies Inc., the Awards Director is Layna Fischer in collaboration with judges drawn from the ranks of WfMC, OMG and BPM.com. General information and guidelines may be found at www.bpmf.org or contact:

Layna Fischer, Layna@FutStrat.com
Future Strategies Inc., www.FutStrat.com

Contents and Chapter Abstracts

Guest Chapters:

BUSINESS PROCESS AS A SERVICE: ENTERPRISE CLOUD COMPUTING
Jon Pyke, CIMtrek, United Kingdom

The big buzz at the moment is around Enterprise Cloud Computing (ECC) and its impact on processes and the management of processes. ECC is the special case of utilizing Cloud computing for competitive advantage through breakout opportunities for both cost savings and, more importantly, for business innovation in terms of unprecedented speed and agility and vastly improved collaboration with business partners and customers. Once you understand what ECC is, there is a far more important question; why does it matter? The author discusses three key points that define why ECC matters to the world of BPM and where the competitive advantage kicks in.

THE DIFFERENCE BETWEEN BPM AND ADAPTIVE CASE MANAGEMENT
Nathaniel Palmer, WfMC, USA

In the half-century since Peter Drucker first identified and coined the phrase "knowledge worker," the share of the work force represented by this group has grown considerably, to as much as half of all workers by some measures. So, too, have grown investments targeting knowledge worker productivity, with global IT spending reaching $4.35 trillion in 2010, according to Global Technology Index author Dr. Howard A. Rubin.

Yet we are far from realizing the level of improvement seen in manual labor over the course of the last century. Traditionally, IT investments targeting business productivity have focused on one of two areas. The first is automation technologies, such as enterprise resource planning (ERP) or the more contemporary technology of business process management (BPM). Those address repeatable, predictable modes of work and are designed to enforce a command and control management model, where efficiency gains are sought through standardizing how work is performed.

ADVANTAGES OF AGILE BPM
Keith D. Swenson, Fujitsu America Inc., USA

Agile BPM represents the next generation of business process management—designed to flexibly address all types of processes to support all forms of work. It combines traditional Business Process Management (BPM) style predefined processes, along with Adaptive Case Management (ACM) style dynamic work support.

Agile BPM is designed to flexibly address all types of processes used to conduct business: structured, unstructured, and hybrid process types to support all forms of work.

In recent years many organizations have come to the understanding that their business processes are proprietary business assets that can yield competitive differentiation and advantage. This recognition has led to the adoption of first-generation BPM technologies to automate fixed, repetitive processes for efficiency and cost-effectiveness.

The author discusses how the next generation of BPM, Agile BPM, will incorporate product capabilities that extend well beyond the system integration and fixed process automation initiatives that characterized first-generation BPM.

BUSINESS DRIVEN ARCHITECTURE: COMBINING BPMN 2.0 AND SEMANTIC TECHNOLOGIES
Ralf Mueller, Linus Chow, Jean Prater, Oracle, USA

A business process management (BPM) suite includes tools for business analysts and developers to use in modeling entities, such as business processes, business rules, human workflow, and complex events. Modern BPM operates using the common tenants of an underlying Service Oriented Architecture (SOA) runtime infrastructure based on the Service Component Architecture (SCA) and supports the BPMN 2.0 OMG standard. Oracle BPM is a comprehensive, preintegrated, and hot-pluggable example of such a suite for dynamic businesses.

This paper presents an ontology for BPM based upon BPMN 2.0, Service Component Architecture (SCA) and the Web Ontology Language (OWL 2). The implementation of this ontology supports a wide range of use cases in the areas of process analysis, governance, business intelligence and systems management. It also has the potential to bring together stakeholders across an enterprise, for a true agile end-to-end enterprise architecture. We start with a 90-day Proof of Delivery conducted for the DoD DCMO in 2011.

Section 1: Europe

EPA CONNECT GMBH, GERMANY
Finalist, Europe, Nominated by Adobe Systems Inc., USA

epa connect GmbH supports the technology systems for its sister company, impuls Finanzmanagement, a market leader in independent consulting and procurement of private health insurance contracts. Several complex processes are involved with impuls Finanzmanagement's day-to-day business as the company compares offers from several insurance companies, analyzes the coverage and calculates price-performance benefits. The company also guarantees acceptance by the insurance companies from which they receive offers and provides advisors who council customers through the whole process.

INSTITUTO DE CRÉDITO OFICIAL (ICO), SPAIN
Gold Award: Europe. Nominated by BizAgi, United Kingdom

Due to the severe crisis that the global financial sector recently faced, the small and medium sized companies (SMBs) in Spain experienced limited access to their normal lines of credit. This represented a serious threat to the sector that generates the most employment in that country. As a response to this challenge, the Spanish government decided to provide, through the Instituto de Crédito Oficial (ICO) the Financial Facilitator, an analytical and consulting tool that facilitates access to the small and medium sized companies and the self-employed, to sources of finance enabling them to undertake their corporate and professional projects.

LSC GROUP, BABCOCK & MINISTRY OF DEFENCE, UK
Silver Award: Europe. Nominated by TIBCO Software, USA

During 1999, the UK Ministry of Defence (MoD) Submarine Support Integrated Project Team (SubIPT) was faced with the issue of the cost of submarine ownership and in partnership with Babcock (then DML) set out to realize significant programme savings during HMS Vanguard's 1st Long Overhaul Period Refuel (LOP(R)). One of several steps in achieving this objective was to establish a joint initiative between Babcock, SubIPT (MoD) and its chosen technology partner, LSC Group, to transform the business using workflow technology. To support this approach a Collaborative Working Environment (CWE) was developed by LSC Group to improve collaboration and communication between all stakeholders involved in the submarine refit across the UK. To transform the business the latest workflow technology was adopted to replace paper-based business processes and to enable much greater process integration with existing MoD and industry systems, thereby enabling efficiency and cost reduction.

Section 2: Middle East and Africa

NOKIA SIEMENS NETWORKS, GLOBAL NETWORK IMPLEMENTATION CENTERS, UNITED ARAB EMIRATES
Gold Award: Middle East-Africa. Nominated by Appian, USA

Nokia Siemens Networks (NSN) is one of the largest telecommunications hardware, software and services companies in the world, with more than 60,000 people in over 150 countries. NSN offers a complete portfolio of mobile, fixed and converged network technologies as well as professional services (consulting and systems integration, network implementation, maintenance and care, and managed services) to more than 600 Communications Service Providers around the world.

NSN's initial foray into Business Process Management (BPM) was the award-winning "Zeus" project which thoroughly transformed its Consulting & Systems Integration division and delivered an estimated €6 million annual productivity savings. Based on this success, NSN has now deployed a sophisticated, pan-organizational BPM Program, leveraging and extending the success of "Zeus" through one of the most mature Center of Excellence organizations in the BPM industry.

Section 3: North America

UNITED STATES DEPARTMENT OF ENERGY LOAN PROGRAMS OFFICE
Gold Award, North America. Nominated by Accenture/HandySoft, USA

The primary mission of the U.S. Department of Energy (DOE) is to advance the national, economic and energy security of the United States. DOE's Loan Programs Office (LPO) was created to accelerate the domestic commercial deployment of innovative and advanced clean energy technologies at a scale sufficient to contribute meaningfully to this mission. LPO is able to accomplish its goals by guaranteeing loans to eligible clean energy projects (i.e., agreeing to repay the borrower's debt obligation in the event of a default) and by providing direct loans to eligible manufacturers of advanced technology vehicles and components. The LPO also has a fiduciary obligation to U.S. taxpayers, and must ensure that the loans and loan guarantees provided have a reasonable prospect of repayment.

FARMERS INSURANCE GROUP, UNITED STATES
Gold Award: North America. Nominated by Pegasystems, USA

To leverage the power of their many recent acquisitions, Farmers Insurance Group assembled a road map of activities encompassing more than 300 separate initiatives to be accomplished through cooperative efforts between business teams and IT. Farmers' challenge was integrating the technology of legacy customer services systems from their acquired companies and, in doing so, ensure a unified consistent standard of quality of customer service for all Farmers customers.

The road map provided the guiding vision so that existing technology investments could be further leveraged and that the most critical business needs could be met first. This provided immediate value to the business because of the relatively short time between concept and delivery. The result: drastic improvements in both productivity and customer satisfaction. Farmers also saw significant reduction in the time required for both training of new CSRs and adoption of the new methods. Finally the company experienced new higher levels of improved quality, accuracy, consistency and speed in the processing of claims.

LINCOLN TRUST COMPANY, USA
Silver Award: North America. Nominated by Lincoln Trust Company, USA

Lincoln Trust Company constituted a BPM program in 2007 with the initial goals focused on operational efficiency and going paperless in our back office processes. The overall program has been widely acknowledged for its tremendous success and directly contributed to Lincoln Trust Company's survival in the face of the global financial crisis. This paper discusses the continuation of the program and specifically describes our experiences implementing one of our most evolved BPM processes to date.

Over the past year Lincoln Trust Company has faced a new, better, and very significant challenge—growth! One of Lincoln Trust Company's most strategic business channels has developed a partner channel that has resulted in a 100% increase in sales from last year and is anticipating 1000% increases in new plan establishment. Thrilled with the prospects, but concerned with the impact to new customers, staff, and budget, Lincoln Trust Company executive management decided to leverage our BPM competencies to achieve a vision to provide "white glove" treatment to our new customers, automate the process, and significantly reduce the need for additional staffing within the business unit.

Section 4: Pacific Rim

'US' - UTILITY SERVICES; AN ALLIANCE BETWEEN SOUTH EAST WATER LTD, THIESS SERVICES AND SIEMENS, AUSTRALIA

Gold Award: Pacific Rim. Nominated by Interfacing Technologies Corporation, Canada

The 2009 executive team's strategic review of the **'us'**—Utility Services IT projects identified an opportunity to increase the value that its projects were delivering by taking a more holistic approach. Many of our IT projects, as is likely the case in many companies, were very focused and delivered value to a single business group or function but not necessarily across the business. This reality was amplified in our case because we not only work across departments, but also across multiple companies within the Program Alliance. The review concluded that value would be significantly increased by integrating solutions across functions and business groups through a better understanding of our end-to-end processes.

In response to these findings, we established an innovative Business Process Management (BPM) Centre of Excellence (CoE) to 1) gain that understanding, and 2) integrate it into IT projects where appropriate. The CoE has positively affected several projects since its creation but the farthest reaching of them, and the focus of this study, is the *Job Costing Improvement* project. Herein referred to as *Job Costing*, the project has delivered reductions in cost and increases in data quality for financial and operational reporting through improvements across our core operations and maintenance processes.

INDUSIND BANK, INDIA

Silver Award, Pacific Rim. Newgen Software Technologies Ltd., India

IndusInd bank is among the first of the new-generation private-sector banks granted licenses in the mid-nineties, driven by the process of reform in the banking sector in India. The bank found out that there is a wide business growth potential for the various banking and security products along with other services it offered, provided they could become customer centric, scale up their operations and at the same time maintain cost efficiencies and targeted service levels.

The bank reaped huge benefits by tapping the growth potential through Newgen's scalable solution which enabled improved turn-around-times (TATs), enhanced operational efficiencies and adherence to regulatory compliance.

Section 5: South and Central America

UNIMED PORTO ALEGRE MEDICAL CO-OPERATIVE LTD, BRAZIL
Gold Award, South America. Nominated by BPM Soluções, Brazil

Proper monitoring of the contractual instruments which govern relations between clients and providers is a prerequisite for the efficient management of an organization. Unimed Porto Alegre, the leading medical co-operative in the south of Brazil, recognizes the importance of optimizing the management of its contracts both with corporate clients and providers. Our priorities are standardization, monitoring, speed of response and risk reduction. Through the use of the BPM approach and the automation of processes we have been able not only to revolutionize the way in which we monitor and manage our contracts but also to open the way for a wide number of automation and optimization initiatives in other departments.

ARCELLORMITTAL FOUNDATION, BRAZIL
Silver Award, South America. Nominated by AuraPortal, USA

ArcelorMittal Foundation (AMF) is responsible for managing and sponsoring cultural projects for any local social organization interested in promoting them. As a result of its BPM initiative, within the Foundation, 100 percent of their project proposals can be submitted and evaluated via electronic forms. This represents an increase of 50 percent in the number of project responses. Also, a 50 percent reduction in the time to evaluate each proposal was achieved. As a result of this BPM initiative, which included a tightly integrated SOA environment, a new and improved AMF system was launched called the "CTRL Cultura" system.

TELECARRIER, PANAMA
Silver Award: South & Central America. Nominated by PECTRA Technology Inc., USA

Created in the year 2000 with the purpose of commercially developing the Central America region by rendering services of International Data Center, data and voice transmission, basic telephone and long distance, wholesale, and Internet, Telecarrier is a leading company in the telecommunications industry within the LATAM region. At a technological level, proposals for customized development, and CRM (Customer Relationship Management) were analyzed as short–term solutions, or the adoption of a work philosophy based on process management, and the incorporation of BPM (Business Process Management) technology as a mid-term and long-term alternative; the latter having been chosen on account of its flexibility, scalability, and core-process traceability.

The implementation of the project took twelve months, and it involved the whole organization as well as the CEO's full commitment, as it was a corporate project designed on five pillars on which the work was initially carried out.

Section 6 Appendix

AWARD WINNERS AND NOMINATORS CONTACT DIRECTORY

FURTHER READING, ASSOCIATIONS,

Section 1

Guest Chapters

Business Process as a Service: Enterprise Cloud Computing

Jon Pyke, CIMtrek, United Kingdom

The big buzz at the moment is around Enterprise Cloud Computing (ECC) and its impact on processes and the management of processes. ECC is the special case of utilizing Cloud computing for competitive advantage through breakout opportunities for both cost savings and, more importantly, for business innovation in terms of unprecedented speed and agility and vastly improved collaboration with business partners and customers.

Once you understand what ECC is, there is a far more important question; why does it matter? Here are three key points that define why ECC matters to the world of BPM and where the competitive advantage kicks in.

1. On the cost side of the equation, many, but not all IT and data center costs can be reduced and tied directly to usage, up or down as needs go up or down.

2. But there's more, much more on the revenue side. Risk and startup expenses for innovation initiatives can be cut dramatically, letting companies take more small bets and test out more new ideas. With no upfront capital expense, new projects can be scaled up instantly if they take off, or shut down quickly if they fail. For example; startup Animoto.com, which renders animated MTV-like photos matched to music, scaled from five virtual servers to 7,500 in six days when they got explosive traction at Facebook. Massive scalability and up-or-down elasticity give companies a whole new sandbox for testing new business ideas and growing them if they take off.

3. Companies don't work alone, and, on average, over 20 companies make up today's value chains. Cloud computing allows a company to collaborate in new ways with its trading partners, and collaboration is the key to gaining competitive advantage. By establishing shared workspaces in "Community Clouds" employees from multiple companies work together as "virtual enterprise network" and function as though they were a single company. They all participate in the same value delivery system, sharing computing, communication and information resources. This is especially important as no one company "owns" the overall value chain.

So is this a new idea; is Cloud computing new? The short answer is NO, Cloud computing is *not* a new technology or architecture or methodology. But it *is* a new "delivery model" where all computing and networking resources are delivered as "services" that are elastic (use as much or as little as you need at any given time), massively scalable, and are available on-demand with self-service, pay-as-you-go variable cost subscriptions.

Ok, so we now know what Cloud Computing is and we have a pretty good idea as to the benefits derived from taking the Cloud route—how do you know if you are using the Cloud? Well, Cloud computing has a number of basic; some might say, essential, characteristics:

1. *On-demand self-service.* A consumer can provision computing capabilities, such as server time and network storage, as needed automatically.
2. *Ubiquitous network access.* Capabilities are available over the network and accessed through standard thin or thick client platforms (e.g., mobile phones, laptops, and PDAs).
3. *Location independent resource pooling.* The provider's computing resources are pooled to serve all consumers using a multi-tenant model, with different physical and virtual resources dynamically assigned and reassigned according to consumer demand.
4. *Rapid elasticity.* Capabilities can be rapidly and elastically provisioned to quickly scale up and rapidly released to quickly scale down.
5. *Measured Service.* Cloud systems automatically control and optimize resource use by leveraging a metering capability at some level of abstraction appropriate to the type of service (e.g., storage, processing, bandwidth, and active user accounts

What you will notice is that everything relating to Cloud uses the notation XaaS this is because the whole concept and language used for Cloud computing essentially relates to supplying "Everything as a Service." Let's examine them in a little more detail:

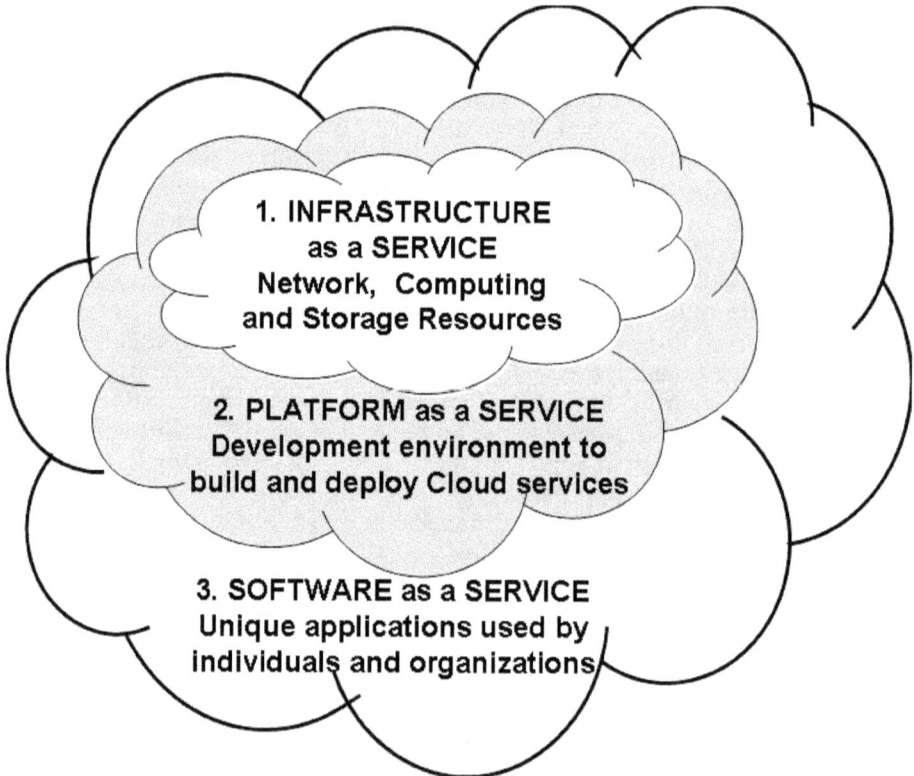

1. INFRASTRUCTURE as a SERVICE
Network, Computing and Storage Resources

2. PLATFORM as a SERVICE
Development environment to build and deploy Cloud services

3. SOFTWARE as a SERVICE
Unique applications used by individuals and organizations

Everything as a Service

1. *Cloud Infrastructure as a Service (IaaS).* The capability provided to the consumer is to provision processing, storage, networks, and other fundamental computing resources.

2. *Cloud Platform as a Service (PaaS).* The capability provided to the consumer is to deploy onto the Cloud infrastructure consumer-created applications using programming languages and tools supported by the provider. The consumer does not manage or control the underlying Cloud infrastructure, network, servers, operating systems, or storage, but the consumer has control over the deployed applications and possibly application hosting environment configurations.

3. *Cloud Software as a Service (SaaS)* The capability provided to the consumer is to use the provider's applications running on a Cloud infrastructure and accessible from various client devices through a thin client interface such as a Web.

But there's more to the three Software-Platform-Infrastructure (SPI) layers that NIST addresses when it comes to **Enterprise Cloud Computing**.

There is an expanded delivery model that helps business users understand how Cloud computing can help them take full advantage of what the new delivery paradigm has to offer.

Number 4 on my list is *Business Process Management (BPM) as a Service (BPMaaS).* Sometimes referred to as Process as a Service (PraaS) or Business Process as a Service (BPaaS), BPM services represent the highest level in the Cloud services hierarchy. These services provide the complete end-to-end business process management needed for the creation and follow-on management of unique business processes.

And finally we have *Management Controls as a Service (MCaaS).* MCaaS offers services such as monitoring service-level agreements with Cloud providers, security management, distributed policy management, role-based authentication and authorization, and other foundation services needed by all layers in the Cloud stack. The lower down the Software-Platform-Infrastructure (SPI) stack the more security and other capabilities consumers are responsible for implementing and managing themselves. On the other hand, the further up the stack, the less the consumer needs to be concerned about how each of the lower levels works. Regardless of where the consumer participates in the stack, management controls are essential whether or mpt they are the responsibility of the consumer of the Cloud Service Provider (CSP).

To take full advantage of the cloud, organizations must realize that they have to create a *process layer* that decouples the control of business processes from underlying applications. In other words, process segments buried in traditional computer applications need to be rendered as "services"; services that can be bundled, unbundled and rebundled as end-to-end business processes. In the same way that middleware provides a data abstraction layer, a Business Operations Platform provides a process abstraction layer that delivers business services when and where they are needed. This process abstraction layer can be best described as a Business Operations Platform (BOP) and really defines what BPMaaS is all about. After all, if you're going to put things in the cloud, you'd better have something to stand on.

A well-defined platform can help businesses deploy, execute, measure, manage and optimize their business processes in the Cloud. Properly implemented, BPMaaS can help organizations pin-point and resolve process bottlenecks, monitor and anticipate business activity and quickly react to the constantly changing business environment.

Many industry analysts recognize process technology as one of the most important software technologies needed for deploying effective Cloud solutions. There are two clear reasons for needing process technology to underpin the provisioning of business systems in the Cloud:

1. *Rapid Innovation:* As we have seen, the Cloud is the ideal mechanism for utilizing extensive computing power—be that storage or specific applications such as CRM, ERP or SCM. As it stands, running a given application in the Cloud—also known as Software as a Service (SaaS)—saves money. But SaaS solutions don't help a business innovate as because companies using a SaaS application are using the same software. SaaS solutions don't enable companies to build unique applications that differentiate them from their competitors. Process management technology, on the other hand, lets you do this in an easy and flexible way. A BOP can orchestrate the interaction and integration of services to create and manage unique business processes.

2. *Compliance:* Cloud deployments can be very disruptive and lead to anarchy and a breakdown of corporate governance and compliance. Think of the myriad Excel spreadsheets that are used to run most businesses—no control, no compliance, no ownership. Process enablement of these types of applications can provide ownership, control and auditability, making them compliant with the corporate governance demands without stifling innovation and change.

Before the BPM was available, enterprise applications typically would be in charge of their localized sets of processes, with the subjugation of adjacent applications to these processes. With every application handling a given process differently, clearly this wouldn't a workable solution in the Cloud. This means that, with a BOP, the control of business processes is externalized away from individual applications. The BOP controls the execution of the processes, the provisioning of services and the delegation of tasks or activities to the individual applications according to their specific uses and needs. In order to do this effectively, the BOP must be able to support the following:

- Manage applications in parallel as well as in series.
- Manage people-intensive applications.
- Decouple the process from the application.
- Work both inside and outside the organization.
- Be both continuous and discrete, and allow processes to change over time.
- Put the control of business processes into the hands of the business user.

Finally, here is an environment that allows and *encourages* the business world and the technology world to align. Given that the business process is where these two worlds come together, the BOP becomes the place where the two worlds can achieve the most in terms of collaborative development and common understanding—eliminating decades of misunderstanding.

The Business Operations Platform does six main jobs:

1. It puts existing and new application software under the direct control of business managers.
2. It facilitates communication between business and IT.
3. It makes it easier for the business to improve existing processes and create new ones.
4. It enables the automation of processes across the entire organization—and beyond.
5. It gives managers real-time information on the performance of processes.
6. It allows organizations to take full advantage of new computing services.

Unlike early BPM offerings that were stitched together from fragments of technologies past, BPMaaS must be built on a standards-based, modern architecture. With a service-oriented architecture (SOA) and full BPM capabilities companies can create a complete business operations environment that can drive innovation, efficiency and agility.

It is essential that any product purporting to offer BPMaaS must include business process design, execution, monitoring and improvement capabilities. It must be designed to help business managers directly align business process implementations with business goals, while facilitating process improvement via control and visibility into process metrics and real-time business activity. At the same time, it must help IT managers and developers to model and integrate the entire enterprise business process landscape, while ensuring that existing IT assets are fully leveraged.

The user interface should completely web-based to make collaboration much easier, especially if business and IT professionals reside in multiple geographical locations. A shared process model defines the "contract" for process implementation, which is fulfilled by connecting top-down business process design components to bottom-up technical services. This approach puts the business firmly in charge, by empowering business professionals to directly influence and control IT implementations. Furthermore, the BOP approach gives business managers and business analysts complete confidence that their models are up to date and reflect actual deployed processes.

On top of these capabilities, the platform should also provide a Composite Application Framework (CAF) and enterprise Master Data Management (MDM) to establish a single view of the business that can then be continuously and effectively monitored via the platform's integrated Business Activity Monitoring (BAM). This level of visibility makes continuous business process improvement a reality. It helps the organization to reach operational excellence via analysis of non-performing processes and reduction of process-related friction across the extended supply chain. If all of the above is not enough to contend with the platform must also provide dynamic Case Management capabilities and hook into the *social networking* aspects of today's business environment.

Last, and by no means least, it needs to include comprehensive process auditing that helps decision makers to achieve better process governance is essential. This is necessary to better comply with external and internal regulations and quality initiatives, such as SOX, Six Sigma, HIPAA, or Basel II. From an architectural perspective the platform must be fully Cloud-enabled and have ways of metering and monitoring *what's* happening and *where* it is happening. In short a BPMaaS must be fully deployable in private, public and hybrid Clouds.

The Cloud does offer you a new way to develop and deliver cost effective IT services and solutions, but it is vital you learn from the lessons of the past. The take-up of PC Networks was started and driven by users in a series of individual user-driven projects. This caused serious problems as it became clear that it was one environment: client server.

Getting a grip now of what is happening and how it will impact business processes is important if we are to prevent some of the problems from the past happening again.

The Difference Between BPM and Adaptive Case Management
Nathaniel Palmer, WfMC, USA

INTRODUCTION

In the half-century since Peter Drucker first identified and coined the phrase "knowledge worker," the share of the work force represented by this group has grown considerably, to as much as half of all workers by some measures. So, too, have grown investments targeting knowledge worker productivity, with global IT spending reaching $4.35 trillion in 2010, according to Global Technology Index author Dr. Howard A. Rubin.

Yet we are far from realizing the level of improvement seen in manual labor over the course of the last century. Traditionally, IT investments targeting business productivity have focused on one of two areas. The first is automation technologies, such as enterprise resource planning (ERP) or the more contemporary technology of business process management (BPM). Those address repeatable, predictable modes of work and are designed to enforce a command and control management model, where efficiency gains are sought through standardizing how work is performed.

Yet scripting work processes in advance, as is presented through work automation, offers little benefit for increasing knowledge worker productivity, without the ability to adapt to changes in the business environment. Much of the knowledge worker's daily activities cannot be accurately defined in advance, at least not with the precision necessary to code into IT applications, and therefore they most often take place outside the realm of ERP and BPM. Where it does occur, it is in the other common target area of IT investments—the tools and infrastructure that enable communication and information sharing, such as networking, e-mail, content management and increasingly social media.

As IT investments have advanced their footprint in the workplace, a gap has emerged. It can be found between e-mail and ad hoc communication tools, which, while used in one form or another by all knowledge workers, offer little with regard to task management, and the ERP/BPM realm, premised on predictable work patterns defined in advance. What has emerged to fill this void is Adaptive Case Management (ACM).

WHAT IS KNOWLEDGE WORK?

Knowledge work as a concept was really introduced just in the last 50 years; ancient in IT years, yet relatively new in the history of mankind. In "Management Challenges for the 21st Century," Drucker posits that during the 20th century the greatest contribution for management was the fifty-fold increase on productivity of manual work or the manual worker, particularly in manufacturing. That had been the goal from the beginning of the industrial revolution, and even before, with Adam Smith's allegorical pin factory onto Frederick Taylor's Scientific Method. Throughout the 20th century what could have been thought of as "knowledge work" was most often limited to coordination of manual workers. While there were doctors, lawyers, bankers and other knowledge-based professionals, they represented a relative small percent of the workforce. It was not until the 21st century that the shift had begun, to the point where today so much more of what we do is inarguably knowledge work. So much more is about leveraging our know-how in intellectual capital. As Drucker writes, "in the 21st century the absolute imperative for management is productivity of the knowledge worker."

Recently we took a survey of two hundred organizations and asked about the hurdles and pain points that knowledge workers face relative to productivity. What keeps them from being productive? Curiously, it is not the knowledge-intensive activities, it is not the stuff that really requires their know-how, such as determining what steps to take, or who to collaborate with or getting together a team of collaborators. Ultimately, the greatest productivity traps are found in the more mundane activities, simply tracking who's doing what, where they have dependencies on co-workers. Where are they in the course of their work, what's the state of their work? How are they managing the documentation that they need, the information and documents that they need to support a given task? These are the things that knowledge workers find the most challenging.

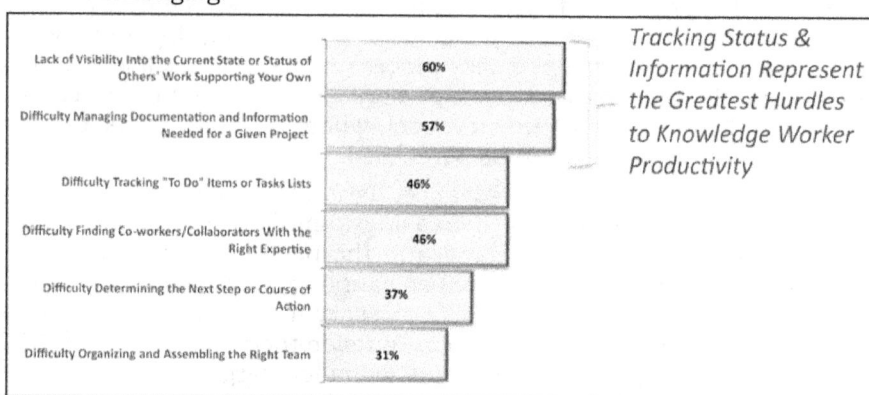

Source: 2011 ACM Survey

Common Productivity Hurdles Faced by Knowledge Workers

Looking at the how knowledge workers spend their day, the same group reported overwhelmingly that it's in unstructured and most often unpredictable work patterns. As shown above, only a third of their time is spent structured work that can be most easily can be or already has been automated. In most organizations, low hanging fruits have already been plucked, leaving few remaining opportunities. Yet for specific structured-but-not-automated processes that remain, they nonetheless add up to comparatively little of any given workers day and thus not an ideal target.

Where knowledge workers do spend most of their time is either in the purely ad-hoc space where nothing ever happens the same way twice, or otherwise within *barely repeatable processes*. The latter is involves specifically defined goals and milestones, but inevitably the sequence to realize these changes from day-to-day.

Barely repeatable processes are often those where the pathways are relatively complex with different variations and different decision points. Often with these types of processes it is possible to define and apply policies and specific business logic around how that work is performed (read "business rules") as well as high level patterns of how the process is going to flow (read "milestones") yet still be impossible to determine in advance the exact sequence of tasks and activities. For example, such a process may involve an electronic form or something that is launched by the BPM system, otherwise achieving the same milestone may instead involve a purely human task occurring entirely outside of this system. In each case, a series of activities is involved, as well as predefined outcomes required, yet that exact combination and sequence of activities is determined by the unique circumstances of a given case.

This pattern (described above) fits well with ACM, but not BPM. With BPM, all the possible paths and permutations are defined in advance, and as each activity occurs, the state of the process changes. As the state changes and is transferred from one activity to the next, control flows similarly from one activity to the next. So the business process map shows the flow of control or specifically who has management of the process at any given time.

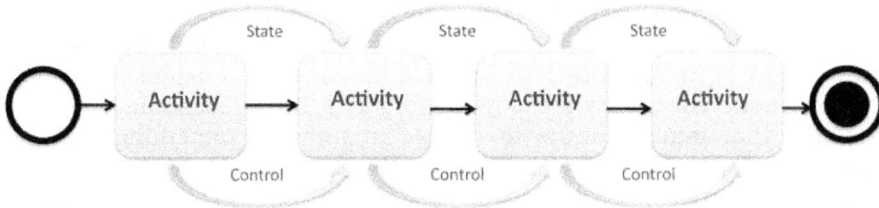

BPM Involves the Flow of Control and the Sequencing of State Changes

Contrast this with ACM, which really focuses on events and outcomes. An event occurs, a case file is opened, and then the end point is known. The circumstances, which define how and when the case is completed is known, but the means to reach that is not predetermined. A series of activities will occur, information will be created and added to the case, as that information and the context around it is added to the case, that's what determines the state of the case ultimately. And it's only when that goal is reached that the case is completed. There may be any number of processes that are kicked off during that time, but the sequence for those activities, the activities themselves may be predetermined but the sequence, how the work is performed and how it flows, that can't be determined in advance.

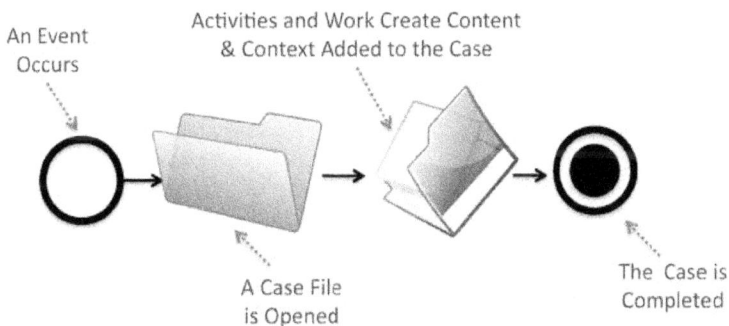

ACM is Event-Driven, Content- and Context-Aware

Comparing BPM and ACM exposes the difference between deterministic and non-deterministic processes. Deterministic processes are determined in advance. The actual pathways may be very complex, yet the decision points, the business logic, the business rules—all the attributes that determine how a process can flow are predefined. State is determined by whatever activity just occurred and how that relates to the process going forward.

ACM, in contrast, is inherently non-deterministic, where the end point is known but the pathway for reaching the outcome is determined by each stage, each milestone in the management of that case. The state of the case is not determined by where it fits on a particular flow chart or process map, but by the content and the context within the case.

Considered a basic process where an event occurs, here's a simplistic example; a customer reports a problem, a case is opened and then what happens next is the movement toward realizing and resolving the goal, but exactly *what* happens is not determined in advance. In this case an issue is investigated, could be that potential solutions are tried, maybe successfully, maybe un-successfully. No doubt there is correspondence with the customer, whether that is an external customer or an internal customer, where it's supplied unsuccessfully, alternatives are going to be researched. It may be something that takes months to resolve, it may be something that takes hours to resolve.

Yet unlike a BPM process where sequence is predetermined, with ACM all that is known is what the goal is, what the end state is defined as, and the policies, the rules, the resources, the players that are involved in that case, but not exactly how it's going to transpire. For that reason, because ACM is goal driven, it is also inherently nonlinear. A case evolves over time, toward achieving that goal, but often in unpredictable directions. It requires the ability to jump ahead, jump back, to go to any point based on the circumstances of that case. It is not a sequence that can be determined in advance.

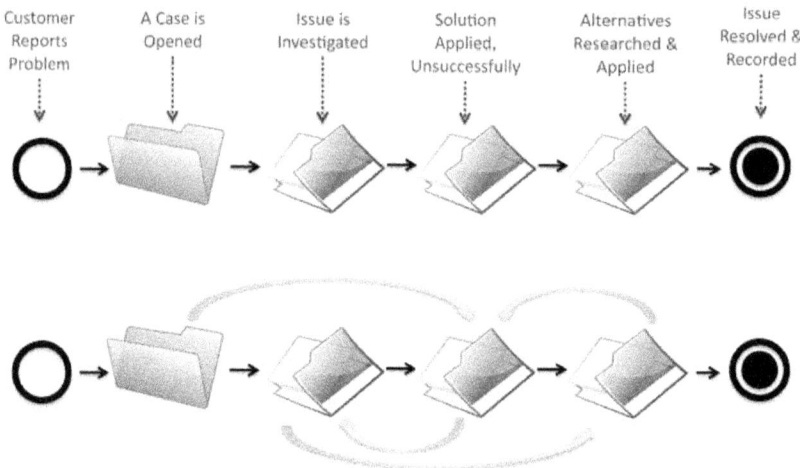

With ACM Goals Are Predetermined, Sequence and Pathways Are Not

With a BPM process, at any given point you are launching a process that has to run its course and be completed and that maybe that there are several processes that are involved. For example, managing the lifecycle of a relationship of a customer, using ACM you're managing that from beginning to end, without predetermining when that relationship is going to end. Rather, over the course of that relationship you will be advancing toward specific goals, such as on-boarding steps and product or services provisioning, as well as other specific milestones which in all likelihood do follow a managed or even automated process, yet the specific sequencing of these are predetermined. In all reality, all organizations have patterns of work that fall into the categories consistent with both traditional BPM and ACM. It is not an "either/or" proposition of "BPM vs ACM" exclusively, but rather a matter of when to apply which approach.

ACM PATTERNS: TAMING THE UNPREDICTABLE

We asked organizations about the type of work patterns that are consistent with ACM but that apply to their organization, whether or not they feel that today that they are doing ACM. Certainly there are ones that have a very mature notion of ACM, in the process or work pattern as it is managed today. A great example of this is adjudication or investigative case management. In these work patterns, it is not about the process per se, it is about the case— i.e., achieving the outcome and capturing how it was realized, rather than automating that process in a predefined way.

Here the notion of long-lived may indeed apply, as an investigative process, such as a background check or a criminal investigation that needs to live until that goal is reached, until the case is resolved. With background checks performed by government agencies, for example, backlogs of in-process and thus incomplete investigations are widespread. The role of ACM is to streamline these expediting that process, which requires improvement of both the quality of the information that is being captured as well as efficient as possible. Because the information capture in this process must be of evidentiary quality (something that can be proven in court if it's ever challenged) it is processes involved cannot be fully automated, but require considerable oversight by the professionals involved (e.g., knowledge workers.).

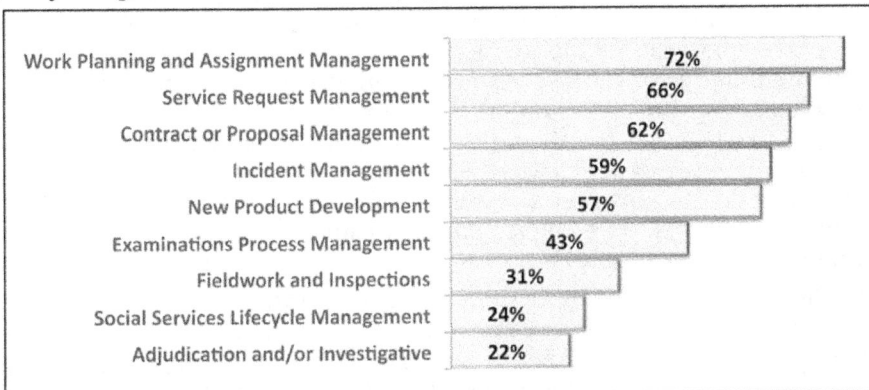

Work Planning and Assignment Management	72%
Service Request Management	66%
Contract or Proposal Management	62%
Incident Management	59%
New Product Development	57%
Examinations Process Management	43%
Fieldwork and Inspections	31%
Social Services Lifecycle Management	24%
Adjudication and/or Investigative	22%

Source: 2011 ACM Survey

ACM Patterns Applicable to Surveyed Firms

Another example common to government agencies is "Social Services Life-cycle Management" involving the end-to-end interaction between the services provider (be it a government agency or non-profit organization) and their relationship with the beneficiary of those services. That cycle might last a single individual's lifetime, or it may be short-lived. In either case it will follow the lifecycle of the relationship, not any particular task or process or single activity. This is probably the most commonly understood pattern of case management.

"Work Planning and Assignment Management" was cited as being applicable to 72 percent of survey respondents. This pattern involves circumstances of managing and tracking who performs work, what their assignments are, and the interplay between projects and resources, not specifically managing the work itself. This presents a compelling example of the benefits of ACM as it can be either short-or long-lived with little opportunity to define this at the outset. It's something that very often will run over the relationship with a particular employee which may go on for decades, or in some cases, it may be a matter of weeks or months.

In contrast, "Service Request Management" presents a use case or work pattern where by its definition, the process should not be long-lived. The service incident, whether via an internal help desk or external customer, originates with an event or issue where the goal inevitably to be resolved as expeditiously as possible. The pathway realizing this will likely follow standard procedures, including predefined processes at various points, yet will also involve some degree of unpredictability. There will be investigation, things that are tried; you can't determine in advance exactly how that's going to unfold. What is required is to capture all the interaction, while also providing the tools to guide those involved to resolve the issue as quickly as possible. This is an ideal application of ACM—capturing context, guiding knowledge workers, but aiding rather than automating that which requires human intervention.

RETHINKING KNOWLEDGE WORK

In a recent McKinsey Quarterly article entitled "Rethinking Knowledge Work," Tom Davenport defines case management (going forward referred to as "ACM") as a combination of workflow, content management, business rules, portal and collaboration tools, which collectively allow for the completion of an entire "case" or unit of work. In other words, it is the orchestration of those tools together that support the entire lifecycle of a case, from end-to-end. ACM ties together the tools that support knowledge work, as single application and environment, whether virtually or physically, with a single point of access. That involves the integration of external tools and social media (think "mashups") to facilitate communication and assist with data visualization, with various information sources or repositories.

ACM differs from tools such as BPM and ECM because it is not simply a parallel silo, but rather a superset or master system of record, capturing both the "what" (data, files, records or most often links to the physical sources of those) and the "how" (metadata, audit trail, as well as the context of decisions and actions). As a result, adaptive ACM facilitates better data and records management through the ability to identify and organize content distinctly from other cases—whether shared or unique, it is connected to the specific business context in which it was used.

In this way, an ACM system, the case folder and the case itself is a system of record. This is in contrast with BPM; even though it is connected with ECM or other information management abilities, the function of BPM is to provide a transactional thread across multiple systems of record.

Case management, by its definition, is a system of record of what happened. It captures the context as well as links the information as the case evolves. It can include email, voice mail, traditional documents, GIS documents and video. All the content and the related context are edited around that which is required to have a 360-degree understanding of what has happened with that case. The files of that media may reside outside and, in fact, may be used by multiple cases but the ACM system pulls it all together in a virtual folder to have one version of the truth, ultimately providing the permanent record of that case.

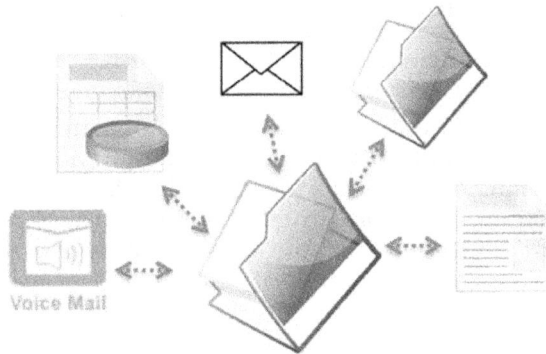

Virtual or Physical, ACM is System of Record For All Forms of Content

Davenport writes, "[ACM] can create value whenever some degree of structure or process can be imposed on information-intensive work. Until recently, structured provision approaches have been applied mostly to lower-level information tasks that are repetitive, predictable and thus easier to automate." ACM offers the chance to improve the productivity of knowledge work by allowing knowledge workers to make smart choices and apply best practices, not to simply automate decisions for them.

Productivity improvements, measured in both financial and non-financial terms, come from reduced re-work, as well as improved customer and employee satisfaction. In part, that results from greater visibility into areas of work previously "under the radar" when performed in purely ad hoc environments, offering the ability to prioritize activities across multiple cases, balancing workloads, as well as monitoring quality, timeliness and speed.

BUSINESS IS DRIVEN BY GOALS

Supporting the dynamic nature of today's business environments and the self-directed, non-repetitive nature of knowledge worker processes requires the ability to assemble structured and unstructured processes from basic predefined business entities, content, social interactions and business rules. It requires capturing actionable information and supporting decisions without having to model or reengineer processes in advance, but instead based on patterns defined by business users. Unlike traditional BPM systems, where the focus is the process route along which the item of work or case information follows a predefined path, with ACM the case itself that is the focus.

Drucker has labeled this orientation or management practice as "management by objectives" or MBO. With this approach, knowledge workers and management establish specific goals or objectives within the organization so that the outcome is mutually understood, but the specific course of action and the decision-making are left to the knowledge worker. ACM provides guidance and measurement of outcomes, as well as the long-term maintenance of data surrounding the process to demonstrate how objectives were realized and decisions were made.

Highly predictable work is easy to support using traditional programming techniques, while unpredictable work cannot be accurately scripted in advance, and so requires the involvement of the workers themselves. Aiding knowledge workers, enabling real productivity gains, would logically come from both automating repetitive work where possible, while facilitating the less predictable, more dynamic work modes requiring the flexibility to be defined according the circumstances and context of a given moment in time.

Consistent with this, in our recent survey respondents reported that knowledge workers spent two-thirds of any given day in activities which did not follow a predetermined path and were unpredictable in nature, but much of this also involved specific goals. In other words, most of a knowledge worker's day is spent working toward an identified outcome, yet the means for achieving this cannot be predetermined.

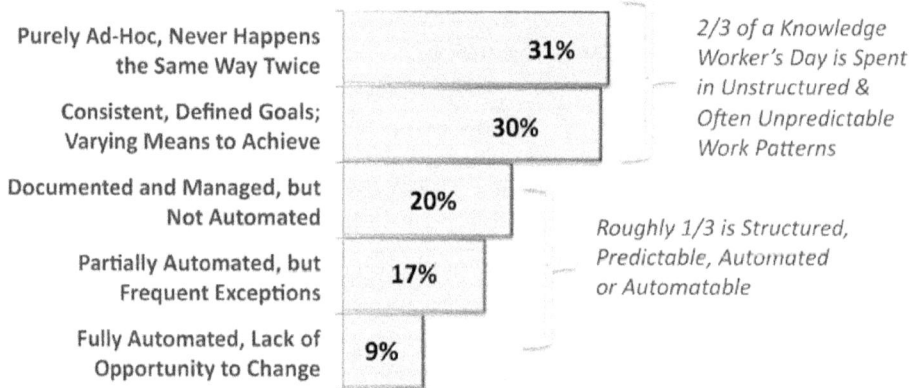

Work Mode	Percent	
Purely Ad-Hoc, Never Happens the Same Way Twice	31%	*2/3 of a Knowledge Worker's Day is Spent in Unstructured & Often Unpredictable Work Patterns*
Consistent, Defined Goals; Varying Means to Achieve	30%	
Documented and Managed, but Not Automated	20%	*Roughly 1/3 is Structured, Predictable, Automated or Automatable*
Partially Automated, but Frequent Exceptions	17%	
Fully Automated, Lack of Opportunity to Change	9%	

Source: 2011 ACM Survey

Percent of Day Spent in Different Work Modes

ACM assists the knowledge worker to apply know-how and make decisions. ACM addresses those issues in the productivity hurdles, the mundane activities and transaction costs involved in managing work such as having visibility into the state of affairs and current activities, managing and capturing information in context—as well as having business rules and analytics to be able to apply to that.

Providing guidance in the form of help in knowledge management functions and to be able to provide that in context; that's where the notion of adaptability applies—adapting to circumstances of the case as it evolves rather than simply predetermining at any given time what is supposed to be occurring. It has to occur, it has to adapt based on where that state is, where that case is. State is determined based on the information in the case.

Adaptive, Not Ad Hoc

The use of "adaptive" in *Adaptive* Case Management refers to the need for knowledge worker support systems that are not explicated, programmed or hand-coded by specialists as they have been in the past, but instead can be dynamically modified by ordinary users in the course of their work.

This orientation frames the definition of ACM systems that are not simply ad hoc and devoid of any manageability, but are able to support decision-making and data capture, while allowing the freedom for knowledge workers to apply their own understanding and subject matter expertise to respond to unique or changing circumstances within the business environment.

One core quality of ACM is support for goal-seeking and goal-driven processes, where goals can be modified "in flight" by the knowledge worker. Similarly, knowledge captured during the performance of the case can support the identification and creation of new processes or case rules, without requiring IT/developer involvement.

Ultimately, adaptability is defined as more than simply the ability to change, but how the change is facilitated. It can be measured through a reduced need for training and change management of knowledge workers, as a result of guidance provided by the system. With ACM, this is based on the current context of the work and what needs to be done, including the ability to identify and initiate collaboration with specific subject matter experts. If this is starting to sound like knowledge management, it should. Although not designed as a repository for codifying implicit knowledge in the traditional spirit of knowledge management, it should provide an effective means for identifying know-how by capturing the context in which knowledge work is performed.

Other examples of adaptability in ACM include providing access to reusable templates for initiating new cases, including the use of completed cases as templates. That allows knowledge workers to take advantage of automated tasks, while controlling if and when they are invoked, for example, having the ability to create standard correspondence (letters, e-mails, etc.) at any point in the case, with the system automatically capturing context of interaction and responses.

BUILDING RESPONSIVE SYSTEMS

In many ways, emergence of ACM represents the shift from adapting business practices to the design of IT systems, to building systems that reflect how work is actually performed. The latter is the way all IT projects should be approached, yet the former spotlights the traditional gap between business and IT understanding. Accurately assessing the business impact of IT is often difficult because the introduction of software changes the way people work, as well as the way they are organized.

In this way, the case may live on in perpetuity, retaining this last state until another event occurs to launch it or it may be specifically or officially put into a suspense state, able to be restarted at any time. But it can also be used to launch another case.

So the case itself can be a template for a new case instance. For example, with a costumer resolution scenario, it may be that a particular customer issue now has become a best practice for unrelated issues, related issues, or other occurrences of that issue and that case can then be the template for how that's is going to be solved going forward.

Enabling Knowledge Workers to Work The Way They Work Best

ACM enables better records and data management by connecting context and outcomes with the actual information. The ability to identify cases, to be able to access that information based on the case, based on the context of what occurred, as well as to manage that separately so the different files can be cross referenced and linked between cases, ultimately this allows for capturing and managing the context and the know how-from what has occurred in the course of the performance of that case.

ACM is ultimately about allowing knowledge workers to work the way that they work the best. To provide them the tools and information they need to do their job in the way that they want to work. Increasingly, this means having access to social media and outside information sources. There is a significant amount of work currently conducted through LinkedIn, Twitter and other social sources as well as resources selected by individual workers that create input and contextual information that's a critical part of the case record, but is not part of any centrally managed IT infrastructure. ACM provides the ability not only to pull that in as part of the case record, but also to be a platform for enabling mash-ups and to work in the chosen environment.

Similarly, extending the transactional management of traditional BPM with the adaptable goal driven benefits of ACM, provides the ability for delivering work and managing where and the way the work is done today. Rather than creating yet another island of automation, ACM allows us to work the way we work best.

The direction for ACM allows the work to follow the worker, providing the cohesiveness of a single point of access. ACM does not impose whether this work is virtual or physical but pulls all the end points, information, environments and provides that long-term record of how work is done, as well as the guidance, rules, visibility and input that enable knowledge workers to be more productive.

Advantages of Agile BPM

Keith D. Swenson, Fujitsu America Inc., USA

Agile BPM represents the next generation of business process management—designed to flexibly address all types of processes to support all forms of work. It combines traditional Business Process Management (BPM) style predefined processes, along with Adaptive Case Management (ACM) style dynamic work support.

INTRODUCTION

Agile BPM is designed to flexibly address all types of processes used to conduct business: structured, unstructured, and hybrid process types to support all forms of work.

In recent years many organizations have come to the understanding that their business processes are proprietary business assets that can yield competitive differentiation and advantage. This recognition has led to the adoption of first-generation BPM technologies to automate fixed, repetitive processes for efficiency and cost-effectiveness.

But the next generation of BPM, Agile BPM, will incorporate product capabilities that extend well beyond the system integration and fixed process automation initiatives that characterized first-generation BPM.

Three essential areas constitute Agile BPM:
- Continuous Process Optimization
- Collaboration and Social Networking
- Extending Enterprise Ecosystems

CONTINUOUS PROCESS OPTIMIZATION

An issue that lies at the heart of process automation is the lack of agility in many BPM implementations and technologies, putting process automation initiatives and technologies out of synch with the dynamically changing business conditions they are supposed to reflect and support. There exists a critical need for continuous process visibility and analysis to ensure that key business processes are performing effectively to support the business as its practices and requirements evolve.

But process discovery and visualization are challenging for most organizations. In fact, industry research has stated that in the conventional BPM cycle of Discover-Model-Simulate-Automate-Optimize, the Discovery phase consumes over 40 percent of the time and effort to implement BPM. This is because discovery of existing processes is largely a manual, time-consuming exercise conducted through meetings and human interactions. Most workers lack a holistic view of processes, even processes they are involved in. Typically they know the immediate previous and subsequent step of any process in which they are participants. As a result, identifying and modeling existing processes is, at best, anecdotal and inefficient, and at worst, highly inaccurate. The consequence of this is that most organizations that have automated business processes do not perform continuous visualization, analysis, and optimization of existing key business processes that may be out-of-date.

What is needed is evidence-based process detection and verification that provides insight to both IT and the business side of how well or poorly existing business processes are delivering efficiency and business advantage. Process Mining, also known as Automated Process Discovery (APD), performs off-production analysis of existing business processes—uncovering typical flows, repetitions, and loopbacks to highlight process inefficiencies and bottlenecks where they exist and identifying the right processes for improvement and continuous optimization.

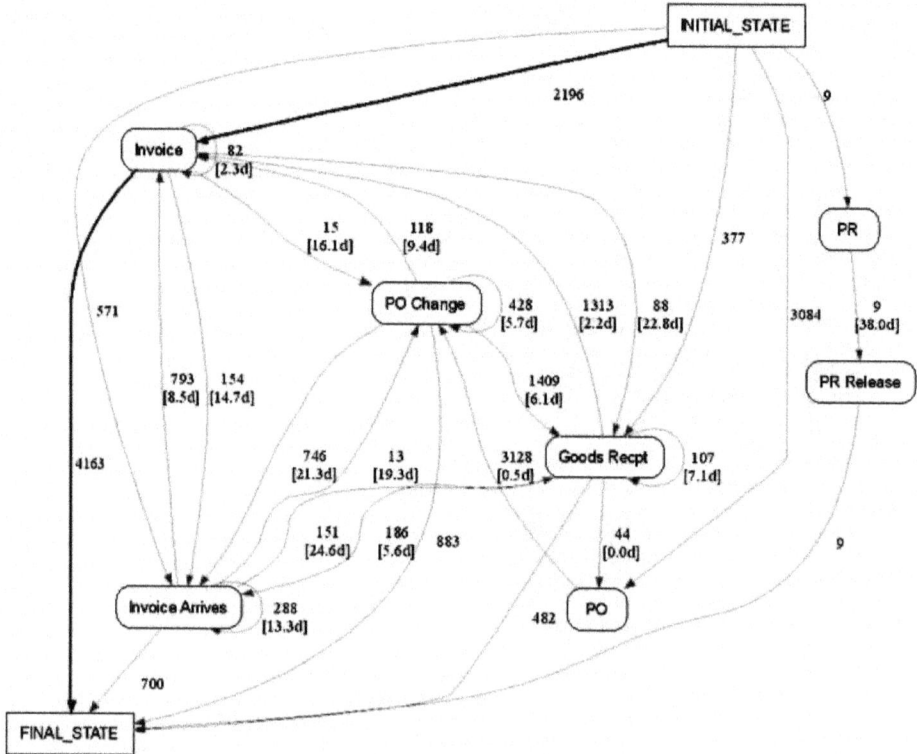

Figure 1: Automated Process Discovery visualizes actual process paths, identifying the most critical processes for improvement.

With system-based evidence on the true "as it really is" state of existing business processes, IT and business management can collaboratively identify and prioritize the key processes for improvement. Armed with actionable process insight, processes can then be optimized and automated. Where too many or overlapping processes exist, APD can help rationalize them and create lean process profiles.

APD highlights the most commonly traversed process paths, the least common paths, repeated steps, loopbacks, and the cost of each process. By identifying the most common business process patterns, it provides end users with the opportunity to standardize on existing common processes that are effective.

This process mining works in combination with traditional BPM to identify the critical process intersections and stages that affect business performance. Once identified, the traditional BPM can use analytics techniques to set performance thresholds and monitor these Key Performance Indicators (KPIs) for any potential deviations in process that could degrade business performance.

Process owners and business executives require this management view on process latencies or redundancies. The system can monitors process performance and issues alerts corresponding to business conditions requiring corrective action. This delivers real-time business intelligence for continuous process performance and optimization.

Figure 2: sets performance thresholds and monitors Key Performance Indicators for any potential deviations.

COLLABORATIVE AND SOCIAL

The next capability of Agile BPM is accommodating and managing semi- and completely unpredictable business processes that involve collaboration among teams.

The first generation of BPM technologies has been traditionally applied to manage routine, repeatable business processes within a company. These processes—such as invoicing or order processing—typically follow exact steps that are normally repeated without exception. But there is another area of work—*knowledge work*—that is conducted in nearly all forms of business. This type of work involves judgment, can involve team collaboration, and almost never follows predictable, identical, repeated patterns.

Knowledge work and collaborative work represents the most valuable and differentiated work performed in an organization and as such, it tends to involve the highest value business initiatives and most expensive and highly trained workers in the company. Yet this work is not immune from inefficiency. The challenge has been how to provide system automation to track, measure, monitor, and manage processes and steps that cannot be defined in advance.

Agile BPM includes capabilities to address these ad hoc process flows necessary for knowledge-work, allowing process participants to punch out of structured processes and to task others for additional insight, input and approvals. Or they can instantiate a process outside of a defined process model, one whose course will proceed along dynamic, unpredictable steps to completion. Interstage BPM provides dynamic routing, workload balancing, and creation of processes on the fly. And it addresses the hybrid process scenarios where a structured process can spawn the need for collaboration or where a dynamic process can invoke structured process fragments.

When using Agile BPM, users can easily veer from previously defined, structured processes to respond to business change by extending existing processes dynamically with new tasks or by creating new processes from scratch to address these situations. Business users create completely new processes by simply creating a list of activities—a process outline—and Interstage automatically converts it into a sequence of tasks. In this way, business team members implicitly participate together in defining processes based on actual work.

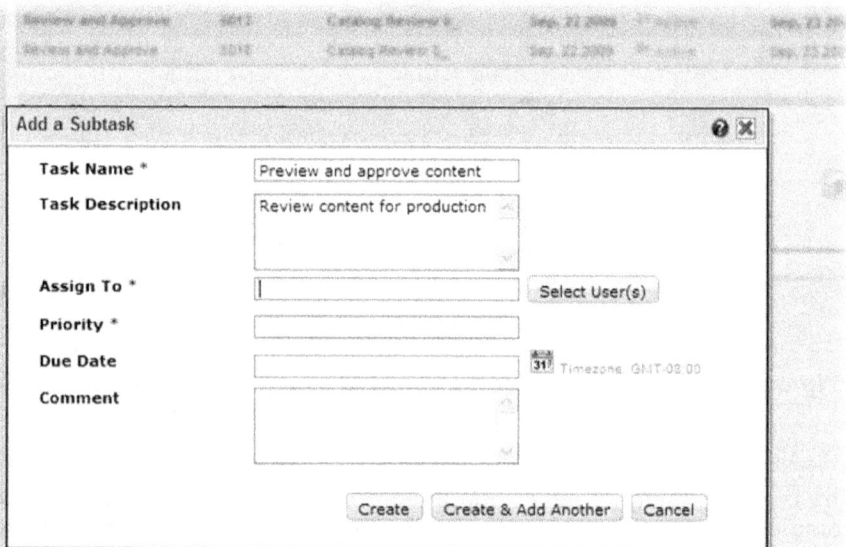

Figure 3: dynamic tasking lets users address and manage all forms of work, including ad hoc tasks and activities.

In this way, one can support collaborative, unstructured, and dynamic business processes needed for knowledge work. This is also known as case management in specific industries such as legal, healthcare, and insurance. Addressing individual business situations and work types that are unique, case management is now a relevant and commonly occurring work pattern in numerous other pursuits including mergers and acquisitions, financial portfolio management, and customer exception handling scenarios.

Dynamic process support allows users to model and manage a process where the starting point is known but the end point is not. It also lets users modify processes at runtime to accommodate necessary changes in process to support the work objective. It even lets people retroactively start processes for the case that work got started before the case manager realized that a process would be needed.

Collaborative work models and social media are teaching us that self-direction for teams and individuals are superior to the old "command and control" work models in nearly all situations involving knowledge work. Controls are moving downward in organizations. The world is moving too fast for centralized control. Decisions need to be made at ever more autonomous points, involving information exchanges and consultations in unforeseen, unplanned, and impromptu ways.

Increasingly, social interaction is figuring prominently in the development of a participatory culture for collaboratively producing work. The concepts of online communities where team members can contribute ideas, share information, and obtain information are central to next-generation Agile BPM. It includes social, collaborative capabilities for decentralized communication and immediate information updates to keep broad-based teams current and in possession of all of the facts related to a process-based work initiative.

Business processes involve numerous people, tasks, and decisions. Users need to be able to collaborate with each other via instant messaging, exchange knowledge through wikis to help complete tasks, and even sign up for RSS feeds so that they remain up-to-date on the status of tasks.

Users need a workplace that forms a dynamic, Web-based community framework for collaboration. They need tools for organizing people and information assets involved in work projects and provides information about the status of Workplace members and their tasks. And users should be able to leverage the process wikis and outlining capabilities to enable better collaboration and sharing of process knowledge.

EXTENDING ENTERPRISE ECOSYSTEMS

Today's business processes are not exclusively native to one entity. Now they span corporate boundaries to connect multiple, different audiences including customers, suppliers, partners, and other constituent parties. These extended corporate ecosystems increasingly involve shared business processes and as such need the capability to streamline, monitor, measure, and manage workflows that cross individual company and organizational boundaries.

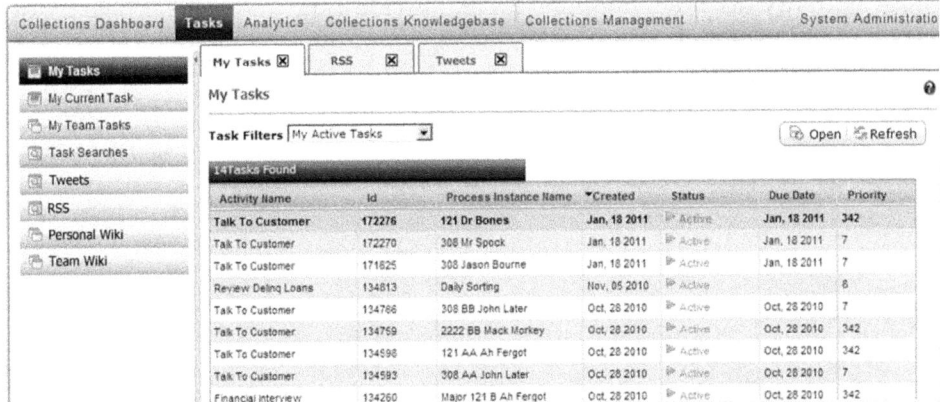

Figure 4: supporting social interactions – sharing knowledge, insight, and best practices to accomplish work more effectively.

An Agile BPM approach is ideal for linking process participants across these boundaries. Because it is Web-based, deployments can easily link to any process participants, regardless of where they are situated. The benefits of this approach include reduced capital costs, the ability to design and run processes from anywhere, and the capacity to easily extend processes to and among varied constituent parties.

CONCLUSION

A fact that is sometimes overlooked is that the point of Business Process Management is to improve the way that people perform and complete their work. Users demand capabilities to make it easy to have a pulse on business or project-based work performance. Unified dashboards present real-time access and detail of all tasks, processes, reports, KPIs, and alerts. Team leaders can quickly drill down into the specifics of an issue, compare team members' performances, identify the right person to assign to a task based on past performance, and even examine potential workload scenarios for particular team members before reshuffling assignments to get work done optimally. Empowered to quickly and flexibly sub-task work to different team members in response to dynamic conditions, managers are able to optimize all forms of process—structured, unstructured, hybrid—in support of accomplishing work and overall business performance.

Next-generation Agile BPM is designed to address all of the requirements of managing work in today's enterprise: from streamlining routine, repeated business processes to managing dynamically evolving business cases involving teamwork, collaboration, and judgment across and among diverse sets of process participants.

ABOUT FUJITSU AMERICA

Fujitsu America, Inc. is a leading ICT solutions provider for organizations in the U.S., Canada and the Caribbean. Fujitsu enables clients to meet their business objectives through integrated offerings including consulting, systems integration, managed services and outsourcing for enterprise applications, data center and field services operations, based on server, software, storage and mobile technologies. Interstage BPM is Fujitsu's leading edge product that presents powerful Agile BPM capabilities, combining both traditional BPM and ACM capabilities into a single unified approach. Fujitsu provides industry-oriented solutions for manufacturing, retail, healthcare, government, education, financial services and communications sectors.

For more information, please visit: http://solutions.us.fujitsu.com/

Business Driven Architecture: Combining BPMN 2.0 and Semantic Technologies

Ralf Mueller, Linus Chow, Jean Prater, Oracle, USA

1. EXECUTIVE SUMMARY / ABSTRACT

A business process management (BPM) suite includes tools for business analysts and developers to use in modeling entities, such as business processes, business rules, human workflow, and complex events. Modern BPM operates using the common tenants of an underlying Service Oriented Architecture (SOA) runtime infrastructure based on the Service Component Architecture (SCA) and supports the BPMN 2.0 OMG standard. Oracle BPM is a comprehensive, preintegrated, and hot-pluggable example of such a suite for dynamic businesses.

Semantically-enabling all artifacts of BPM, from the high-level design of a business process diagram to the deployment and runtime model of a BPM application, promotes continuous process refinement, comprehensive impact analysis, and reuse to minimize unnecessary proliferation of processes and services. A database capable of storing semantic data can be used to mange semantically-enabled BPM ontologies and models, inference with rules to discover implicit relationships in the models, and perform pattern-matching queries to find associations. Oracle Database Semantic Technologies is an example of such a database with support for W3C standards (RDF, OWL, SKOS, and SPARQL), and scalability and security for enterprise-scale semantic applications.

This paper presents an ontology for BPM based upon BPMN 2.0, Service Component Architecture (SCA) and the Web Ontology Language (OWL 2). The implementation of this ontology supports a wide range of use cases in the areas of process analysis, governance, business intelligence and systems management. It also has the potential to bring together stakeholders across an enterprise, for a true agile end-to-end enterprise architecture. We will start with a 90 day Proof of Delivery conducted for the DoD DCMO in 2011.

2. PROOF OF DELIVERY

The Advance of Standards in BPM/SOA, Semantic, and Analytics Technologies provides Enterprises with a unique opportunity for greater transparency, agility, and collaboration. We wanted to demonstrate that these technologies can be used in a real life Enterprise environment that supports current Department of Defense Standards (BPMN 2.0 Primitives Conformance Class Modeling and Execution, RDF, and OWL) in a true end to end execution environment. The value of this is summarized in the video: http://www.youtube.com/watch?v=OzW3Gc_yA9A [8]

Guided by the DoD Architectural Framework (DoDAF v2) and directives on the Use of End-to-End (E2E) Business Models and Ontology in DoD Business Architectures, and following the open standards set by the World-Wide Web Consortium (W3C) and the Object Management Group (OMG) we piloted a process that executes a BPMN 2.0 Primitives compliant process that reads and updates an RDF database. This RDF Database has an OWL ontology used for standard

SPARQL queries used by a Business Intelligence Tool. Additionally, the BPMN 2.0 Primitives Process Definition has been converted and stored in RDF with a specific BPMN 2.0 Ontology for further analysis.

This Pilot successfully proves that the DCMO vision is truly implementable with standards based, leading edge, and off-the-shelf products today. Additionally, this pilot also proves that bringing together all the standard technologies (BPMN 2.0 Primitives, Semantic Technologies, Business Analytics/Intelligence) is not only possible, but shows that the combination is greater than the individual parts. The vision of a shared, transparent, and actionable business processes across a large enterprise is possible and will dramatically increase the efficiency and effectiveness of operations.

Semantic E2E Architecture

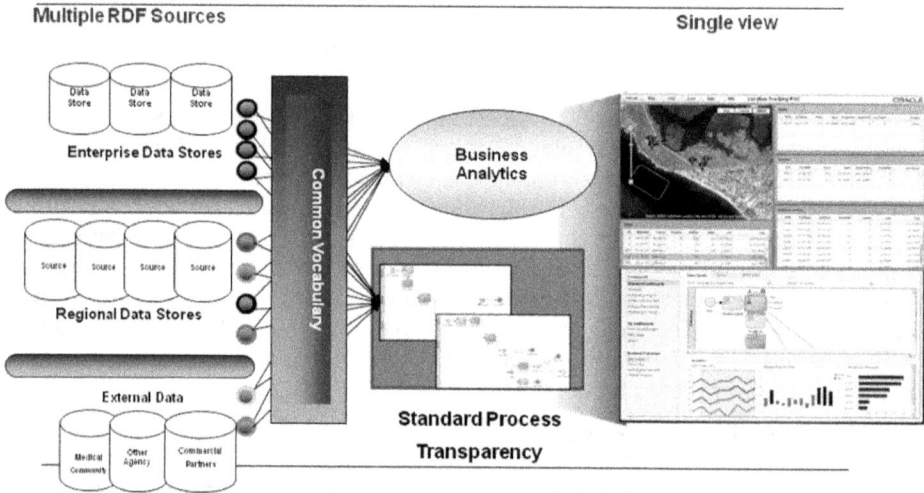

Source Business Mission Area CTO/CA Office of the DCMO

Combining BPMN 2.0 Primitives compliant processes with Semantic Technologies can enhance the Agility of the Enterprise through standardization, collaboration and transparency.

We took a Primitives Compliant BPMN 2.0 process that is fully executable and stored it in the RDF Triplestore based on the BPMN 2.0 Ontology and queried this using SPARQL.

Example Triples from the process showed the relationship between the Exclusive Gateway and the User Task. It also shows the object property for "inLane".

The executing process reads and writes to the RDF Triplestore. This was tested using SPARQL.

The runtime BPMN 2.0 Primitives process instance provides state and audit information while reading and writing to the RDF Triplestore. It also provides metadata that can be used by Business Intelligence Software via a SPARQL Gateway.

3. SUMMARY RESULTS OF E2E PILOT:

We were successful in completing a BPMN 2.0 Primitives compliant executable

Purchasing Review Process

BPMN 2.0 Stored Semantically

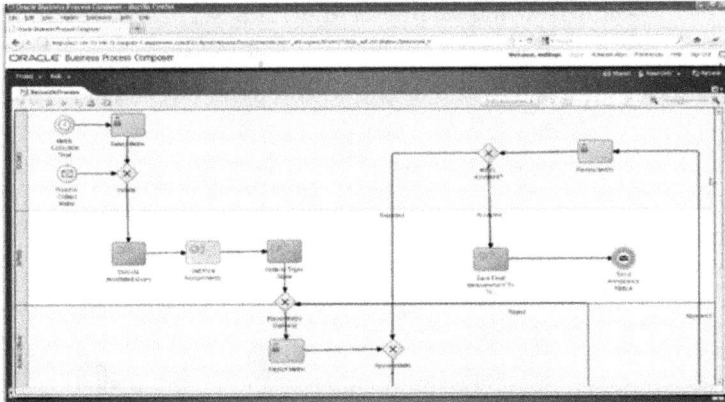

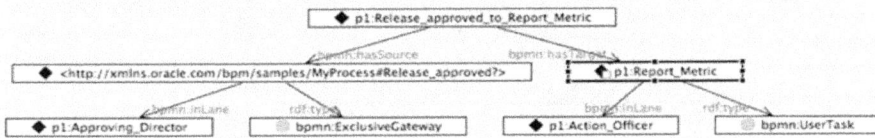

process that reads and writes to an RDF Triplestore. We validate the results using SPARQL queries. Furthermore we integrated Business Intelligence, for Business Analytics, using a SPARQL Gateway. Finally, we stored the BPMN 2.0 Primitives compliant process in RDF Triplestore using the BPMN 2.0 Ontology and tested the results using SPARQL.

SELECT ?usertask ?lane

WHERE

{ ?usertask rdf:type bpmn:UserTask . ?usertask bpmn:inLane ?lane }

Oracle SPARQL Endpoint Query Results

usertask	lane
<http://xmlns.oracle.com/bpm/samples/MyProcess#Approve_Metric_for_Release>	<http://xmlns.oracle.com/bpm/samples/MyProcess#Approving_Director>
<http://xmlns.oracle.com/bpm/samples/MyProcess#Review_Reported_Metric>	<http://xmlns.oracle.com/bpm/samples/MyProcess#DCMO>
<http://xmlns.oracle.com/bpm/samples/MyProcess#Report_Metric>	<http://xmlns.oracle.com/bpm/samples/MyProcess#Action_Officer>

We are continuing research in combining BPMN 2.0 Primitives and Semantic Technology standards to influence the development of standards and potential use in E2E applications.

The US Department of Defense (DoD) is leading the way in the Federal Government for Architecture-driven Business Operations Transformation. A vital tenet for success is ensuring that business process models are based on a standardized representation, thus enabling the analysis and comparison of end to end business processes. This will lead to the re-use of the most efficient and effective process patterns (Style Guide), comprised of elements (Primitives), throughout the DoD Business Mission Area (BMA).

Running BPMN 2.0 Primitives Process with Audit Trail and Business Analytics

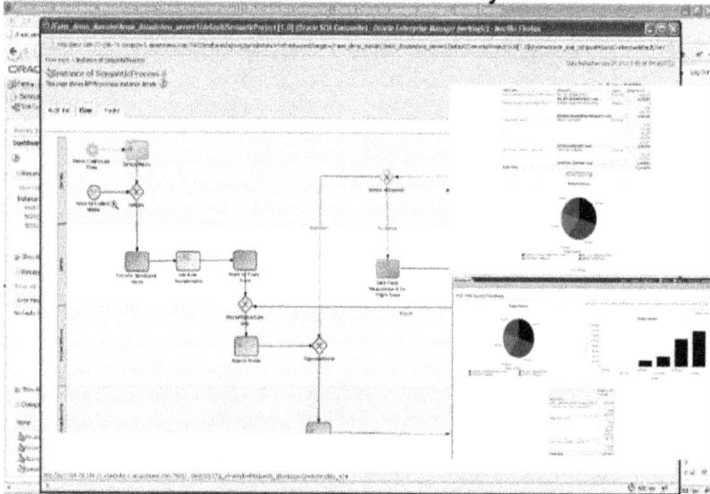

4. ACKNOWLEDGEMENTS

We'd like to thank Dennis Wisnosky and his team at the US DoD DCMO, Lloyd Dugan, Sudeer Bhoja, Xavier Lopez, Bhagat Nainani and Zhe Wu for their contributions to the paper and valuable comments.

5. REFERENCES

[1] Business Process Model and Notation (BPMN) Version 2.0, http://www.omg.org/spec/BPMN/2.0/

[2] Ghidini Ch., Rospocher M., Serafini L.: BPMN Ontology, https://dkm.fbk.eu/index.php/BPMN_Ontology

[3] Oracle Database Semantic Technologies, http://www.oracle.com/technetwork/database/options/semantic-tech/

[4] Service Component Architecture (SCA), http://www.osoa.org

[5] Kolovski V., Wu Z., Eadon G.: Optimizing Enterprise-Scale OWL 2 RL Reasoning in a Relational Database System, ISWC 2010, page 436-452

[6] "Primitives and Style: A Common Vocabulary for BPM across the Enterprise"; Dennis Wisnosky, Chief Architect & CTO ODCMO and Linus Chow Oracle; BPM Excellence in Practice 2010; Published by Future Strategies, 2010

[7] Web Ontology Language (OWL), http://www.w3.org/owl

[8] Intro to Semantic Technology in the DoD Business Mission Area: http://www.youtube.com/watch?v=OzW3Gc_yA9A, UD DoD Office of the DCMO, Dennis Wisnosky, DCMO Chief Architect and CTO, 2011

Section 2

Europe

epa connect GmbH, Germany

Finalist, Europe
Nominated by Adobe Systems Inc., USA

1. Executive Summary / Abstract

epa connect GmbH supports the technology systems for its sister company, impuls Finanzmanagement, a market leader in independent consulting and procurement of private health insurance contracts. Several complex processes are involved with impuls Finanzmanagement's day-to-day business as the company compares offers from several insurance companies, analyzes the coverage and calculates price-performance benefits. The company also guarantees acceptance by the insurance companies from which they receive offers and provides advisors who council customers through the whole process.

About two years ago, sales representatives and IT experts set the goal of expediting and simplifying the company's processes by implementing a BPM system to virtualize services. In response, epa connect developed a solution that allows customers and representatives to meet, complete and sign necessary paperwork and forward contracts to the insurance carriers, all online. All the while, the system safeguards sensitive information and manages legal requirements involved. Benefits gained from the implementation include expanded customer access to services, reduced demands on staff, a new competitive edge in reaching and meeting with new customers and improved quality and timeliness of materials available to customers.

2. Overview

impuls Finanzmanagement decided that in order to gain an edge over its competitors, the company would leverage the reach of the web to enable dynamic, interactive sessions between insurance agents and clients. The goal was to support a fully digital process for signing up customers for new services. The types of information exchanged posed a challenge with regard to handling sensitive customer information and insurance data and meeting legal requirements. It was imperative that the exchange of personal, medical, and lifestyle information be adequately managed. In addition to supporting easy online interactions, the system had to enable staff and customers to electronically complete and sign legally-binding contracts, all while enabling staff to still have engaging and personalized interactions with customers. At the end of the process, customers needed to receive a copy of the insurance contract, while duplicate copies were to be automatically archived.

There are many benefits to the new system implemented by impuls. For example, during online meetings, advisors can use multimedia content such as flyers, videos, and presentations, facilitating collaboration with customers and making customer interactions more powerful. The system enables people to fill out secure electronic insurance documents and sign them with digital signatures. epa connect developed miniature applications called Pods to simplify and organize the screen layout of its customer-facing application. The Pods display audio, video, or presentation fields and the contract forms, providing customers a richer, more engaging experience. Once the terms of the agreement are reached, the contracts can be electronically sent to the customer and a second copy is automatically archived. The backend system helps ensure seamless data exchange. Also, from the archives, all insurance documents can be accessed securely through the impuls customer portal, supporting customer self service.

Overall, the advantages were clear: Expanded customer access to services, reduced demands on staff, significantly lower travel costs, a new competitive edge in reaching and meeting with new customers, higher closing quotas and improved quality and timeliness of materials available to customers.

3. BUSINESS CONTEXT

The German financial services market is extremely competitive—there are many insurance brokers and carriers. As the largest insurance broker in Germany, impuls Finanzmanagement knows the market can only be won by delivering standout customer experiences. However, with all the paperwork and legalities involved, this can seem like a daunting task for financial services providers. For example, impuls Finanzmangement compares offers from up to 40 different insurance companies with more than 20,000 fee variations in order to find their customers the best possible deals. They then analyze the coverage and calculate price-performance benefits. And all of this takes place before the contract and paperwork signing even begins.

Before the BPM system was implemented all processes were manual and had to take place in person. A typical enrollment transaction involved an agent visiting potential customers' homes with a briefcase full of paperwork, or the customer making time for in-person appointments at the agent's office. It wasn't rare for multiple appointments to be necessary to complete a single enrolment, along with mailing and/or faxing back and forth of signed documents. This process was not only time consuming for both agents and customers, it also left considerable room for human error. A number of things could go wrong: The agent may realize that they have the wrong forms or not enough copies; the customer may not have all the necessary information at hand; the completed paperwork may have errors and have to be resent; errors may occur when the agent enters/processes the customers' information into the backend systems, etc. Such delays could prove costly to impuls, especially if it ultimately drove the customer to look for services elsewhere.

4. THE KEY INNOVATIONS

4.2 Business

impuls customers see many benefits from the new BPM system. With the implementation, impuls is able to streamline the complex insurance enrollment process, cutting out the need for travel and filling, mailing and faxing paper documents. The potential for human error is also virtually eliminated by the new system so significant back-and-forth is avoided. And although transactions on the new system take place online, the technology allows for real-time web meetings and dynamic presentations through which agents can guide customers from start to finish—the personal and engaging feeling of in-person meetings isn't lost. Agents can provide the same quality service when and where it's convenient for customers.

Enrollments on the new BPM system happen at least two to three times more efficiently than through in-person transactions and the system boasts a 90 percent closure rate. Faster transactions mean more time to close more sales, which is a win not only for impuls, but also for the insurance companies they work with.

Further, the insurance companies can feel assured that final paperwork and contracts will be delivered quickly and error-free.

4.3 Process

Prior to the implementation of impuls direct, impuls' business was strictly based on outbound sales. Agents would call prospective clients on the telephone and then travel to the home or office of any potential leads to discuss the details of various offers, bringing with them a stack of papers including forms, contracts and informational materials. It wasn't rare for it to take more than one visit before a customer made up their minds about wanting to enroll and about what services they preferred. At this point, agents would walk customers through the contracts and paperwork either by yet another in-person meeting, or over the phone (which could lead to confusion and time-consuming errors). Once the customer's paperwork was completed, the agent had to manually enter it into their backend system for archiving and send it to the adequate insurance company, once again, leaving considerable room for mistakes.

impuls direct reduced a process which previously took several days down to a few hours (at most). After agents learn of a potential lead, they can now arrange for an online meeting where they can provide informative materials, easy to understand visuals and demonstrations digitally. Once a customer is ready to enroll, agents can—in real time—walk customers step-by-step through each digital form and contact which customers can fill out, sign and submit online. Once a customer submits a form, it is automatically processed, archived and delivered to the adequate insurance company by an integrated backend system.

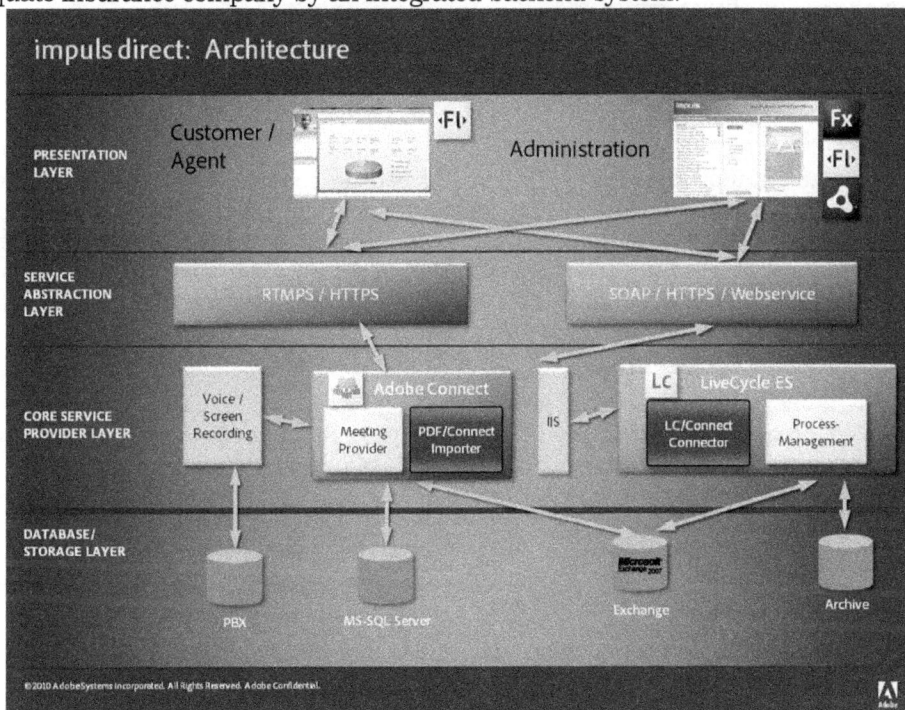

PROCESS SCHEMATIC

4.4 Organization

impuls direct has dramatically changed and enhanced the jobs of impuls sales agents. Most obviously perhaps are the financial benefits. Agents are paid on commission and with a system that's two-to-three times more efficient and has a 90 percent close rate, their earnings increase dramatically. The system has created an ideal situation for agents because they are able to process transactions much faster and more accurately, while still being able to interact directly and build rapport with customers through online meetings. Although an outbound sales force still exists, they are able to focus on customers with special needs that require in person visits. Over the past two years impuls Finanzmanagement has gone from zero to 140 online sales agents located in three call centers throughout Germany.

impuls direct is managed by epa connect GmbH , impuls Finanzmanagement's sister company. Executives at impuls Finanzmanagement founded epa connect GmbH as their full-time IT systems support group. Having the team of IT experts at epa connect GmbH enable agents and staff at impuls Finanzmanagement to focus their time and energy on the business aspect of insurance, without having to worry about technology issues and IT projects.

5. HURDLES OVERCOME

Management:

One major issue that impuls management had to resolve was concerns from employees that with the implementation of impuls direct outbound sales agents might lose commission as online sales increase. In order to address concerns impuls's management implemented a policy which stated that outbound sales agents would keep the full commission resulting from any lead that they passed along to online sales agents.

impuls's management founded sister company, epa connect GmbH, to manage all of impuls Finanzmangement's IT projects. This freed them from having to deal with potential hurdles associated with IT and technology issues.

Business:

The implementation of a new BPM system can be costly. However, impuls saw ROI from impuls direct within 11 months of the implementation. Beyond the high success rate of the new online sales meetings, the online system requires no travel and no paper, greatly reducing the cost of resources associated to sales as well. The new tech-savvy sales force tends to be of a younger demographic as well, which helps impuls reduce employment salary costs.

Organization Adoption

impuls implemented a training program for employees using impuls direct. The complete program takes only ten days to complete. Since the system is automated and very intuitive, it has been easy for impuls's sales force to adopt.

6. BENEFITS

6.1 Cost Savings

With the implementation of impuls direct, impuls Finanzmangement has seen cost savings associated with each of the following categories:

Employee Salaries —The new tech-savvy sales force tends to be of a younger demographic which requires lower base salaries. Since meetings with customers happen online rather than in person, potential concerns about customers feeling uncomfortable working with a younger insurance agent are eliminated.

Travel—Since impuls's online sales agents don't travel, they have no travel costs to expense.

Paper and printing materials—impuls direct eliminates the need for paper-based materials and forms and dramatically reduces printing and mailing needs.

6.2 Time Reductions

With a no need for travel, faxing, mailing, significantly reduced error margins and a fully automated digital system, impuls direct has converted a sales process that previously took several days to one that takes a few hours at most.

6.3 Increased Revenues

impuls direct has helped drive revenues at impuls Finanzmangement through its efficiency and effectiveness. The cost and time saving discussed above combined with its easy adoptability and 90 percent closure rate lead the company to see ROI within 11 months of the implementation.

7. BEST PRACTICES, LEARNING POINTS AND PITFALLS

Best Practices and Learning Points

- ✓ Involve all company stake holders in communications and trainings associated with the new implementation
- ✓ Establish a committed IT support team that is separate from business and sales staff
- ✓ Maintain a close relationship with vendor for technical support
- ✓ When transferring a sales process that was previously face-to-face to an online system, the system should have capabilities that can deliver a stellar customer experience. Clients should feel engaged and the quality of service should not be compromised.

7.2 Pitfalls

- ✗ Do not leave any stake holders out of the loop in terms of the new implementation. Be particularly cautious that employees that will continue to operate within the original business model have a thorough understanding of the new system and what it implies, even if they will not operate the system directly.
- ✗ When possible, avoid overlap between business staff and operations and IT.
- ✗ For online sales, video conferencing is not always an appropriate action. Customers should be focused on the product and the agents' presentations, not on agents' appearances.

8. COMPETITIVE ADVANTAGES

Through its implementation of impuls direct, impuls Finanzmangement took the old tried-and-true insurance sales tactic of working closely with and engaging the customer, and made it much more efficient, effective, flexible and less prone to error. The 140 new online sales agents and three new call centers that impuls has opened since the implementation certainly help maintain the company's position as the leading and largest insurance broker in Germany.

To maintain their competitive edge impuls finanzmangement is currently expanding impuls direct's capabilities to integrate with new electronic identity cards that will be issued to German citizens in 2011.

9. TECHNOLOGY

In an effort to find the right technology to automate the complex and document intensive insurance enrollment process, epa connect surveyed several enterprise technology vendors and discovered Adobe offered technology that fit their needs from end-to-end.

During online meetings using Adobe Connect, agents can use multimedia content such as flyers, videos, and presentations—similar to what mobile sales teams use, except it can now be handled virtually. epa connect developed miniature applications called Pods to simplify and organize the screen layout of its customer facing application. The Pods display audio, video, or presentation fields and the contract forms. To allow for the exchange of personal, medical, and lifestyle information from customers, epa connect GmbH established legal and technical requirements, and created a plug-in for Adobe Connect to collect data securely over the Internet. The system lets customers fill out insurance contracts electronically, sign them digitally, submit them to impuls who can then forward contracts to the insurance carrier. Upon submission, the customer receives a copy of the insurance contract and a second copy is automatically archived.

Interactions between the Adobe Connect Pro user application and Adobe Live-Cycle Enterprise Suite (ES) on the back end help ensure seamless data exchange. Adobe LiveCycle ES modules are used to manage updates to contract forms received from more than 40 insurance providers on a regular basis. impuls receives most of the contract forms in Portable Document Format (PDF) and developed a converter to read the PDF forms and publish them online in individualized Adobe Connect Pro securely hosted web "meeting rooms." Here, people can fill out the contracts. After completion, the contracts in PDF are submitted to a LiveCycle workflow process that handles digital signatures input and submission to a revision-safe archival solution managed by EASY software AG.

All insurance documents can be accessed securely through the impuls customer portal. The IT experts managed to combine Adobe Connect Pro, LiveCycle ES, and EASY ARCHIVE software into a seamless workflow.

10. THE TECHNOLOGY AND SERVICE PROVIDERS

Adobe Systems Inc., www.adobe.com

Instituto de Crédito Oficial (ICO), Spain

Gold Award: Europe
Nominated by Bizagi, United Kingdom

1. EXECUTIVE SUMMARY / ABSTRACT

Due to the severe crisis that the global financial sector recently faced, the small and medium sized companies (SMBs) in Spain experienced limited access to their normal lines of credit. This represented a serious threat to the sector that generates the most employment in that country. As a response to this challenge, the Spanish government decided to provide, through the Instituto de Crédito Oficial (ICO) the **Financial Facilitator**, an analytical and consulting tool that facilitates access to the small and medium sized companies and the self-employed, to sources of finance enabling them to undertake their corporate and professional projects.

On November 2009, ICO initiated a project for the creation of a tool to model and automate their credit application management process, for the small and medium sized companies and self-employed group. The said process covers from receipt of the original credit application until it is presented to the financial entities, including intermediate credit analysis and pre-approval activities.

2. OVERVIEW

One of the most devastating effects of the recent global financial crisis was the freezing of corporate credit. As a response to face and overcome this challenge, the Spanish government decided to provide, through the Instituto de Crédito Oficial (ICO) the "Financial Facilitator", a new and innovative analytical and consulting tool which facilitates access to the small and medium sized businesses (SMBs) and the self-employed, to sources of finance to enable them to undertake their corporate and professional projects. Each day lost could lead to the bankruptcy of another small or medium sized business, and so it was imperative that the proposed solution was implemented as soon as possible.

The solution included the integration and management of several processes and systems involving three main actors, the SMBs wanting to apply for credit, the ICO, and the external Spanish banks and financial entities. The ICO does not have offices with direct service to the public, meaning that their line of attention had to be via the internet. Therefore, the SMB and the self-employed needed to upload their applications through the network. Once the application is registered, it would enter a formal but thorough corporate credit evaluation and pre-approval process interacting with risk analysis systems and credit analysts. If the application is pre-approved, the ICO then presents it to the major Spanish financial entities (Santander, BBVA, Banesto, among others) by giving them access to the system. The financial entities would then continue with the internal processing of the pre-approved application, counting with the additional support of the Spanish government. The complete end to end process also needed to be integrated through SOA to other legacy systems and supported by a Call Center for customer service.

The technological infrastructure for this process had to be implemented very quickly (less than 7 weeks), and it had to be robust, secure and modern, offering the necessary flexibility to enable easy modification and expansion in the future. These results could only be delivered in the timescale and with the quality expected, with a sound knowledge of the financial sector and with a powerful platform for process management.

In November 2009, a project was initiated for the creation of a tool for the modeling and automation of ICO's management process for credit applications from the SMB and self-employed group. The said process covered from receipt of the original credit application via internet until it was presented to the financial entities, including all the middle back office processes such as the credit evaluation, analysis of the operation and interaction with the call center and legacy applications.

On December 2009 and in record implementation time, the system was launched for general use by the corporate sector to which it was aimed. Since that date, a widespread publicity campaign to promote the "Financial Facilitator" has been under way. In its first days, the "Financial Facilitator" processed hundreds of applications, thus satisfying its initial objective.

3. BUSINESS CONTEXT

The Financial Facilitator was a radically new and innovative idea, resulting from a circumstantial necessity to help a whole nation to survive the financial crisis. The freeze in corporate credit affected, disproportionately, the small and medium sized companies as their reduced capital reserves are dependent on credit in order to maintain their operational viability. With some sectors that generate large volumes of employment affected by the recession, like that of the construction industry, Spain could not afford to let down its bastion of economic resistance, i.e. the small and medium sized industries.

As a result, the credit application process as implemented in the Financial Facilitator had to be conceived from beginning to end. However, its quick implementation time and positive usage response brought several benefits to ICO and to the Spanish government in general.

4. THE KEY INNOVATIONS

4.2 Business

Not only the new concept of the "Financial Facilitator", but the integration and automation of several processes and activities, made the whole system manageable and made it easier for the Spanish government to expand, control and support the lines of credit, helping to reactivate the financial sector in that country.

Key benefits and innovations of the Financial Facilitator include faster and easier credit application process (anywhere, anytime from the internet), automation of credit analysis and evaluation processes, wider access to lines of credit and support from the Spanish government. These all helped to increase the number of SMBs and self-employed applying for credit.

The tool also made it possible to manage a pre-approval process, enabling the financial entities to receive preapproved applications that carried the additional support of the Spanish government. ICO assumed the responsibility of part of the interest that the debtor would normally pay; also, part of the capital of the loan was guaranteed by the ICO, should the debtor get behind in the payments. In this way the government was assuming part of the inherent risk involved in the system. This resulted in an increase in the chance of applicants actually getting a final credit approval because of the reduced risk presented to the financial entities.

The ICO also improved its national recognition, customer service and productivity in a significant way by being able to implement a complex solution in record time, reacting with agility to face the financial crisis. Also, as soon as the system was launched, the ICO was able to receive and process hundreds of credit applications at the same time, helping to unblock the flow of credit in the country and looking forward to stabilize the macroeconomic model.

4.3 Process

Before the Financial Facilitator there wasn´t really a specialized system put in place for credit requests backed by the Spanish government. Credit requests had to be done in the traditional way, directly at the bank or financial institution office and there was less visibility and general control over the different lines of credit in the country for SMBs and self-employed. Also, the credit request process was not as easy and straightforward for requestors.

The Financial Facilitator included the integration of internal and external applications, systems and people to, as its name says, facilitate the request and approval process for financial credit to both applicants and authorizing entities. This case presented a complex challenge, such as the creation and integration of an internet application (Web portal) for credit requests, back office processes for credit analysis and evaluation, extranet applications for the presentation of pre-approved applications to major financial entities, call center systems across the whole end to end process and other legacy systems.

The following diagram shows a general scheme of the process:

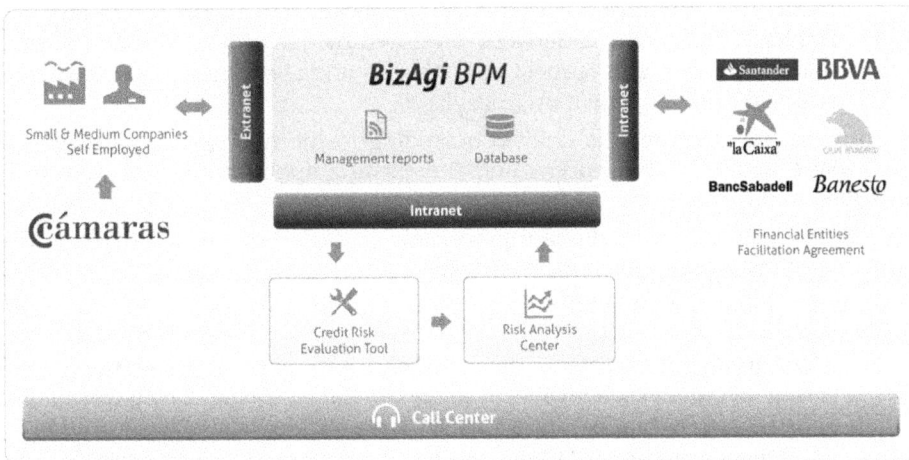

The system allows and tracks the following activities:
- Online introduction of financial data by requestors (SMB or self-employed)
- Annotations about the state of risk of the operation
- Attaching required documentation
- Annotations about the negotiation status with the financial institutions
- Verification of the payment of the credit to the client
- Security of the stored data, using secure protocols for data transfer

The Web Portal supports the following operations and functionalities.

Operations (via Bizagi SOA):
- Creation/Update of user accounts for clients
- Creation of new operations
- View all existing operations
- Advance on existing operations

Functionalities (Bizagi embedded)
- Information/data entry

On the other hand, analysts or financial agents connect to the system via internet or intranet, depending on their geographical location and infrastructure. They perform the following activities:
- Study and analysis of the provided documentation
- Risk evaluation using external applications
- Establish contact with the banks and financial entities and present the cases
- Attach guarantees originated by the guarantors

The Financial Facilitator had to be integrated with the following applications and legacy systems:
- Experian: Contains information about fulfillment or breach of money obligations.
- CIRBE (Central de Información de Riesgos del Banco de España): This is a confidential database containing the risks that credit entities have with their clients. It contains information like the total pending balance of a credit or credits on their name.
- Rating (Scoring): It performs a client evaluation and gives a punctuation mark. This application was created specifically for this project by PwC.
- Banks: A group of web Services developed by this project to send information about the credit request to the banks and allow them to perform queries to the BPM application (Bizagi).

The process architecture was defined according to the role and requirements of the involved actors in the process and the existing applications that were to be integrated to the system.

The Financial Facilitator could be reproduced or adapted as needed by other governments or financial institutions worldwide.

Recently the Financial Facilitator project has expanded to cover 3 lines of credit as follows:
- ICO-Advising: ICO receives the credit request and performs all the processing and analysis activities to make the final decision. The payment is done by private banks that ICO has previously made agreements with.
- ICO-Direct: same as ICO-Advising but the final credit payment is done by ICO itself.
- ICO-SGR: like ICO-Direct but the guarantor is a SGR (Sociedad de Garantía Recíproca)

4.4 Organization

The Financial Facilitator was quickly adopted by all stakeholders and actors, and the credit request process for SMBs and self-employed was able to run smoothly in a very short period of time after implementation.

The Financial Facilitator also made the job of credit analysts easier by being able to centralize all requests and application information into one system and visualize the status of all pending requests in a more efficient manner. Tracking and case management helped ICO and its employees to be more productive and to improve their operational efficiency. Through reports and indicators, they were also able to show real time results and conversion metrics.

5. HURDLES OVERCOME

The major challenges of this project were more technical rather than business related because of the short period of time for implementation. However, although the system was conceived from new and the necessity of implementation was imminent, ICO and the other external actors were very keen to help to put it in place and launch it to production as quickly as possible.

6. BENEFITS

6.1 Cost Savings

Cost savings are not really measurable in this project because the tool did not exist before. The only cost comparison that can be done is towards the credit request processes made in the traditional way. Following this, we can say that the costs associated to the credit request process managed through the Financial Facilitator are significantly less if compared to a non-web and non-automated credit request application process. There is much less paperwork involved and no human resources needed to receive the applications (they are all received online). Centralized management of incoming requests also resulted in a better and more optimum use of the resources.

6.2 Time Reductions

The system helped to reduce time in the submittal of credit request applications (online) and reduced the cycle times (from application to credit pre-approval). Banks and financial entities were able to get a greater amount of pre-approved credit requests in a reduced period of time, shortening as well the completion of their own final approval process.

6.3 Increased Revenues

ICO is a public entity that works for the development and improvement of national wealth. The activities supported by ICO cannot be measured in terms of revenue as with any other company or enterprise. However, we can mention the following facts which could help to determine the size of the project and that of the transactions managed by the Financial Facilitator.

- More than 65000 credit requests received since the first launch to production up to now (9 months)
- The system has been able to received more than 5000 credit requests in 1 day

6.4 Productivity Improvements

As previously mentioned, having all credit requests centralized in a single system made it easier for credit analysts at ICO to manage, track and control all the incoming requests. They were also able to review and evaluate the applicant´s information and documentation in a more organized manner and were able to make decisions on pre-approved credits much faster, increasing the level of operational efficiency and productivity. Banks and financial entities also experienced productivity improvements as they received more and quicker pre-approved credits backed by the Spanish government, which helped them to perform their final credit approval in a shorter period of time.

7. BEST PRACTICES, LEARNING POINTS AND PITFALLS

7.1 Best Practices and Learning Points

✓ Pay special attention to customer needs and requirements
✓ Work together with all stakeholders to design the best solution possible
✓ Spend enough time in planning and solution design/architecture to reduce the chance of errors or issues in the implementation process and allow assigning the right and precise amount of resources to the project
✓ Use your experience in other similar or industry-related projects to help to improve the trust that the customer puts in you
✓ Consider the size, complexity, and other key characteristics of your project to build and use the right project management activities and skills

7.2 Pitfalls

✗ Avoid accelerating project activities too much (specially planning and design) due to customer pressure for a fast implementation
✗ Avoid solving problems on the go, try to previously identify possible issues and scenarios and be attentive for warning signs

8. COMPETITIVE ADVANTAGES

The competitive advantage gained by ICO with the implementation of the Financial Facilitator was that it was perceived as the only credit and financial entity that was able to react with agility to solve the financial crisis in Spain. Although the recession is said to become to an end, this system still holds an important national recognition as an effective tool to help to maintain the economic flow in this country. The Financial Facilitator is still promoted nationwide and will probably continue to be an innovative and worthy solution for a long time.

Other advantages include:

- Creation of new lines of credit for SMBs and the self-employed
- Internet as main channel
- Quick implementation

9. TECHNOLOGY

ICO selected Bizagi and Price Waterhouse Coopers (PwC) for the implementation of the Financial Facilitator.

ICO used the three main modules of Bizagi BPM Suite to manage the complete process life cycle: The Bizagi Process Modeler (to diagram/model all the processes and generate documentation), The Bizagi Studio (to transform processes designed in the Bizagi Modeler into applications without the need of programming) and The Bizagi BPM Server (to execute and control the business processes automated with Bizagi Studio). This confirms that Bizagi is an integrated and complete BPM solution, robust enough to integrate and automate internet processes, back office processes, extranet processes, call center systems and other legacy applications through SOA.

As previously described, this case presented a complex technical challenge, such as the creation and integration of several applications. In addition, what could also be considered a challenge was the fact that the solution needed to be implemented and delivered in record time (less than 7 weeks).

The solution offered was able to overcome these challenges with the following activities and functionalities:

- Creation of a web portal with Bizagi embedded to enable online credit application requests
- Internet access with security and authentication
- Design and implementation of the process workflow
- Automation of processes with Bizagi BPM Suite
- Virtual server farm
- Development of an application with load balancing using Windows Server Enterprise Edition
- Solution for database failover using a SQL Server Cluster Enterprise Edition
- SOA integration with four legacy systems (1 - Blacklist and applicant information at the Spanish Central Bank, 2 - Credit Scoring, 3 - Credit Reporting (Experian) and 4 - Call center)

In a more technical perspective, the solution consisted of 2 web servers (for the web portal), 1 application server (Bizagi) and 1 server for Bizagi´s database in cluster, each server with 4 CPUs. The system featured high availability, high reliability, load balancing clusters and failover cluster.

Full implementation up to system launch was done in seven weeks with the following phases:

1. Development of the Financial Facilitator tool and negotiation with the various agents involved in the process

2. Pilot Test (Initial launch of the tool and integration with financial entities)

3. Implementation and Deployment (Production environment)

Consultants from Bizagi and PWC were able to work together and in parallel to be able to deliver the expected quality and level of functionality of the solution. Although time was short, the solution was planned and studied in depth together with the involved parties in order to select the most efficient and optimized solutions to overcome every single challenge. The satisfactory result is supported by the fact that the project was launched on time and within the first days of operation the ICO was able to process hundreds of applications without any inconvenient or issue.

10. THE TECHNOLOGY AND SERVICE PROVIDERS

ICO selected Bizagi BPM Suite (http://www.bizagi.com) and Price Waterhouse Coopers (http://www.pwc.com) for the implementation of the Financial Facilitator. PWC is a company that combines a vast knowledge in the credit approval processes with extensive experience in the implementation of Bizagi BPM. Bizagi is a leading BPM solution capable of empowering businesses of all types and industries around the world, providing them with unprecedented adaptability to changing market conditions through optimal business process automation and continuous improvement solutions.

The functionalities and ease of use of Bizagi BPM Suite, together with the expertise of Price Waterhouse Coopers, was the perfect combination to make the system work.

LSC Group, Babcock & Ministry of Defence, UK

Silver Award: Europe
Nominated by TIBCO Software, USA

1. EXECUTIVE SUMMARY / ABSTRACT

During 1999, the UK Ministry of Defence (MoD) Submarine Support Integrated Project Team (SubIPT) was faced with the issue of the cost of submarine ownership and in partnership with Babcock (then DML) set out to realize significant programme savings during HMS Vanguard's 1st Long Overhaul Period Refuel (LOP(R)). One of several steps in achieving this objective was to establish a joint initiative between Babcock, SubIPT (MoD) and its chosen technology partner, LSC Group, to transform the business using workflow technology. To support this approach a Collaborative Working Environment (CWE) was developed by LSC Group to improve collaboration and communication between all stakeholders involved in the submarine refit across the UK. To transform the business the latest workflow technology was adopted to replace paper-based business processes and to enable much greater process integration with existing MoD and industry systems, thereby enabling efficiency and cost reduction.

Driven by a suite of bespoke and commercial off the shelf (COTS) applications, including a custom-built business process automation (workflow) solution from TIBCO, the CWE has delivered a trusted secure web-based workspace, enabling members from disparate organizations to work together and share information within a single secure environment. Its prime users consist of all submarine MoD departments and the major Tier 1 industry partners in Naval Defence, including Babcock, Rolls Royce and BAE Systems. TIBCO's workflow component allows automation of business processes, integration with existing applications across MoD and industry boundaries, to replace inefficient and sometimes out of date paper-based processes. The newly automated business processes have resulted in time and cost savings, which have directly contributed to the MoD and Babcock achieving its goal to reduce the cost of submarine ownership, de-risk the LOP(R) programme and to achieve positive share line contract performance.

2. OVERVIEW

Initiated in 1999, the purpose of the CWE has been to improve collaboration and communication between all stakeholders – both MoD and industry – in the submarine refit programme in order to de-risk the LOP(R) programme, and to ensure the submarines availability whilst driving down refit costs. The workflow solution component of the CWE has fully automated business processes that were previously done manually whilst integrating with existing MoD and industry systems to drive out non value added tasks improving efficiency, quality and safety.

Benefits of the workflow solution include:
- The ability to capture and automate business processes and much greater flexibility and lower costs to enable continuous improvement
- Significant reduction of non value added tasks, administrative effort and reduction of posts
- Greater governance over the business process and improved quality and safety.

- Closer MoD and industry relationships as a result of the transformation project and the stakeholder workshop sessions held throughout the project so far
- The ability to expand incrementally the workflow technology to transform twelve business process applications. (SCIs, surveys, concessions, DRS, IPCs, change requests, A&As, engineering helpdesk, VOs, minor trials, worked out concessions, DA review concessions)
- Greater visibility of the end-to-end process with step-by-step measurement, enabling identification and resolution of bottlenecks.
- Removal of rework costs of re-raising lost items (CWE automated processes replaced original paper based processes)
- Creation of a Submarine Enterprise Information and Knowledge repository
- Removal of paper processes and storage facilities that need to be maintained

The CWE and workflow solution also have great potential to be scaled to include other areas of the business. The initial deployment was 80 CWE seats and is now approaching 3500 users as other Maritime and Equipment programmes are added.

The main challenges relating to the workflow element of the CWE were around analysis and governance.

Analysis

The initial project definition study identified enterprise business process constraints and proposed improvements that would return quick wins in reducing cost, improving quality and giving greater efficiency. Issues to overcome included stakeholders with their own processes, systems and applications, which needed to be integrated at different stages of the business process lifecycle. Cultural differences and resistance to change had to be delicately addressed and facilitated to develop coherent processes and more efficient and effective communication.

Governance

In order to ensure compliance with the nuclear safety case and the business process rules, the workflow technology had to provide a full audit trail that could prove which Suitably Qualified and Experienced Personnel (SQEP) resources had undertaken the decisions throughout the business process and had a historical log of the details. Introduction of a governance structure to enable endorsement and prioritisation of resources was fundamental in our ability to rapidly transform the business and realise business benefits.

3. BUSINESS CONTEXT

During 1999 both MoD and industry relied heavily on conventional paper-based systems at a time when team sizes could not be maintained and where the volume of paper for HMS Vanguard's LOP(R) could not be contained within the programme. These issues were a strong motivation to change and due to the additional demands of driving down the cost of submarine ownership, this provided an ideal climate for change.

The driving motivation of the CWE was its people and their ability to harness the power of workflow technology to enable inefficiencies and risk to be reduced and managed and to facilitate a reduction in costs. Workflow technology provided a new innovative tool to address some of the following long standing issues:

- How to manage an increasing workload with decreasing resources

- How to improve the decision making turnaround timescales without the loss of quality whilst de-risking the LOP(R) programme
- Failure to ensure adherence to the business process
- The inefficiencies of managing paper and the long term storage costs
- How to improve quality and safety

4. THE KEY INNOVATIONS

4.2 Business

There are many different stakeholders involved in a submarine refit, from large engineering companies through to smaller more specialist partners. As a result of the ongoing transformation we have established much closer enterprise working relationships and a greater spirit of openness and sharing.

The processes involved in the submarine refit programme are now automated and fully integrated with MoD and industry systems. This has removed significant non value added time and has embedded knowledge into the workflow systems so that key stakeholders can focus their attention on decision making. Stakeholders are now simply required to complete their task when it arrives in their actions list and the system will decide what happens next i.e. who/which process is next in line.

The CWE means all stakeholders have access to exactly the same information and has enabled a culture of collaboration and sharing to be realized. Introduction of workflow and electronic approvals was a first for the submarine enterprise and has ensured a much greater level of control and safety.

SubIPT, Babcock and LSC Group have worked in partnership to continuously improve the CWE to meet evolving user requirements, using our innovative technical and domain experts. Workflow has enabled the submarine enterprise to manage a much higher level of volume with much smaller teams which would not have been achievable under the paper-based processes.

Turnaround timescales were important to the submarine enterprise and workflow has delivered between 70 and 80 percent improvement in turnaround timescales. This has significantly de-risked the LOP(R) programme.

4.3 Process

Processes for incorporation into the CWE are identified by the user community on a priority basis. As has been described elsewhere, the process begins with a series of workshops to identify the optimum process flow to be developed, and the identification of existing applications which need to form part of the process as either a feeder or receiver (or both) of data.

Developed processes can vary considerably in their complexity and volume. Key steps within the processes vary from 2 to 24 with many of these steps being important, often safety-critical, approval steps.

The schematic below provides a simplified view of one of the 21 processes now in use within the CWE. It reflects the action of carrying out a 'Survey' of a submarine which is an activity used to assess the state of the vessel before deciding on what work needs carrying out. As can be seen, the survey process is instigated by data feeds from four other applications used by various stakeholders in the overall management and maintenance of the submarine, follows a process of data capture, assessment and various approvals, and finishes by updating appropriate source applications with the results and approvals.

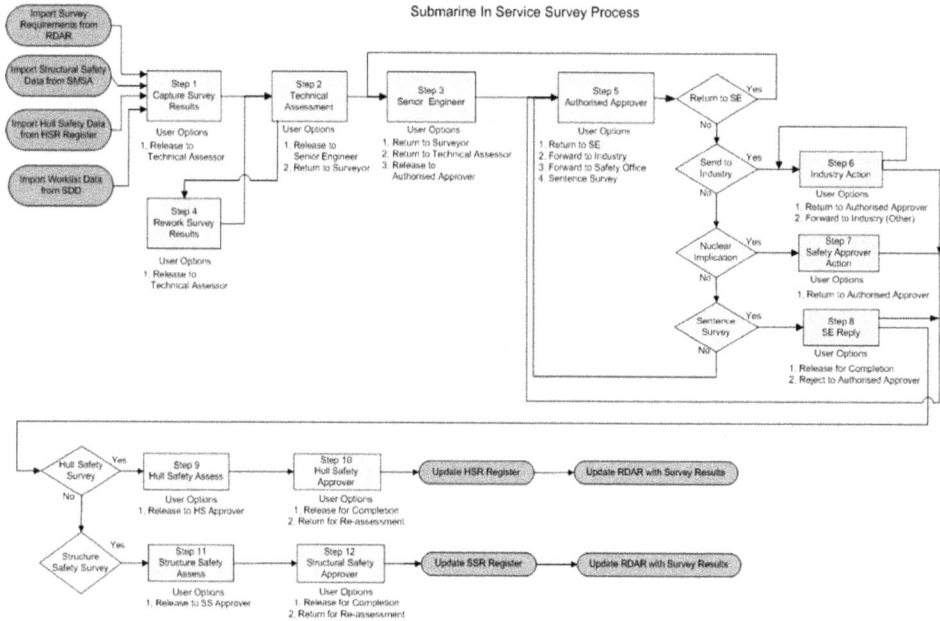

Submarine In Service Survey Process

Import Survey Requirements from RDAR

Import Structural Safety Data from SMSA

Import Hull Safety Data from HSR Register

Import Worklist Data from SDD

Step 1 Capture Survey Results
User Options
1. Release to Technical Assessor

Step 2 Technical Assessment
User Options
1. Release to Senior Engineer
2. Return to Surveyor

Step 3 Senior Engineer
User Options
1. Return to Surveyor
2. Return to Technical Assessor
3. Release to Authorised Approver

Step 5 Authorised Approver
User Options
1. Return to SE
2. Forward to Industry
3. Forward to Safety Office
4. Sentence Survey

Step 4 Rework Survey Results
User Options
1. Release to Technical Assessor

Return to SE — Yes / No

Send to Industry — Yes / No

Step 6 Industry Action
User Options
1. Return to Authorised Approver
2. Forward to Industry (Other)

Nuclear Safety Implication — Yes / No

Step 7 Safety Approver Action
User Options
1. Return to Authorised Approver

Sentence Survey — Yes / No

Step 8 SE Reply
User Options
1. Release for Completion
2. Reject to Authorised Approver

Hull Safety Survey — Yes / No

Step 9 Hull Safety Assess
User Options
1. Release to HS Approver

Step 10 Hull Safety Approver
User Options
1. Release for Completion
2. Return for Re-assessment

Update HSR Register

Update RDAR with Survey Results

Structure Safety Survey — Yes / No

Step 11 Structure Safety Assess
User Options
1. Release to SS Approver

Step 12 Structural Safety Approver
User Options
1. Release for Completion
2. Return for Re-assessment

Update SSR Register

Update RDAR with Survey Results

Schematic

While a specific refit or maintenance period on a submarine is usually the catalyst for the development of a process, over time this process is then often adapted for use on other types of submarine, or for different types of maintenance. While similar in activity, many factors mean that these process instances are different, and one of the benefits of having developed the process within the iProcess Suite is that new variances of the process can be delivered with minimal effort while maximizing reuse of the work already carried out.

4.4 Organization

The move from a paper-based system to automated workflow has had a positive impact on both MoD and industry staff. They are no longer burdened with inefficient paper processes, as workflow has enabled them to manage more with less resources, whilst providing improved quality and safety.

The lessons learned and knowledge and experience gained in the CWE have enabled the wider deployment of variants of the CWE across the defence sector, resulting in a greater return on investment.

The CWE is now widely used by a growing number of UK Defence Sector communities (currently approaching 3,500 users among the maritime user-base including MoD project teams, naval bases, platforms and industrial contractors) and more recently abroad by the Babcock led Canadian Submarine Management Group (CSMG). Driven by business needs, the CWE is continually improving its functionality and capability, and is now being applied to new design and build programmes, such as the Successor Trident replacement programme.

5. HURDLES OVERCOME

Management

Issues to overcome included stakeholders with their own processes, systems and applications, which needed to be integrated at different stages of the business process lifecycle. Cultural differences and resistance to change had to be delicately addressed and facilitated to develop coherent processes and more efficient and effective communication.

Introduction of a governance structure to enable endorsement and prioritisation of resources was fundamental in our ability to rapidly transform the business and realise business benefits.

We were very keen that the new workflow processes be seen as business driven and not as an IT project. This enabled a much greater level of buy in from the stakeholders as they took ownership and pride in what was produced.

Stakeholder analysis was key in order to identify key individuals who may either be blockers or supporters of business change. By targeting these individuals we were able to achieve much greater 'buy in' of the final solution and embed change management thinking as part of normal business.

Organization Adoption

Education was an important factor in the acceptance of the automated workflow solution by staff, especially those at a lower level. A major flaw of the previous paper-based system allowed users to ignore parts of a particular process that may not have suited them but had an important purpose i.e. safety or financial implication. The workflow solution applies governance and rules that prevent this from happening. Education was also key to helping users understand the importance of these processes and why they are in place, rather than just training in the software application.

6. BENEFITS

The Collaborative Working Environment (CWE) has been operating across the Submarine Support Environment (SSE) for over 10 years. A study of the impact of the CWE on the timeliness and quality of the submarine refits over a five-year period identified a range of benefits that can be directly attributed to the deployment of the CWE. Where a realistic and relevant baseline of current activity costs was available, it was possible to quantify the associated benefit after CWE implementation; however, where such baselines could not be established, the acknowledged but unquantifiable benefits were not claimed. Whilst the CWE benefits, both quantitative and qualitative, were specifically identified across a five-year period, it is widely recognised that they are enduring and have been increasingly adopted by other maritime engineering programmes, contributing towards an ongoing cheaper and more efficient maritime refit programme.

6.1 Cost Savings

Based on the findings of Babcock's Marine Division the SSE identified quantitative benefits amounting to £7.8M over a 5 year period, accruing from two main areas:

- Cash savings of approximately **£5M** resulting from:
- An up-front reduction in contract costs to the MoD for two refits based on the confidence that the refits would be delivered in a more efficient and effective manner. This totalled **£2.1M**.
- A reduction in administrative and no-longer relevant process activities resulting from the introduction of automated business processes. These savings amounted to **£2.4M**.
- Efficiency savings associated with the improved method of delivery of one specific business process – reporting and approval of engineering concessions. This realised over **£400K** of direct savings to the customer over the five-year period.

- Opportunity cost savings of £2.8M achieved through the diversion of staff from non-value adding activities incorporated into automated business processes. (This included the time and material costs associated with the mundane task of photocopying and handling of thousands of hard copy documents).
- Another class of submarine, namely the Astute, avoided the cost of developing its own through life support solution by adopting the submarine enterprise approach, saving many millions on a new IT solution.
- The CWE and workflow continues to provide a 2:1 return on investment.

6.2 Time Reductions

Overall process times have been significantly reduced with an 80 percent improvement in turnaround timescales (See graph below – the graph shows the gradual improvement in turnaround times for a key process automated as part of the Vanguard Submarine refit).

- Workflow has allowed twelve key business processes to be quickly re-engineered across the MoD/industry boundary without the need to customise expensive IT systems
- The CWE has allowed quick identification of process bottlenecks that would impact platform delivery.
- Reduction of overall submarine refit time

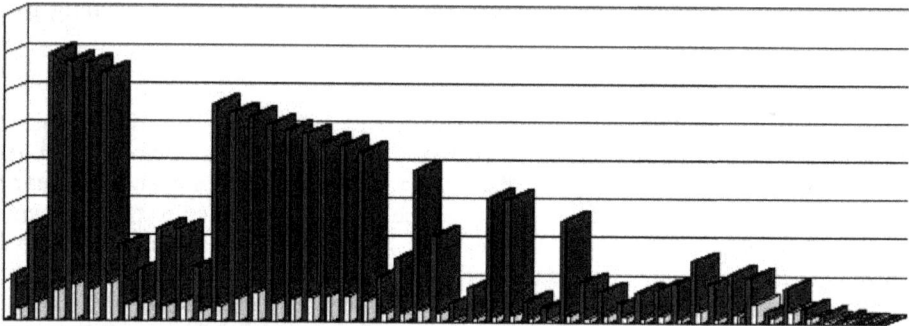

6.3 Productivity Improvements

The major qualitative benefit to emerge is the forging of a true enterprise culture across the major stakeholders engaged in the refit of submarines. The adoption of business process automation to capture end-to-end processes that span the traditional customer/supplier contractual boundaries helped to establish enterprise-wide working relationships. Working as key players in a single process brought the stakeholders together to discuss problems and to work together to reach mutually acceptable solutions that addressed each other's needs. Other qualitative benefits that emerged as a result of this collaborative culture were:

Adoption of an optimised and standardised approach to engineering processes across Devonport Dockyard, with the intention of rolling these out to Faslane Dockyard.

- The capture, automation and mandating of agreed processes that incorporate local business rules, authorisations and delegated powers.
- Faster process turnaround timescales with fully metricated and auditable process performance, enabling the identification and correction of process bottlenecks.
- Provided access to new sources of information and exploitation of legacy databases and information sources
- Reduced information search costs

- Improved information and knowledge management

Two processes in the refit programme that significantly improved were the 'specification change enquiry' (SCI) and 'concessions approval'. For SCI, the cycle time was reduced from 125 days to 28 days, process steps and cost were reduced, with improved reporting and safety. The cycle time for concessions approval was reduced from 186 days to 21 on average. Process steps and cost were reduced and decision making and material state management improved.

7. BEST PRACTICES, LEARNING POINTS AND PITFALLS

7.1 Best Practices and Learning Points

✓ *IT training was not enough. LSC Group used Babcock and MoD business experts to win 'hearts & minds' by providing process training and on the ground support*

✓ *Acknowledging the real-life process helped users to understand the importance of the businesses processes and why they are in place*

✓ *Lots of minor tweaks to the CWE provided real benefit and increased buy in/credibility. For this, a fund for continuous improvement is required as well as a business-led board to initiate and support change*

✓ *A 90 day programme for incremental changes allowed the business culture to improve and become more proactive*

✓ *Taking each improvement opportunity to progressively build an integrated solution has led to a stronger CWE*

8. COMPETITIVE ADVANTAGES

Our approach to continuous involvement in the CWE in order to continually improve, change and enhance the solution is a major USP and a part of its immediate and long-term strategy to sustain competitive advantage. The CWE's focus on the workflow component and its ability to bring disparate stakeholders together are other key competitive advantages. It also has the ability to reengineer processes, meaning that once stakeholders have decided on what is the correct process, it can be reengineered or 'leaned' to improve it further and bring further business benefits i.e. further cost and time savings. Hosting of the CWE within the MoD environment at restricted and secret level means that both MoD and Industry can share the tool. Similar competitive solutions to the CWE haven't addressed the workflow/business process management element. The CWE addresses complex engineering processes, which is a distinct USP in the selling environment.

9. TECHNOLOGY

TIBCO's iProcess™ Suite is a comprehensive customised business process management suite that enables enterprises to automate, manage and improve their business processes to maximize operational efficiency and effectiveness.

iProcess Suite provides a complete end-to-end process management solution for all parts of the business process lifecycle – from process modelling, automation of people and system activities, visibility into running process, and optimization. It is simple enough that companies can start with a single departmental process and powerful enough to scale to hundreds of processes across an enterprise.

Its benefits include:

- Improved operational management and decision making by providing business managers with insight into process performance and the ability to compare current results to historical data and required levels of performance.

- Improved business agility by enabling the rapid adaptation of processes in response to changing conditions.
- Reduced operating costs by automating time-consuming and error-prone manual tasks.
- Improved productivity by giving business users the information and direction they need to do their jobs most effectively.
- Enables continuous process improvement based on actual process behaviour to maximize operational effectiveness and efficiency.
- Fosters business and IT collaboration. Business experts model the process and IT staff then implement the process leveraging the enterprise's IT infrastructure.

LSC Group considers the TIBCO workflow the heartbeat of the CWE solution. The workflow element gives them competitive advantage and a key reason that TIBCO was chosen over other BPM technology providers is because of its scalability and ability to roll out to other areas of the business, beyond submarines.

10. THE TECHNOLOGY AND SERVICE PROVIDERS

UK MoD

MOD is both a policy-making Department of State - like any other central government department - as well as being the highest level military headquarters in the UK, providing political control of all military operations. It controls resources for the Armed Forces of some £30 billion per year. Within and across the MOD, military and civilian personnel work closely together to deliver Britain's defence. Its headquarters are in Whitehall, London.

http://www.mod.uk/DefenceInternet/Home/

LSC Group

LSC Group is a solutions, services and management consulting company, dedicated to the delivery of efficient and effective services to meet the business transformation challenges of today and tomorrow. LSC Group is a subsidiary of Babcock International.

http://www.lsc.co.uk/

Babcock International

Babcock is an engineering support services organisation, operating in the defence, energy, telecommunications, transport and education sectors. Babcock International is the parent company of LSC Group.

http://www.babcock.co.uk/default.aspx

TIBCO Software

TIBCO's infrastructure software gives customers the ability to constantly innovate by connecting applications and data in a service-oriented architecture, streamlining activities through business process management, and giving people the information and intelligence tools they need to make faster and smarter decisions.

http://www.tibco.com/

In addition to TIBCO's bespoke business process automation (workflow) solution, the CWE comprises the following COTS solutions from third-party vendors:
- A portal, including collaboration tools
- A database
- A project vault (document management)
- Business intelligence (business tools and applications)

Section 3

Middle East-Africa

Nokia Siemens Networks, Global Network Implementation Centers United Arab Emirates

Gold Award: Middle East-Africa
Nominated by Appian, USA

1. EXECUTIVE SUMMARY / ABSTRACT

Nokia Siemens Networks (NSN) is one of the largest telecommunications hardware, software and services companies in the world, with more than 60,000 people in over 150 countries. NSN offers a complete portfolio of mobile, fixed and converged network technologies as well as professional services (consulting and systems integration, network implementation, maintenance and care, and managed services) to more than 600 Communications Service Providers around the world.

NSN's initial foray into Business Process Management (BPM) was the award-winning "Zeus" project which thoroughly transformed its Consulting & Systems Integration division and delivered an estimated €6 million annual productivity savings. Based on this success, NSN has now deployed a sophisticated, pan-organizational BPM Program, leveraging and extending the success of "Zeus" through one of the most mature Center of Excellence organizations in the BPM industry. The single BPM platform has been leveraged to provide a multitude of BPMS 'Apps', delivering process automation, process governance and consistency, to many areas of the NSN's business, from its Business Solutions & Operations to its Managed Services and its Global Network Implementation Centers. Ultimately, through the effective use of BPMS, NSN now have enhanced levels of business visibility for managers and executives, supported by dedicated socio-business networking functionality (integrated collaboration within process).

2. OVERVIEW

Conventional BPM wisdom is to "start small and think big." Nick Deacon, NSN's Global Head of BPM, defied that convention by "starting big and thinking even bigger."

Nokia Siemens Networks was created in 2007 through the merger of the former Networks Business Group of Nokia and the carrier-related businesses of Siemens. As a result of the merger, NSN had a heterogeneous technology and tools landscape that did not meet the needs of its dynamic business. Nick assumed leadership of NSN's Consulting & Systems Integration (CSI) division at the company's founding. Having had first-hand experience with working environments that lacked robust processes and tools aligned to a process framework, he immediately set out to get CSI speaking one common process language, utilizing a Business Process Management suite to manage the division effectively and support growth.

Through a modular delivery approach, Nick targeted initial BPMS services rollout in 4-6 months and complete end-to-end division operational management within one year. The resulting BPM solution, named "ZEUS" after the Greek God of Control, has delivered a benchmarked €6 million in annual productivity savings. NSN estimates that Y/Y cost savings may double (or more) in the future.

While he started somewhat "under the radar" in the CSI division, Nick's true vision was always to use BPM to transform the way NSN operates as a global organization. The basic tenet of this vision is that a competitive, industry-leading business needs to have full end-to-end visibility into its fundamental business components (Sales, Delivery and Resources), as well as the ability to drive and maximize its business performance through effective portfolio management, knowledge management, remote capability and overall business management. This data needs to be accessible in a holistic environment that supports not only business management but also Consultant's, Engineers, Project Managers, and other employees. NSN's infrastructure housed large enterprise systems such as ERP from SAP, and other rigid and disconnected sales workflow, resource and knowledge management applications. This enterprise tools landscape did not provide the flexibility or cohesion NSN needed to conduct its dynamic business, placing limitations on real-time business management and Future Planning capabilities, while also creating data inaccuracy and redundancy, and significant overhead wasted on reporting, training and data entry.

Timing being everything, the transformational value of "Zeus" within the CSI division began gaining the attention of the larger NSN organization just as global economic indicators began to fall, and the world's major economies headed into recession. In conjunction with a reorganization of NSN's business units, BPM began to flourish across the company.

Today, NSN's 10,000+ employees in the Business Solutions & Operations division are supported by an expanded version of "Zeus," managing aspects of Sales, Service Delivery, Remote Operations and delivery, Resource & Competency Management, Solution Management, and overall Business Management. The NSN BPM CoE has subsequently been able to re-use much of the ZEUS functionality to deliver a fast business solution to NSN's Managed Services division. This functionality, housed again on the single platform is badged "Apollo" and delivers Project Management, Global Delivery and Sales support. Significant cost benefits have been immediately realized through this re-use and platform sharing. "Apollo" has been benchmarked as delivering €1.5 million in annual productivity savings.

The BPM CoE has recently delivered the next solution, this time for NSN's Global Network Implementation Centers. "Cronos", as it's referred to, is focused on the automation and management of the deployment, maintenance and upgrading of roughly 150,000 of NSN's network sites around the world. The original quote for a similar solution was 1.1 M Euros and a delivery time of 9-12 months. The BPM CoE delivered the initial solution in 3 months at a cost of 60K Euros.

All three of these systems are front-ended by a common, LinkedIn/MySpace-like collaborative portal known as "Hermes" that features personalized home-pages, communities of interest, messaging and more. In addition, the BPM CoE has developed "Athena," a centralized process and tools management portal with status dashboards and reports for all NSN employees.

The BPM CoE is now building the reputation for fast, effective delivery of customized process automation solutions which means the demand for it's services within NSN is growing by the day.

3. BUSINESS CONTEXT

NSN inherited an array of inflexible and disconnected tools – SAP for logistics, a workflow solution for Sales, COTS solutions for Resource Management and Financial functions, and primarily local hard drives for knowledge management. Areas such as Delivery, Technical Support, and Reporting had no systems support at all. Individual divisions were forced to use EXCEL to off-set the limitations of the enterprise systems, and to fill the large gaps. In addition, divisions had limited ownership of data entry and were often reliant on others to populate required data sources. This created poor visibility across units, and across the organization as a whole, into areas such as Sales and Forecasted Revenue, Project and Service Delivery, Cost and Margin, and Demand and Supply Planning. The lack of embedded process and an underlying cohesive technology platform created an inability to govern effectively, and poor visibility of business data led to inaccurate decision making and planning.

4. THE KEY INNOVATIONS

Customers:

NSN's comprehensive BPM Program encompasses multiple process solutions targeted at all core elements of the global business: Sales, Delivery, Resources, Technical Support, Competency Management, Remote Delivery/Offshoring and overall Business Management.

NSN's customers are directly and positively impacted by the company's BPM Program. By allowing all divisions and employees to collaborate more effectively, easily access the tools and systems they need, and focus their time on effective task completion, and by giving management the real-time data required to make faster and better decisions, the BPM Program ensures that customers receive consistent, high-quality service. With CRONOS, customers receive automated daily reports informing them as to their respective site status and monthly summary reports documenting KPI and SLA status against agreed standards.

Process:

"Zeus," "Apollo" and "Cronos" span a multitude of processes across numerous NSN divisions. On the whole, definitions for these core processes were either buried in large, complex binders of information that were collecting dust on shelves, or simply held in employees' heads. An important first step at every stage of NSN's BPM journey has been to clearly define both current and ideal-state processes using simple, BPMN-standards based process modelling. After the initial rollout of an improved process, NSN then focuses on process optimization based on real-world, in-production experience.

This optimization is greatly enabled by real-time process architecture and "on-the-fly" process modification capabilities of the Appian BPM Suite, upon which NSN's entire BPM Program is built. Real-time data visibility on process performance and bottlenecks is used to modify process models in-flight, with the changes deployed in real-time into the production application.

Appian's 100 percent web-based software and Service Oriented Architecture are also important factors in achieving NSN's BPM vision. Both significantly ease the integration challenges posed by such a large-scale BPM program. Appian's "Smart Services" also make SOA a useful tool outside of IT, giving end users drag-and-drop simplicity in employing web service components within their composite applications and mash-up portals.

Just two examples of NSN's BPM-based process innovations include:

The Resource & Competency Management application: allows Resource Managers (RMs) to understand, for the first time, the skill sets of all employees, forecast accurate project close dates, and identify the required resources. All employees now rate themselves against the NSN portfolio of service products and general skills. A custom interface allows RMs to search this user store, filtering by skill sets and other criteria. Extended user profiles and reports give RMs a 360-degree view of resources and competencies, and detailed SQL Reporting delivers insight into current and predicted staffing needs, staff availability, and allocation ratios segmented by regions and sub-regions.

The Project Management application: enables Project Managers to track and manage all of their projects against agreed milestones and against a well-defined series of quality gates. The application tracks the financial elements of each project, alerting PMs and senior managers to deviations in cost accuracy and delivery accuracy enabling the business to accurately monitor progress and revenue against targets. Throughout the delivery process, resource needs are monitored for current needs and for anticipated potential new projects born out of new requirements which can then be requested using the **Resource Management application**. Other functionality now available within this module includes Risk Management, Change Management, control of Non-Conformance costs and full Project Schedule capabilities.

Organization:

The BPM platform, referred to as the 'BPM Universe' touches and supports many areas of company operations around the globe, including its development teams in India, as well as suppliers and customers. The universe provides one holistic process/data environment with Single Sign-On across the organization. All NSN employees now benefit from the efficiencies and lowered learning curve of standardized and repeatable workflow processes, managed by exception. Recorded video training files are built into the workflows, known as WALTs (Watch and Learn today) to minimize the overhead of training and to ensure users are able to use existing and new functionality with minimal delay.

Through the cockpits, portals and full reporting portfolio, NSN management now has improved its business-critical decision making based on real-time data.

- "Zeus" has roughly 5,000 users, and about 2,000 logins per week within the BSO division
- "Apollo" has roughly 3,000 users within the Managed Services division
- "Cronos" has 500 permanent logins within the Global Network Implementation Center division, with additional ad-hoc system access
- NSN estimates that by the end of CY 2010, the BPM system as a whole will have between 15,000 to 20,000 users and roughly 5,000 logins per week

The "Athena" application provides a centralized process and tools portal for employees, combining the principles of Process Management with communication, commenting and collaboration. Process and IT owners maintain the data through the coordination and oversight of the BPM Center of Excellence. Athena provides dashboards on the aggregated state of all processes and their related IT tools, with drill-down capability to see the status of a particular process, the individuals responsible for it (and related processes) and a Knowledge Center of materials related to it. Additionally, Athena provides a dedicated Collaboration Area for each process, including discussions and email updates for all users subscribed to that specific process or community. All of the Athena functionality available for processes is also available for related IT tools.

All NSN BPM systems are front-ended by a common LinkedIn/MySpace-like portal called "Hermes." "Hermes" provides collaboration tools for all BPM users, such as user profiles, communities of interest, and messaging capabilities. For example, "Zeus" users have "MyZeus" areas – an online environment they can design, build, develop, optimize and maintain for work and networking. This includes:

- My Profile (a professional summary and NSN assignment profile, as well as any personal interests or information they wish to share)
- My Network (LinkedIn-like networking and communities of interest)
- My Message Board (a Facebook-like environment with notifications and collaborative messaging within and outside a user's defined networks)
- My Files (centralized documents and knowledge centers based on user profile)
- My Activities (tasks and assignments from all the dashboards a user has access to)
- "How To" for videos, guides and online Help

The entire BPM Program is driven and orchestrated by one of the most sophisticated BPM Center of Excellence organizations in the BPM industry. It consists of a mature team of 40 people across four dimensions:

- Process Management & Control (overall CoE leadership)
- Demand Management (managing the "bucket list" of business requests), including business analysts who translate the requirements of the business into technical Requirements Specifications which can be used by the developers.
- Build & Deliver, based in the Ukraine, providing fast, agile BPM solutions to the business through efficient development and thorough testing, based on strict development processes and procedures.
- BPM Support (based in India, handles BPM-related user support requests) as well as having the responsibility for Release Management and System Performance and Optimization.

NSN's BPM CoE exists to ensure that business solutions have the required end-to-end processes built an in effect, and to ensure that there is an effective end-to-end IT landscape in place, with appropriate tools aligned to those operational processes. The CoE staff is divided into specializations according to the primary BPM applications ("Zeus," "Apollo," and "Cronos"). At the most strategic level, the CoE oversees the maturing of NSN's overall processes, providing documentation and moving those processes into Athena for access by the global organization. The result is robust processes, developed at relatively low-cost, with fast deployment into the business.

5. HURDLES OVERCOME

When Nick was initially driving "ZEUS" within the Consulting & Systems Integration division only, the primary challenge was to develop and deploy without generating negative attention from IT (with its entrenched reliance on enterprise systems such as SAP) and other business units in the company.

After NSN management saw the success of "Zeus" and began to embrace the value of BPM, the primary challenge shifted to handling the flood of business requests for process improvement solutions. This necessitated a quick ramp-up of BPM expertise and both business and IT representation within a dedicated, and sufficiently staffed, Center of Excellence. Evaluating and prioritizing follow-on BPM solutions, ensuring their successful integration into divisional operations, and promoting those solutions to drive adoption were all crucial elements to the success of the expanding program.

Even with senior leadership buy-in, change management remained an issue across the organization. Moving a global enterprise like NSN towards a process-centric approach is a daunting task. To support the success of the BPM Program, Nick focused on two major campaigns:

- Effective and compelling "marketing" of BPM and the business solutions across division heads and employees
- Effective and accessible training for new BPM system users

Branding the solutions with the Greek god theme names proved catchy and memorable, helping the BPM initiative rise above the rest of the enterprise noise. Creating divisional and regional BPM Champions helped foster awareness. Bringing those Champions together for planning, communications, and brainstorming workshops helped achieve user buy-in and ensure alignment of the program across the complete business – as did regular Steering Board / Change Management Review meetings involving Directors and VPs from across the business. Governance routines are operationalized through repeated communication sessions, the employment of the Champions Community (which is embedded throughout the business), and from having the 100% support of senior management.

System usage among employees was spurred by leveraging the built-in collaboration features of the BPM platform to create personalized user experiences within connected communities of interest. As importantly, a multitude of training resources were made available within each community and for each process (through both "Hermes" and the "Athena" portal). Process supporting brochures and marketing materials are housed within the applications. Touch-points within the workflows explain the processes and provide links to additional materials. Automatic process training (via WebEx sessions) are also available for core processes.

6. Benefits

The BPM system provides one single environment from which to drive the entire NSN business. High-level benefits include:

- Workflow management improving process governance and adherence
- Enhanced function inter-working through visibility and taskings (hand-over of responsibilities, transition of files/data, transition of risks/issues)
- E2E Business Visibility through Live Business Dashboards
  - Full reporting portfolio in place significantly reducing overhead
- Socio-Business Networking
- Integrated collaboration within the processes
  - Management of Business Critical Operational Activities which have high customer focus

Building on the calculated business value of the initial roll-out of "Zeus," NSN estimates that the entire BPM system will generate:

- **"ZEUS": 6M Euros of YoY Productivity savings** through reductions in headcount focused on overhead activities as well as freeing up considerable time from the Solution Consultants, Project Managers and Architects to sell, delivery and support customer business. With wider adoption of the Resource Management and Sales modules (expected over the near-term), **NSN estimates the cost savings driven by "Zeus" will double, or more.**
- **"APOLLO": 1.5M of YoY savings.**
- **"CRONOS":** Initial quotes from alternate suppliers suggested that to deliver such a solution would cost 1.1M and take 9-12 months to deliver.

CRONOS was **delivered by the BPM CoE in 3 months at a cost of 60K Euros**. Through the use of the existing BPM platform, considerable savings have been made on license and support costs as well as the obvious efficiency savings achieved through automation of manual operational processes. That said, **the business value achieved through the increase in the customer perception as a result is almost immeasurable**.

7. BEST PRACTICES, LEARNING POINTS AND PITFALLS

7.1 Best Practices and Learning Points

✓ *Ensure that your BPM Program has executive-level sponsorship*
✓ *Invest the time and resources needed to create a functional BPM Center of Excellence with representation from both the business and IT*
✓ *Create sufficient branding for the solution so that future users can relate / refer to it easily (this enables more effective selling / marketing of the solution)*
✓ *Utilize a BPM suite's built-in collaboration features to create user communities that are invested in using and promoting the solution*
✓ *Make sure the underlying technology platform has the integrated functionality you need, combined with ease-of-use to drive adoption*

7.2 Pitfalls. Avoid:

✗ *Having a Project Lead that isn't 110% committed to delivering the solution and isn't willing to 'fight' to make the solution a success.*
✗ *Thinking small. Have a 'big vision' even if you start off small !*
✗ *Embarking on a BPM project without any BPM experienced personnel within the team (Project Managers / Business Analysts).*
✗ *Delivering solutions which are not fully tested can quickly ruin the user perception and can switch them off completely from using the system*
✗ *Not obtaining the full buy-in and support from key users or influential business users.*
✗ *Trying to deliver a system without senior management buy-in and support;*
✗ *Not having the basics of a Centre of Excellence in place which can be ramped up when required:*
  o *Process Management and Communications*
  o *Demand Management*
  o *Delivery Management*
  o *Support Management*
✗ *Deploying a system on an network which can't cope with the demands of the users as this will only annoy/frustrate the user.*

8. COMPETITIVE ADVANTAGES

NSN's BPM program has enabled the company to drive significant competitive advantage over its competition. Through optimized pan-organizational processes, with strong governance to ensure employee adoption, NSN has increased the speed and agility of its organization, while also improving the consistency of experience and service it can deliver to customers. NSN management is also now armed with a level of end-to-end business visibility and real-time control over all mission-critical business aspects and resources that surpasses the industry standard. BPM now acts as NSN's platform for operational business management, and the ongoing optimization/continuous process improvement inherent in the BPM Program will support continued market advantage.

Additionally, NSN is now seen as embracing modern BPMS technology in order to maximize its performance for benefit of the customer which creates an extremely positive perception when associated with its core deliverables.

9. TECHNOLOGY

The Appian BPM Suite is the technology platform for NSN's BPM program. NSN selected Appian after a thorough vendor evaluation.

NSN was looking for powerful technology, but they were just as focused on working with a vendor who would approach the relationship as a true partnership. Nick Deacon's BPM vision would take the organization into uncharted waters, and he knew he would need an experienced, committed and patient partner on the journey.

Appian satisfied NSN's technical criteria based on its comprehensive and natively-integrated capabilities for process, content management, rules, forms/portal, identity management, collaboration, and more. In addition, Appian's extreme ease-of-use (including tailored user interfaces, personalized portals and information targeting, drag-and-drop process modeling, and ease of user and group administration) was important, as was its flexible architecture (100% web-based with zero client-side downloads, service-oriented architecture and ease of integration). Collaboration and knowledge management are crucial to NSN's program. The Appian platform acts as the single point of management for processes, process artifacts, stored documents and other electronic content (reports, task lists, images, video), plus associated metadata. Appian allows for the collaborative creation of all process artifacts and electronic data, as well as effective distribution, archiving, and protection. Features such as Single Sign-On throughout the entire system, and native search enhanced by integration with Google Search Appliance further extend the ease-of-use. Users interact with a rule- and role-based portal that facilitates NSN's need to capture, share and disseminate information in a flexible yet secure environment.

10. THE TECHNOLOGY AND SERVICE PROVIDERS

Appian is the global innovator in enterprise and on-demand business process management (BPM). Appian provides the fastest way to deploy robust processes, collapsing time to value for new process initiatives. Businesses and governments worldwide use Appian to accelerate process improvement and drive business performance. Appian empowers more than 2.5 million users from large Fortune 100 companies, to the mid-market and small businesses worldwide. Appian is headquartered in the Washington, D.C. region, with professional services and partners around the globe. For more information, visit www.appian.com.

Section 4

North America

United States Department of Energy Loan Programs Office

Gold Award, North America
Nominated by Accenture/HandySoft, USA

1. 1. EXECUTIVE SUMMARY / ABSTRACT

The primary mission of the U.S. Department of Energy (DOE) is to advance the national, economic and energy security of the United States. DOE's Loan Programs Office (LPO) was created to accelerate the domestic commercial deployment of innovative and advanced clean energy technologies at a scale sufficient to contribute meaningfully to this mission. LPO is able to accomplish its goals by guaranteeing loans to eligible clean energy projects (i.e., agreeing to repay the borrower's debt obligation in the event of a default) and by providing direct loans to eligible manufacturers of advanced technology vehicles and components. The LPO also has a fiduciary obligation to U.S. taxpayers, and must ensure that the loans and loan guarantees provided have a reasonable prospect of repayment.

Eligible projects apply to the program and are rigorously evaluated across multiple disciplines, including technical, financial, environmental, legal and regulatory. The LPO initially captured the highly detailed and often sensitive sponsor and project information for the application via paper methods and legacy technology systems. These methods were found to be cumbersome, in some cases, confusing for the applicant and time-consuming for DOE staff reviewing the applications. In an effort to improve efficiencies and provide more transparency to the application process, DOE decided to transform the loan guarantee application and approval process from a series of highly manual steps of data collection and review to a 100 percent Web-based, automated format with front-end data collection and back-end review automation. The new application has been well received by the marketplace, and has resulted in expedited reviews, reduced transaction friction, and greater visibility to both project sponsors and DOE management.

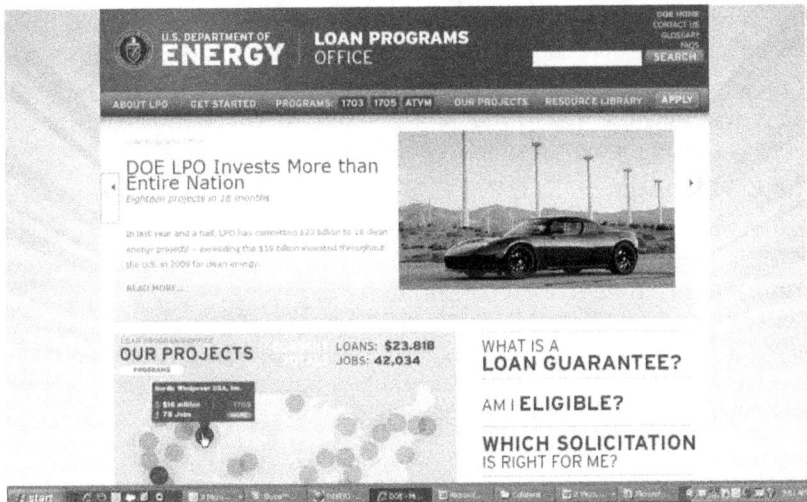

U.S. Department of Energy's Loan Program Office

2. OVERVIEW

The mission of LPO is to accelerate the domestic commercial deployment of innovative and advanced clean energy technologies at a scale sufficient to contribute meaningfully to the achievement of our national clean energy objectives— including job creation; reducing dependency on foreign oil; improving our environmental legacy; and enhancing American competitiveness in the global economy of the 21st century. LPO consists of three separate programs (Section 1703, Section 1705 and Advanced Technology Vehicles Manufacturing Program) managed by two offices, the Loan

Guarantee Program Office (LGP) and the Advanced Technology Vehicles Manufacturing Loan Program Office. Under LGP, loans are available to domestic projects in various clean energy industries, including nuclear, solar, biomass/biofuels, advanced fossil, transmission, wind, geothermal and hydroelectric. As of September 2010, LGP has committed more than $16 billion in loan guarantees to 16 projects. Loan amounts start in the tens of millions and can climb to several billion.

Application fees are consistent with the private sector for similar energy project finance transactions. Sponsor organizations seek such loans because they come with lower interest rates and government backing, resulting in less exposure to risk and greater attractiveness to equity investors.

3. BUSINESS CONTEXT

There were many improvements LPO needed to make in order to comply with governmental regulations and bring greater efficiencies to the application process. Some of those areas of improvements included:

- Create performance goals;
- Revise loan guarantee processes to ensure consistent review; and
- Enable sponsor appeals.

DOE began implementing process changes to address these concerns. For example, LPO established domain expertise amongst the senior staff, engaged in more proactive communications with applicants, and streamlined the evaluation process, As a result of the improvements made, DOE has greatly increased program efficiencies and reduced response time to applicants. However, the application process continued to be paper and time intensive, not to mention it was still viewed as a frustrating roadblock for both applicants and some DOE staff.

As a result of the internal DOE analysis and sponsor feedback, DOE decided to further streamline the application and evaluation process by embarking on a new Web-based application, i.e. the DOE online application portal.

4. THE KEY INNOVATIONS

Business Innovations:

Prior to development of the online application portal, it was not uncommon for sponsors to spend days, even weeks preparing documents, making photocopies and either sending proper documentation via mail or submitting documents through an unreliable legacy system. The development of the online application portal changed all of that. The portal enabled sponsors to create log-ins and submit applications in less than one business day.

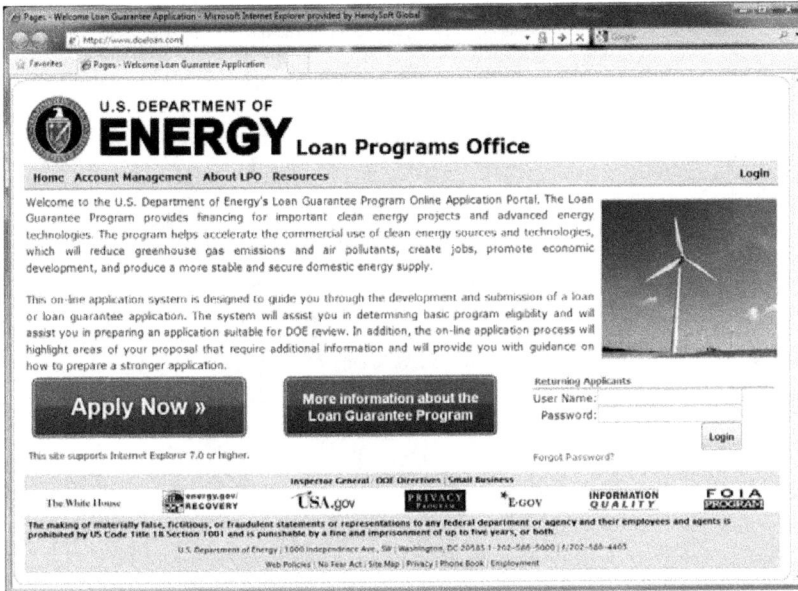

Loan Guarantee Program Application Page

DOE also changed the way it interacted with remote application reviewers. Under the old system, DOE shared project information via paper and mail—an inefficient and time consuming process. Thanks to the portal, DOE provides reviewers secure, direct access to applications through the electronic portal anywhere, anytime provided they have an Internet connection.

Process Innovations:

The application review and approval process has been highly manual and data-intensive. However, what was once a paper-based or flash-drive driven workflow has since been transformed into a Web-based application inside a portal, offering immediate upload, response and feedback.

Figure 1: 2008 Solicitation for Energy Efficiency, Renewable Energy, and Advanced Transmission and Distribution Technologies

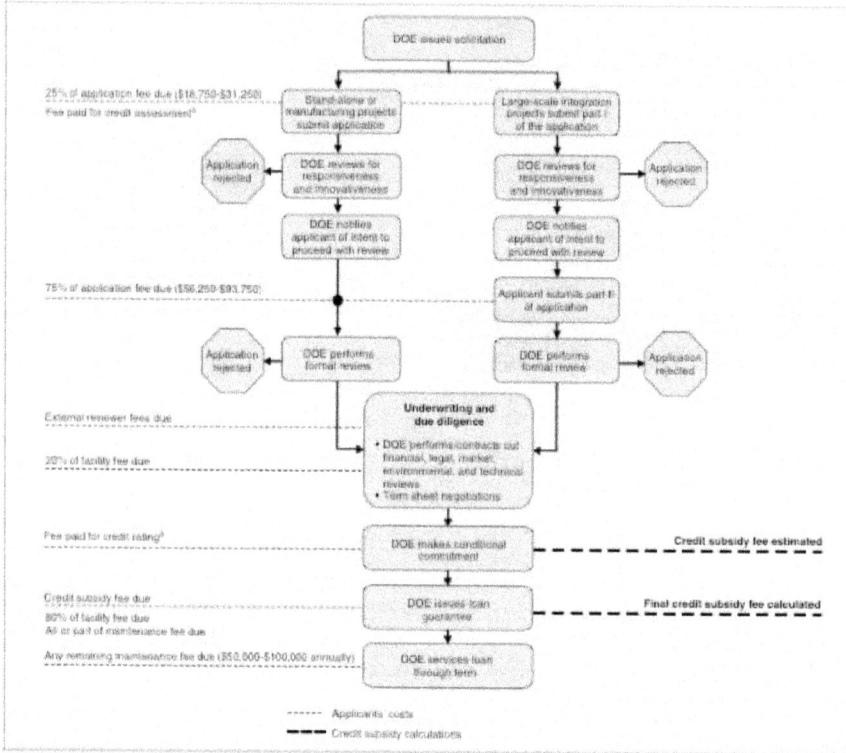

Original Loan Guarantee Workflow

The prototype scenario followed the flow below.

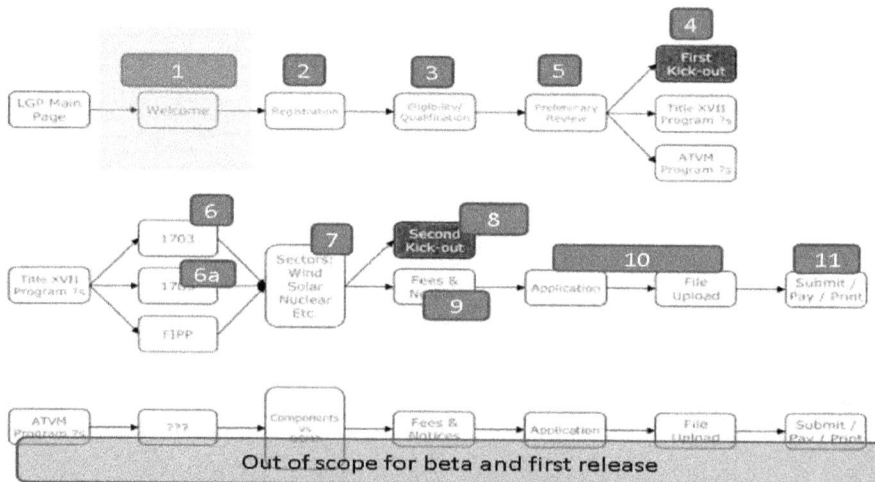

Prototype Screen Flow for Application Portal

Originally, DOE outlined a structure that mirrored the prior serial evaluation process flow. Project sponsors would proceed serially through a multi-step process from the first page to the last. After initial development and feedback, the approach was found halting and rigid. Users needed more flexibility to jump around as data became available to them. Increased flexibility would also help project sponsors justify the application investment.

When choosing a software package for development, the following requirements were deemed necessary: the new business process management (BPM) suite needed to 1) be more flexible and 2) offer integrated modeling and forms environments. Forms would have to adapt to user interests (i.e. differing requirements for different technologies) rather than users adapting to process steps. The user experience trumped the process model.

Ultimately, the project team transformed a highly structured, multi-step process into a more free flowing experience. Steps 1 and 2 (Registration/Fee information and Eligibility) became the only serial activities.

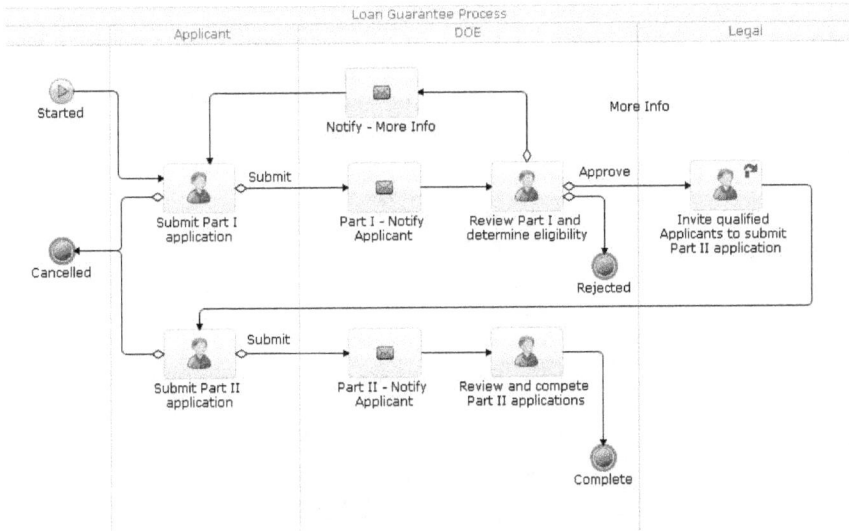

Business Process Definition Offering Greater Flexibility

Process participation includes three core groups: Applicants, Reviewers, and Legal. Each activity is associated with business requirements (e.g., law, policies, procedures, roles, responsibilities, routing, escalations, etc.), screens (aka forms), and data.

For example, the first activity includes the following business rules and forms:

Activity Name	Submit Part I application
Activity Type	Normal Activity
Process Parent:	None
Activity Description:	Applicant fills in the Forms in the part 1 and uploads documents
Response Group:	N/S
Participant:	Initiator (Applicant)

Application:	<ul><li>Forms/Screens</li><li>Solicitation and Fee Information</li><li>Project Eligibility</li><li>Program Questions</li><li>Project Overview</li><li>NEPA Screening</li><li>Sector Questions</li><li>Application Forms</li><li>Upload Supporting Documentation</li><li>Wire Instructions</li><li>Review/Submit</li></ul>Call Web Service to make document library for the Application read-only when the applicant submits the forms in Part 1.
Business Rules:	<ul><li>Specific rules are described in the Form documents.</li><li>User inputs must be eligible for currently open solicitation.</li><li>When Applicant clicks the button 'Start Application' in the BizCove, it brings an ASPX page to create a new project, and redirect to BizFlow workitem.</li><li>The ASPX page calls BizFlow start process web service with process variables update: project_name, applicantName, siteURL.</li><li>Cancel Application (Process flow goes to Cancelled).</li><li>Save for Later (Save current form).</li><li>Save and Proceed (Save current form and mark it as Completed).</li><li>Submit (Process flow goes to "Review Part I and determine eligibility" activity).</li></ul>
Deadline	None
Comments	None

The BPM-based application can be easily adapted to meet new DOE requirements. Administrators or developers can add new solicitation tracks in their entirety, or simply change:

- Portal pages
- Forms
- Form fields
- Questions
- Activities (business rules and process variables)
- Data inputs
- User Interfaces

Questions, for example, can be changed in the database or on the form by following these directions:

- • Change Question in Database
  - Go to the database bizflowlgp.FormQuestionDefinition.

- Find your form id having the question you want to change. See DOE LGP—WebMaker Forms.xls for details.
- Change "QuestionLabel" column value with the new text.

- • Change Questions on Forms

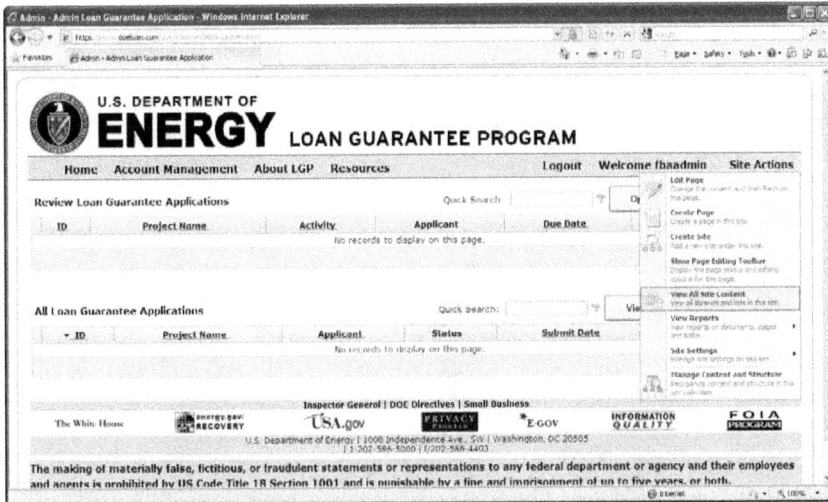

- Open BizFlow project having the form by using BizFlow WebMaker Studio. See DOE LGP—WebMaker Forms.xls for details.
- Change text of the question in the form.
- Generate, deploy, and publish the project to WebMaker server.

Portal Web Parts also can be changed easily by following these directions:

- Log into https://www.doeloan.com portal site as an administrator
- Click on the "Site Action" link at the top left of the page and then click "View All Site Content" to see all libraries and lists in the site.
- Find Document Libraries below: SuperAdmin, Sector Lead, Processor, Reviewer, and Applicant
- Click on the library name to load the library.
- Click the library name or Click on the dropdown menu and click "Edit Properties".
- Click on the "Site Actions" link again, and then Click "Edit Page".
- General page layout of the DOE Loan Guarantee Program portal is as below.
- Click Edit and the Click "Modify Shared Web Part". You will see property edit section of the Page Viewer web part. All BizCove are linked to SharePoint by using "Page Viewer" web part.
- Edit the properties. Most important properties are as below.

- Click "OK" button when done.

User Interfaces are the pages where sponsors and management initiate specific actions (e.g., monitor application). Administrators can easily add/alter/delete user interfaces (aka portlets, BizCoves).

The portal combines BPM and Document Management. The BPM suite includes functionality for process modeling, permission-based architecture, application development (the creation of Web-based forms tied to the process model), process intelligence (user-driven reporting and executive dashboards), and overall process execution.

System Architecture

System components include:

- Web applications that run on Apache Tomcat 6.0 with Sun Microsystems Java SE JDK 1.6.
- Web Server enabling all BizFlow product user interfaces such as BizCoves, Menus, etc.

- BizFlow WebMaker component supporting design, development and execution of web-based forms.
- BizFlow Advanced Reporting component enabling user-driven reporting by retrieving data from databases to generate web-based reports and dashboards.
- BizFlow Form component handling web service calls in process definitions.
- BizFlow SharePoint SSO module handling Single Sign On between SharePoint and BizFlow.

DOE internal user accounts must be created in both SharePoint and BizFlow by using the DOE User Management Tool made available to system Super Administrators. However, applicants (external users) share one BizFlow account.

Organization

The impact to LPO has been monumental. Where paper was once ubiquitous, the portal is now the standard means of application submission, review and validation. Part I reviews used to take upwards of 30-45 days, however, process improvements combined with the application portal have reduced this review period to less than 10 days.

The portal also offers applicants instantaneous guidance as to how they might increase the likelihood that their applications will continue to the next phase. On online glossary helps define terms for project sponsors, making it easier to understand the solicitation Sponsors immediately know whether or not their information has been accepted, and just as importantly whether their application meets very general eligibility parameters. Each document submitted for each application is accessible online for collaboration and review. These enhancements significantly reduce the costs of both submitting and reviewing applications.

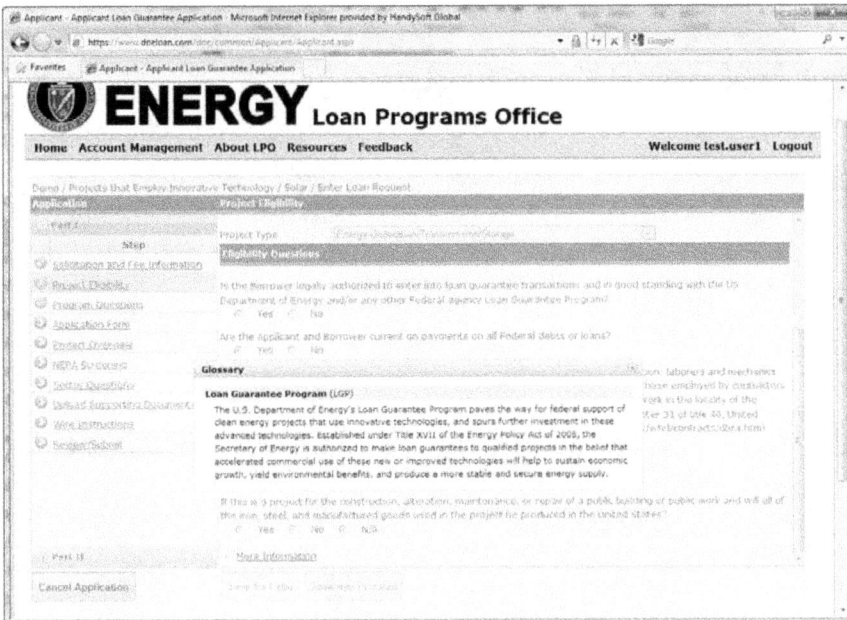

Online Glossary

Web-based Data Entry and Validation

Web-Based Screening

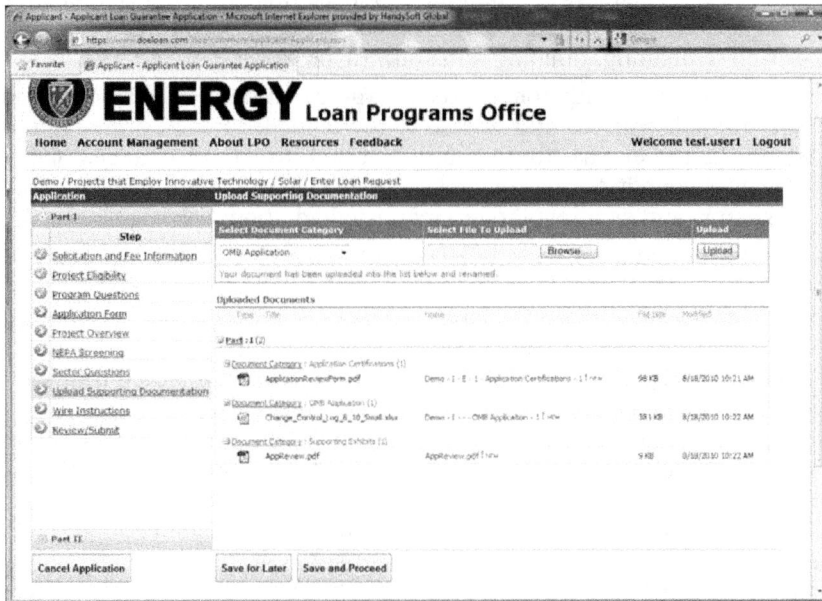

Web-based Document Sharing and Archival

5. HURDLES OVERCOME

At project inception, DOE had complete management buy-in. However, the management team had only limited information to begin the project.

Furthermore, DOE wanted to deliver new functionality in two months. In this time, the system integrator (SI) would have to procure infrastructure and software, create a prototype within three weeks, move into development and ensure proper hosting.

The beta scope included:

- Screening and intake of applications for 1703 and 1705 for Wind (potentially Solar and Geothermal)
- To-do list for complete scope tracked
- Continue development of additional sectors to first release

The project timeline required:

- March 15 start date
- April 6 working prototype
- May 30 launch

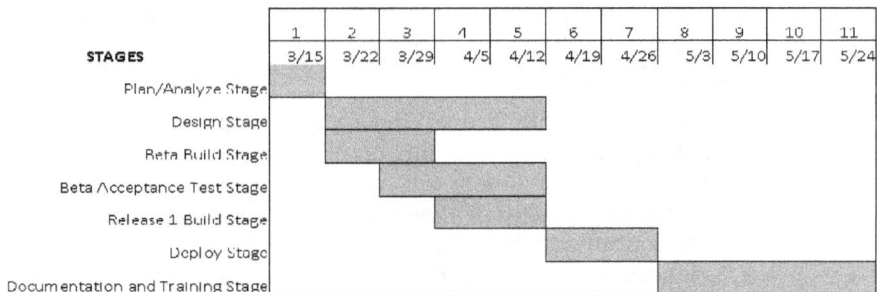

Project Timeline

In order to gather business requirements and technical specifications while ensuring deliver dates, the SI used a methodology called "Speed-2-Market,"an iterative approach to defining, building and showing progress.

The primary challenge with the approach was in obtaining feedback. Feedback came from multiple sources and needed to be reconciled by the primary customer stakeholder. Moreover, as the team continued to show changes (i.e., richer/broader functionality), the customer would discover more efficient and fluid user interactions and as a result often requested additional changes.

- As the project had a two-month delivery objective, the project team made four critical decisions to ensure success:
- Create a senior team of professionals – The DOE portal project is as much about streamlining business processes as it is creating an engaging user experience. Having seasoned professionals on the project ensured that the right questions were asked and scope managed to meet expectations.
- Co-locate the staff – Given the time restraints on the project, it was necessary that team members were co-located to streamline communication. Furthermore, co-location enabled cross pollination of skills and knowledge sharing.
- Manage Scope – The project team created two "buckets" for change management: Immediate Requirements and Deferred Items.
- Require product flexibility – The speed of delivery required a tool suite allowing extreme flexibility with forms development, forms tied together with the process model, a fully exposed API layer and seamless integration with Share-Point.

The project team included:

- Project Manager – 1
- Technical Architect – 1
- System Engineer – 1
- BPM Developers – 2
- Portal/DM Developers – 2
- Testing/Documentation – 1
- Customer Representative – 1

Using this methodology and a flexible product suite, the project team was able to deliver an enterprise portal on-time with more than 150 percent of functionality.

6. BENEFITS

The new online portal is a significant improvement from the previous process. Not only does the new tool make the application submission and review process more efficient, transparent and easier to navigate, the portal also demonstrates DOE's commitment to continuously find ways to improve the program and accelerate important clean energy investments that create jobs, support private markets and transform the way we use and produce energy.

Process enhancements include:

- Design that guides applicants through the application process by making suggestions as to applicable solicitations based on the information the applicant provided.
- Instantaneous guidance as to how they might increase the likelihood that their project will continue to the next phase.
- Comprehensive security features such as encryption algorithms and password protection to ensure that only the applicant and identified department reviewers can access appropriate files.

7. BEST PRACTICES, LEARNING POINTS AND PITFALLS

During the project, the team uncovered many best practices and potential pitfalls.

- Empowered Stakeholder – DOE had one person responsible for the project as the primary point of contact. This person was very involved in gathering and refining business requirements and provided a single point of communication to business users. Where there was no time for lengthy discussion, the employee could make spot decisions that were classified in three buckets: important, important but deferred and not important. This process helped avoid project delays.
- Active Testing – During each stage of delivery, the project team and the customer tested functionality. Field testing revealed holes that internal testing had missed.
- Iterative Approach – With many pending transactions, time is of the essence. Project teams must hold daily reviews with customer to make go/no-go decisions.
- Product Variables – The right tool makes all the difference. Although BPM suites share similar functionality, there are specific capabilities required to rapidly build and deploy Web 2.0 applications, including: integrated modeling and forms studios, codeless development environments, web services integration, dynamic routing, and user-driven reporting.

Most of the challenges faced during the project were related to time constraints and obtaining DOE CIO office approvals. Complexity was never an issue, although hosting the portal externally put some pressure on moving from testing into production.

8. COMPETITIVE ADVANTAGES

The new portal gives sponsors a faster means to commercial success. The portal was designed with an applicant's time value of money in mind, and has enabled DOE reviewers to reduce evaluation time by more than 65 percent.

9. TECHNOLOGY

Category	Development	Test/Production
Environment	• One firewall to protect data and users / simulate Production	• Test first, then becomes Production after beta • Multiple firewalls to protect data and users • Built to support active-active specs
Technology	• Same as production • Source control	• Windows Server 2008 • SharePoint • SQL Server • Active Directory managed accounts • BizFlow BPM
Assumptions	• Can withstand surge capability simulations • Capable of adding additional environments as needed • Virtualization possible in some scenarios	• 300 submissions a year • Surge capabilities as deadlines for submissions loom • Capability to expand for future releases • 99.99% uptime support or greater • Environment to support US Government systems

BizFlow server
- Version: 11.5.0.0

- OS: Microsoft Windows Server 2008 Enterprise 64bit
- Ports
    - Application server: 7201, 8201
    - Web server: 8080

Database

- Microsoft SQL Server 2008 in a clustered environment on SQLDOE (failover mode)
- Port: 1433
- DOE LGP database: bizflowlgp

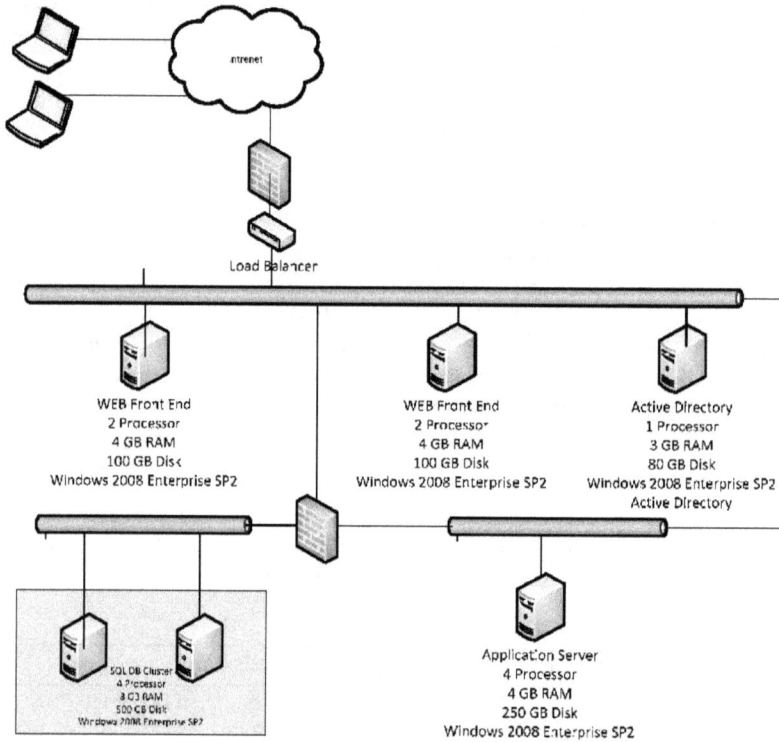

Test/Production Environment

10. THE TECHNOLOGY AND SERVICE PROVIDERS

Services Provider	Product/Service Offering	Website
Accenture	• Management Consulting • Project Management • Application Development • Hosting	www.accenture.com
HandySoft	• BizFlow® BPM Suite • Application Development • Customer Support	www.handysoft.com
USA Energy Advisors	• Department of Energy Loan Guarantee Process Knowledge • Program management	www.usaenergyadvisors.com

Farmers Insurance Group, United States

Gold Award: North America
Nominated by Pegasystems, United States

1. EXECUTIVE SUMMARY / ABSTRACT

To leverage the power of their many recent acquisitions, Farmers Insurance Group assembled a road map of activities encompassing more than 300 separate initiatives to be accomplished through cooperative efforts between business teams and IT. Farmers' challenge was integrating the technology of legacy customer services systems from their acquired companies and, in doing so, ensure a unified consistent standard of quality of customer service for all Farmers customers.

The initiative had three goals:

Business Flexibility
- Create a solution architecture founded on a "decoupled" claims tool that could handle a client's "notices of loss" across all Farmers lines of business. This would create a common intuitive front end that could be deployed across all subsidiaries to promote cross training and balance the workload. It would also aid in the rapid integration of future business acquisitions.

User Productivity Lift
- A tool was needed that would intelligently drive customer service representatives (CSRs) through the maze of State and process specific rules and regulations required to service and adjudicate a claim. Thus creating a significant productivity lift in the effectiveness and efficiency of the customer service team.

Enhanced Quality / Customer Experience
- Finally, Farmers needed a tool that could provide measurement and metrics that would allow a program of continuous improvement leading to sustainable gains in Service Quality and in the total customer experience.

Farmers selected Pegasystems' SmartBPM, a technology that intelligently combines business process, business policy, business rules and reporting into a single integrated package to address these defined needs. Business and IT then worked together to create a single unified solution that transformed the business operation.

The road map provided the guiding vision so that existing technology investments could be further leveraged and that the most critical business needs could be met first. This provided immediate value to the business because of the relatively short time between concept and delivery. The result: drastic improvements in both productivity and customer satisfaction. Farmers also saw significant reduction in the time required for both training of new CSR's and adoption of the new methods. Finally the company experienced new higher levels of improved quality, accuracy, consistency and speed in the processing of claims.

2. OVERVIEW

Farmers Insurance Group Inc., (Farmers Exchanges) headquartered in Los Angeles, Calif., are a wholly owned subsidiary of Zurich Financial Services. The Farmers Insurance Group of companies is a personal lines property and casualty insurance group providing homeowners, auto and life insurance as well as financial services in the United States. The recent acquisition of AIG's US Personal Auto Group, including 21st Century Insurance, strengthened Farmers' position as the third-largest insurance group in the U.S., operating in 49 states and Washington, D.C. The acquisition positions Farmers as the largest auto insurer in several states, including California. Prior to the acquisition, Farmers already provided insurance and financial services to 10.5 million U.S. households.

Farmers Exchanges, serving Farmers Insurance Group, with an industry-leading commitment to customer service, is constantly seeking ways to improve service delivery, particularly claims processing, to customers for all insurance product lines, from auto to personal property.

Driving growth through acquisition of other insurance providers, Farmers faced challenges integrating the customer service systems of acquired companies to ensure quality service for established customers and for customers from acquired companies.

Farmers was processing more than five million inbound and outbound calls annually. They had developed contact centers to centralize operations and created economies of scale to process claims efficiently. They had also developed a primary claims process based on Siebel CRM software in the past, as they acquired more companies; they continued to add other systems to the mix. They soon realized that if they were to continue segregating customer service representatives by the legacy claims system they were accustomed to using, it would **diminish** the return on employee investment and **reduce** their claims-handling capabilities.

Farmers assembled a road map of activities encompassing more than 300 separate initiatives to be accomplished through cooperative efforts between business teams and IT. The overall goals of the initiatives were to introduce standardized business practices, develop standardized business rules, enable faster service capabilities ramp-up, capitalize on functions shared across all business and product lines, and reduce training costs associated with customer service support systems.

Farmers turned to a joint business and IT development process to define the operating requirements of the project. First, the application needed to be easily configurable to maximize use of business and IT resources. Next, it needed to support the current claims application (Siebel). It needed to demonstrate performance and scalability to support large volumes of calls and staff, particularly when Farmers responds to natural disasters or other large-scale catastrophes. Finally, it needed to be an "agnostic" front end that could easily integrate with disparate back office and external applications across all of Farmers Insurance Group as well as potential "to be" acquired companies.

After reviewing offerings from four companies, Farmers selected Pegasystems' SmartBPM as the framework to support FNOL for its auto claims. The powerful SmartBPM engine contains both rules and process to enable intent led interactions bringing the right data and the correct choices to the CSR's screen at the moment they are needed.

The results were significant, including drastic improvements in both productivity and customer satisfaction. Farmers not only reduced training time and costs; it drastically sped up the processing of claims. In a business where hundreds of thousands of claims are in various stages during the course of any given year, streamlining these processes makes a world of difference.

3. BUSINESS CONTEXT

Founded in 1928, Farmers has approximately $18 billion in sales. Today, Farmers Insurance Group of Companies is the third-largest insurer in the U.S. of both private Personal Lines passenger automobile and homeowners insurance, and also provides a wide range of other insurance and financial services products. Farmers operates primarily in 41 states across the country through the efforts of approximately 24,000 employees. Farmers exclusive and independent agents, along with Farmers employees, are responsible for servicing more than 15 million customers.

Farmers' recent acquisition of 21st Century Insurance from AIG placed the company in the top three largest insurance group in the U.S. The acquisition presented Farmers with the challenge of integrating the customer service systems of acquired companies to ensure quality service for established customers and for customers from acquired companies.

Farmers Exchange undertook this project to bring a new degree of order and consistency to their contact center operations. There was an inability to readily integrate the customers of the newly acquired companies with the same level of high quality of service that Farmers was known for offering.

Over time, the multiple acquired systems were not integrating information or performing well together. The training of each system for customer service associates (CSRs) was becoming lengthy and costly for the organization. The segregation of the CSRs to each system was reducing productivity as well.

HERO Vision – a "decoupled" tool to handle First Notices across all LOBs to facilitate cross training and new business acquisitions

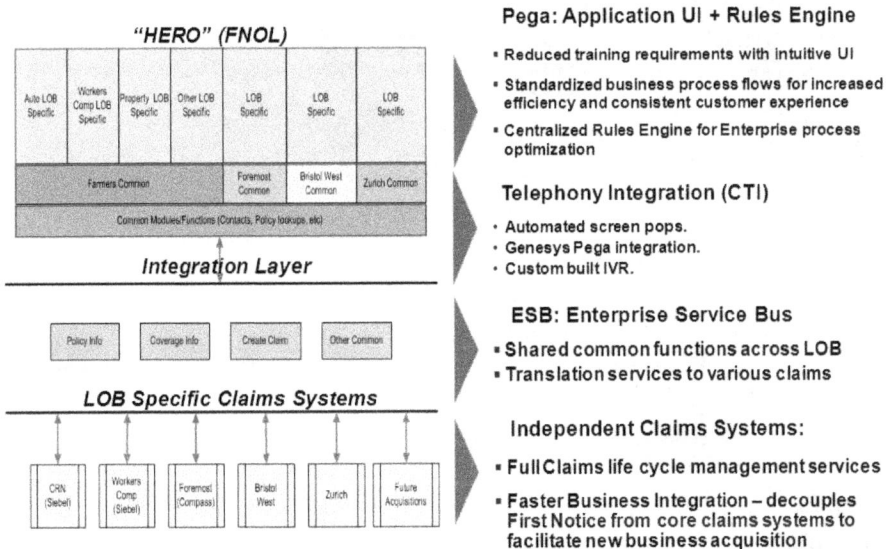

Pega: Application UI + Rules Engine
- Reduced training requirements with intuitive UI
- Standardized business process flows for increased efficiency and consistent customer experience
- Centralized Rules Engine for Enterprise process optimization

Telephony Integration (CTI)
- Automated screen pops.
- Genesys Pega integration.
- Custom built IVR.

ESB: Enterprise Service Bus
- Shared common functions across LOB
- Translation services to various claims

Independent Claims Systems:
- Full Claims life cycle management services
- Faster Business Integration – decouples First Notice from core claims systems to facilitate new business acquisition

Most importantly, it was taking away from Farmers' customer service as well as the CSR job of managing their interactions with multiple systems was becoming more difficult. Turnover was much higher than normal, and higher than what was acceptable. To maintain these old methods were too costly and inefficient to continue.

A solution that could bring together the many disparate systems into a single cohesive platform was needed.

4. THE KEY INNOVATIONS

4.2 Business

Farmers, departed from the typical development model whereby the business side submits requirements and IT reviews those requirements and re-engages the business once having built the solution. They took a different tack, where the business people represented each of the sections for auto and spent eight months with IT at a development center participating in daily sessions analyzing requirements and processes for the project. Throughout the whole phase, iterative development methods allowed team members to witness systematic development of the tools they would be using. This helped to minimize the surprise at the end. It also enabled them to see whether the options for the CSRs within the GUI (graphical user interface) were either overboard or where it might need more functionality.

From this project, Farmers replaced the complex legacy systems with a proprietary application that provided CSRs with an easy-to-use front end dubbed "HERO." HERO presents information and logically sequenced questions to guide customers through the FNOL process. The HERO contact center piece puts all claims first notices and status calls on a common platform so that CSRs only have to train on one system, regardless of the back-end claims or policy system.

Requirements were detailed thru the Elaboration Phase, with the business and Technology teams focusing on Functional Use Cases and Technical Design

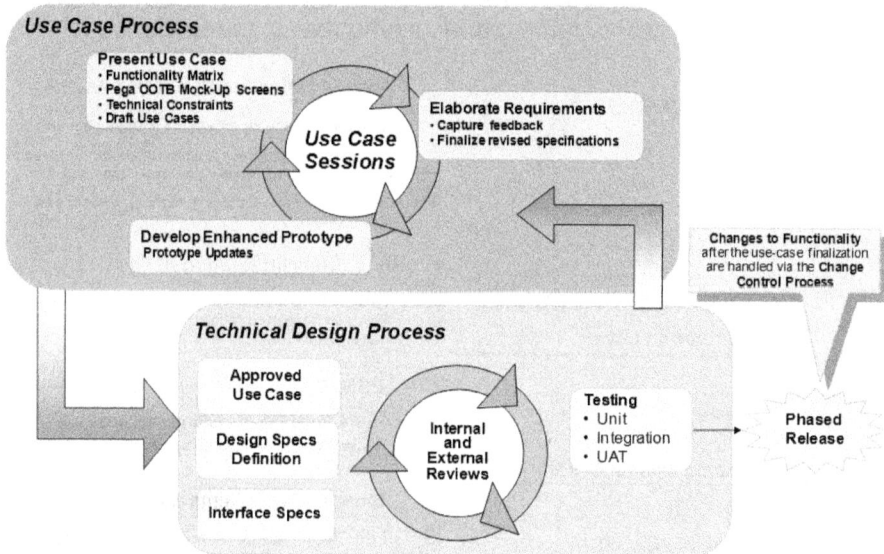

4.3 Process

Process (Before) – The processes were all manual and reflected the knowledge of the individual claims handler and their experience with their respective systems. Multiple call center organizations, across the United States, handled calls in radically different manners. Call loads could not be balanced or shifted as demand changed. Ramp up for emergency situations (e.g., hurricanes, earthquakes, large scale natural disasters) was long and costly.

The CSR's dealt with multiple backend systems in order to service the needs of the caller. Creating inconsistent customer experiences across the board. Much of the call quality depended on the CSR's experience level and knowledge of where to look for information.

Performance reporting was haphazard and lacked standardization. The training cycle was long. Burn-out and turnover were common and help to drive costs upward.

The CSR training cycle was long and costly. Once trained, CSR's still had to spend months and weeks getting proficient in using multiple systems. The skills acquired in training were not fungible across the greater organization.

In summary, the process would not scale and would not support or work for company that was rapidly growing through acquisition.

Process (After) – The claims processes for notice of loss are all automated and reflect best practice of the greater Farmers organization. The collective knowledge of the individual claims handler and their experience has been incorporated into the BPM tool. All calls, through multiple call center organizations, across the United States, are handled in a standard, measurable and repeatable manner. Call loads can be balanced and shifted as demand changes. Ramp up for emergency situations (e.g., hurricanes, earthquakes, large scale natural disasters) can be achieved in a manner of hours. Additional staff can quickly and easily be trained.

The CSR's deal with a single intuitive interface to service the needs of the caller. Creating consistent and informed customer experiences across the board. The call quality emanates from the CSR's ability to listen to the caller's need and the BPM tools ability to lead the process intelligently through context aware computing. As a result, average handling time has been reduced by 20%. This added capacity allows Farmers to take on an increased call load with incurring addition costs.

Performance reporting is consistent and deep with industry accepted standardization. Reporting can be generated at the CSR, unit division or organization level either real time or through an extensive system of reports and charts.

The training cycle is short. It requires one day to become proficient on the system and to immediately take customer calls. Burn-out and turnover have been significantly reduced.

In summary, the current process can scale to meet the business needs, is agile and built for business change. Farmers has continued to pursue an aggressive M&A strategy that has solidified its market leadership and increased revenues.

4.4 Organization

The project impacted the employees by creating a better CSR experience, thus creating a better customer experience overall.

Farmers wanted to allow the CSR to focus on the customer's needs and let the system do the heavy lifting and decisioning based on the responses of the customer. This was accomplished through an approach known as "intent-led" processing. Intent led processing is enabled when processes are sophisticated enough to be content aware. For example, as the CSR works through the call on an accident claim, an event like "car drivable" or "car not drivable" would initiate totally different streams of activities and tasks based on the customer's response. If the car was not drivable the CSR would automatically be presented with lists of towing companies and car rental companies for the applicable area. If the car was drivable the CSR would see the applicable repair shops. The customer's choice would always lead to more context sensitive processes that supported the CSR's ability to service the client, until the call was completed.

The customer experienced a highly customized interaction driven by the situation, the need and the policy coverages. Once the loss data was captured, the claim is then routed to all involved parties (e.g., physician, hospital, car repair, glass replacement, towing, auto rental etc.) and tracked with specific service levels (based on the policy and coverages). At any point in time the claim status (and all parts and pieces) can be determined by the claims manager.

Before this project, the CSRs would have to enter all the data of the customer calling, check multiple systems for information and approval. However, the biggest challenge would be constantly keeping all the elements of the process in their memory. From a management perspective, accurately tracking claim status was a nightmare, particularly on complex claims. The claim event and all the components were very difficult to reconstruct and to visualize.

5. HURDLES OVERCOME

Management

The project had a dedicated VP-level champion who managed the cross-functional project team and served as a catalyst in bringing IT and business together for this corporate-wide success.

The challenge the management faced was navigating and understanding the impact that a collection of acquired systems had on contact center operations, then having the wherewithal to realize that changes must be made.

They overcame this challenge by implementing the project and incorporating all the needs of the employees, management and the customers.

Business

The launch began with a revamping of the first notice of loss (FNOL) system for automobile claims because it is a critical, high-volume point of contact for customers. With the success that the automobile claims line of business, Farmers can now implement it to other areas of the company's vast line of businesses. This one project, the implementation of HERO can be across other lines of business to produce similar results.

Organization Adoption

Adoption has been a "grass roots" phenomenon. Organizational adoption has quickly occurred as this intuitive CSR-centric system has liberated staff at one contact center after another. The challenges that CSRs faced was the fact there were multiple CRM systems to use. The jobs of a CSR were difficult and cumbersome with the multiple systems.

6. BENEFITS

Since going live, HERO has driven up CSR quality assurance scores in terms of both efficiency and file quality, as measured by appropriateness of the claim paid. The application also has driven reductions in overall claims handling times and queue times, enabling more calls to be handled by a representative in a given day. Furthermore, the application facilitates rapid ramp-up in response to catastrophes.

In a catastrophe situation, Farmers can ramp up to service within a couple of hours rather than waiting days trying to figure out how to put more employees on the floor at call centers to answer calls. Because of the intent led processing, HE-

RO also enables CSRs to be trained in a single day rather than over a two-week period, as was necessary with the multiple legacy system.

The application's ease of use drives both efficiency and CSR morale. It was cited in an e-mail from a supervisor that ends with the following statement: "I cannot say how grateful I am to every single developer, every dollar spent and all the people who travelled for so long to make this remarkable product for us to use...This is the Cadillac of claims reporting; it is our future, and it is our HERO!"

6.1 Cost Savings

HERO was able to reduce costs by reducing training hours and costs associated with training. Instead of having multiple systems and training on each, this one easy-to-use system.

Actual training time was reduced from two weeks to one day. This 90% reduction, as incredible as it is, reflects only part of the cost savings. The "intent led" nature of the content aware processes give the new CSR the full benefit of all the best practices used by a seasoned and experienced employee. So the traditional learning curve to achieve effectiveness with customers is dramatically impacted in Farmer's favor.

In addition, staff turnover has been reduced as has employee burn-out.

Finally, the re-use of technical components used to build the Hero BPM solution was evaluated to be at approximately 45%. This re-use factor will speed further development initiatives and continue to lower the total cost of ownership of the technical applications. (A PowerPoint deck is available outlining the technical savings in greater detail)

6.2 Time Reductions

The application has also driven reductions in overall claims handling times and queue times, enabling more calls to be handled by a representative in a given day.

Average Handling Time (AHT) has been reduced by 20%. The equates to adding an additional 20% to the staff at no additional cost. Meaning the current staff can handle higher call volumes without the need to add additional staff.

6.3 Increased Revenues

The application has allowed Farmers to actively engage in M&A activity, bringing new books of business quickly into the standard Farmers HelpPoint© business model. Farmers is no longer constrained in its growth through acquisition strategy.

6.4 Productivity Improvements

Farmers Group delivered a number of business milestones in the first year of this project including an increase in the quality measured in processing claims.

Overall quality scores have improved by 6% indicating improved customer experiences and enhanced service.

The table below indicates other business productivity improvements brought on by the Hero project:

HERO Vision – a "decoupled" tool to handle First Notices across all LOBs to facilitate cross training and new business acquisitions

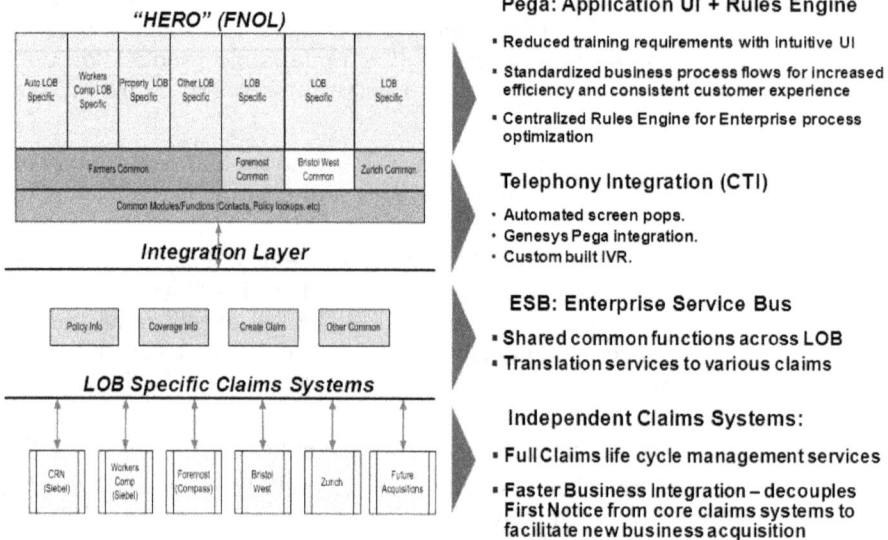

"HERO" (FNOL)

Auto LOB Specific	Workers Comp LOB Specific	Property LOB Specific	Other LOB Specific	LOB Specific	LOB Specific	LOB Specific

Farmers Common			Foremost Common	Bristol West Common	Zurich Common

Common Modules/Functions (Contacts, Policy lookups, etc)

Integration Layer

Policy Info	Coverage Info	Create Claim	Other Common

LOB Specific Claims Systems

CRN (Siebel)	Workers Comp (Siebel)	Foremost (Compass)	Bristol West	Zurich	Future Acquisitions

Pega: Application UI + Rules Engine

- Reduced training requirements with intuitive UI
- Standardized business process flows for increased efficiency and consistent customer experience
- Centralized Rules Engine for Enterprise process optimization

Telephony Integration (CTI)

- Automated screen pops.
- Genesys Pega integration.
- Custom built IVR.

ESB: Enterprise Service Bus

- Shared common functions across LOB
- Translation services to various claims

Independent Claims Systems:

- Full Claims life cycle management services
- Faster Business Integration – decouples First Notice from core claims systems to facilitate new business acquisition

Business Area	Productivity Benefits
State Requirements	All mandatory state specific scripting is included Additional Suggestion/Recommendation scripting is available
Coverage	System will clear more coverage issues behind the scenes (without CSR intervention) Reduced calls to the CCST to validate coverage Early coverage validation results in fewer claims stuck in pending status
Automated File Notes	All required file note information is gathered by the system
Total Loss Screening	More accurate gathering of damage description More accurate point totals System will identify when a vehicle qualifies for total loss
Vendors	No more "missed" vendors System takes CSR through the options in correct order System will not offer a vendor if it does not apply (policy and coverage) All search results will display automatically without CSR intervention or delay

7. BEST PRACTICES, LEARNING POINTS AND PITFALLS

7.1 Best Practices and Learning Points

- ✓ *Focus on the customer as a central point by building the process that gets to where the customer wants to go*
- ✓ *Have IT and business work together to rapidly develop business solutions; Rapidly prototype and iterate the targeted solution*

✓ Eliminate the non-value added process steps

✓ Listen and learn from the current process; focus on key dysfunctional areas

✓ Ensure that all processes achieve a high level of consistency permitting customers to receive the same excellent quality of service

7.2 Pitfalls

✗ Cultural aversion to process; communicate every step of the way with audiences across the organization to make them comfortable with the idea of process

✗ Leading with technology; successful BPM projects are driven by business imperatives

✗ Failing to construct an intuitive process; make sure the process makes practical business sense and delivers real results

8. COMPETITIVE ADVANTAGES

With a new, single-screen interface, structured, fully scripted and question-and-answer based processes, CSRs process more claims, in less time, resulting in improved customer satisfaction and increased productivity.

Because HERO is scalable, and has received a positive response from auto claims CSRs, it's being implemented to support Farmers recent acquisition of 21st Century Insurance (auto) and other lines of business including commercial property, property, specialty, and worker's compensation.

With HERO, Farmers can implement this strategy to other lines of business. Auto was the first business line to benefit from it, and several more lines of business could use an approach that HERO provides. Farmers, for the short and long term, is looking replace the entire core claims application and improve the level and quality of client service, while simultaneously raising productivity and generating cost savings across multiple business lines.

Additional advantages:
- Increased Straight Thru Processing – Claims are handled efficiently and completely. Fewer are set aside for additional review and manual handling. STP reduces operating expense ratios and gives a competitive edge.
- Reduced Training and Call Time – Farmers can ramp up for disaster situations rapidly. The faster claims are resolved, the lower the overall cost of claims.
- Enhanced Coverage Verification – Knowing early in the process whether a claim should even be considered is critical to keeping costs lower than the competition.
- Improved Accuracy of Potential Total Loss – Knowing when to declare a total loss or to attempt salvage is a key differentiation factor. Automating the scoring improves consistency and reduces leakage.

These collective factors will allow Farmers to keep its overall costs to adjudicate a claim low and keep its overall pricing highly competitive in the marketplace.

9. TECHNOLOGY

After reviewing offerings from four companies, Farmers selected Pegasystems' SmartBPM as the framework to support FNOL for its auto claims. The powerful SmartBPM rules engine contains administration rules and enables intelligent interactions according to rules of specific claims transactions. Farmers also chose Pegasystems Process Commander (PRPC) as the framework to their project.

Farmers selected PRPC because of its agility, functionality and because it less costly than purpose-built solutions. It was the only solution that met all of Farmers' requirements. The idea behind Farmer's road map was to decouple certain processes and functions to get the most out of a solution, change its view of technology and the current working environment, as well as move toward a service oriented architecture environment. This technology enabled that to happen.

Based on the SmartBPM tool, HERO triggers the right questions, gathers the right answers and integrates into the claim system itself so that all information becomes part of the case file. Key to the application's functionality is the ability to support scripting through logic for specific loss types reported and to enable intuitive process workflows.

The Pegasystems capabilities within HERO are integrated with back-end applications, including claims and some policy administration systems, through an Oracle BEA Aqualogic Service Bus. Most of the information is passed through the main Oracle Siebel claims system so that the adjusters in the field get everything they need as the Siebel systems knows exactly what has been handed to it. Basic information is also retained within HERO, so if there is a subsequent status call on a given claim, the CSR can present the current status of the claim. It is a true front layer of the main claims application.

The Pega solution delivers a variety of unique features that have impacted the Farmers project and delivered industry-first results. Among these are:

Directly Executable Business Objectives – Business users can input their business objectives, process steps and business rules directly in the system. Additionally, they can change, based on their security profile, rules and tables that run their organizations without the need for programmer intervention or coding.

Unified Policies and Procedures – Business users understand that they can change a rule in one place and they are guaranteed that the rule self-deploys across the business, appropriately

Situational Layer Cake – Business processes can actually share their true commonalities so that rule maintenance is significantly decreased. This allowed Farmers to specialize standard claims reporting processes by state, thus eliminating redundant rules across a standardized process.

Flex Scale Deployment – HERO has been integrated with multiple external and internal legacy systems, eliminating issues with data entry and data integrity. HERO can scale to accommodate additional business users and locations without performance degradation.

Intent-Driven User Experience – The process begins with the end result in mind. The system now asks only those questions that need to be asked in order to get the result intended and the task accomplished, leading to significant time savings and customer satisfaction.

10. THE TECHNOLOGY AND SERVICE PROVIDERS

Pegasystems, the leader in business process management and a leading provider of CRM solutions, helps organizations enhance customer loyalty, generate new business, and improve productivity. Pegasystems' patented Build for Change® technology speeds the delivery of critical business solutions by directly capturing business objectives and eliminating manual programming. Pegasystems enables clients to quickly adapt to changing business conditions in order to outperform the competition. http://www.pega.com

Lincoln Trust Company, USA

Silver Award: North America
Nominated by Lincoln Trust Company, USA

1. EXECUTIVE SUMMARY / ABSTRACT

Lincoln Trust Company constituted a BPM program in 2007 with the initial goals focused on operational efficiency and going paperless in our back office processes. The overall program has been widely acknowledged for its tremendous success and directly contributed to Lincoln Trust Company's survival in the face of the global financial crisis. This paper discusses the continuation of the program and specifically describes our experiences implementing one of our most evolved BPM processes to date.

Over the past year Lincoln Trust Company has faced a new, better, and very significant challenge- growth! One of Lincoln Trust Company's most strategic business channels has developed a partner channel that has resulted in a 100% increase in sales from last year and is anticipating 1000% increases in new plan establishment. Thrilled with the prospects, but concerned with the impact to new customers, staff, and budget, Lincoln Trust Company executive management decided to leverage our BPM competencies to achieve a vision to provide "white glove" treatment to our new customers, automate the process, and significantly reduce the need for additional staffing within the business unit. The new business process is not only allowing us to efficiently establish significant new business, it is also seen as a sales differentiator helping our sales staff win new business. For the first time, IT is being invited by the business on sales presentations to partner in the discussion of superior process and technology for our customers.

2. OVERVIEW

Lincoln Trust Company has had a thriving BPM program since 2007. The executive sponsors have evolved the strategic goals of the program each year as our own corporate strategy has evolved. In prior years, our focus had been on gaining operational efficiencies through an enterprise wide "paperless" process initiative implemented within a BPM framework. As our technology and BPM approach matured, our executive sponsors challenged us to build on the success by conducting BPM projects that would enable a corporate strategy to automate all of our business processes by extending our processes to our customers and using web service technology. By 2009, we had several core business processes for the IRA Services business operating in this manner.

It was in this context that a new and exciting challenge arrived in the form of a massive new business opportunity for the Corporate Retirement Services business of Lincoln Trust Company. It had the potential to generate a 1000% (one thousand percent) increase in monthly new business volume for that team. This opportunity came to Lincoln Trust Company by virtue of a strategic partnership with another firm in the industry that needed a trusted partner to whom they could refer their valued clients when the services they were seeking did not fit into the partner's service model. However, this partner would expect flawless execution immediately upon the start of the partnership. If Lincoln Trust Company failed to provide anything less than "white glove" service, our partner would direct the business elsewhere.

At the same time, the executive leadership of the company was indicating that they were very interested in growing the Corporate Retirement Services department by acquisition. This would present another growth challenge for the department, potentially hitting them at the same time the partnership would ramp up.

As a result, the Corporate Retirement Services department needed to scale its entire business rapidly, starting with its new business process. The on-boarding of new retirement plan business from our strategic partner would be the first touch point with their clients. If this did not go well, then the relationship with the client would be jeopardized from the start. Unfortunately, as described later in the case study, this process is known industry-wide as being very long, arduous and full of opportunities to make mistakes. The Corporate Retirement Services business decided that a rapid transformation in this process was the first priority in their challenge to scale.

3. BUSINESS CONTEXT

After continued success with BPM, we were faced with a tough act to follow, especially dealing with the most complicated business process to date. Although *complete* automation is one of Lincoln Trust's corporate strategies, this particular business process was not a good candidate for typical BPMS implementation. However, the most cost effective way to meet this challenge was to leverage our previously deployed BPMS automation and infrastructure without encumbering the knowledge worker participants in the process by disrupting them with a hailstorm of process tasks. Besides complexity, Lincoln Trust Company had to overcome the best kind of challenge, growth. A wave of incoming new business was imminent, and without impactful automation, the all-important, first impression was at significant risk of falling short of expectations.

Confronted with perplexing business logic and impending corporate growth, we rose to the challenge and delivered a comprehensive solution, which positions the company to handle new clients without hiring new staff. With our business partners, we have built a reusable and reliable foundation on which new business can be added with "white glove" service. Tasks, which were once tedious and error-prone, are now automated and seamless. For example, using automation, we eliminated the manual entry risks associated with keying-in the *same* mutual fund data four different times. The implementation differentiates Lincoln Trust Company in the marketplace. While we believe many competitors are following our lead in automating the New Business process, Lincoln Trust Company has a real competitive advantage- we have designed a solution to efficiently setup new business and created a simplified solution for our customers.

4. THE KEY INNOVATIONS

4.2 Business

We believe Lincoln Trust Company has leapfrogged its larger competitors and addressed one of the most time-consuming, resource-draining parts of the new business process milestones by introducing an electronic, legal document solution in the cloud, and system to system "straight through processing" into the new business process running in our BPMS. This approach to new business has turned the lengthy and complex experience of completing multiple legal documents into a "white glove" experience for new clients and their financial advisors.

The sales team holds one online meeting bringing them all together with pre-filled online documents, walks them through each of them and then coaches them through the electronic signature process. Immediately after the client has electronically signed the documents, system integration with the electronic document software vendor imports it into the BPMS and attaches it to an in-flight BPMS process where the new business specialists are notified of its arrival. The same cloud integration also files the signed PDF into the imaging system.

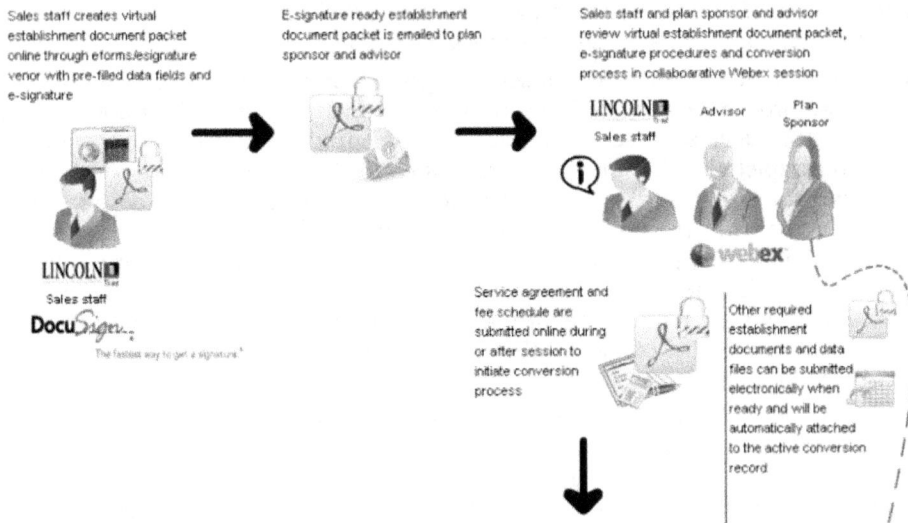

Sales staff creates virtual establishment document packet online through eforms/esignature venor with pre-filled data fields and e-signature

LINCOLN
Sales staff
DocuSign.
The fastest way to get a signature.

E-signature ready establishment document packet is emailed to plan sponsor and advisor

Sales staff and plan sponsor and advisor review virtual establishment document packet, e-signature procedures and conversion process in collaboarative Webex session

LINCOLN   Advisor   Plan Sponsor
Sales staff

webex

Service agreement and fee schedule are submitted online during or after session to initiate conversion process

Other required establishment documents and data files can be submitted electronically when ready and will be automatically attached to the active conversion record

On electronic receipt of web data and documents, a business process management system record is created for the conversion process. All documents and information related to the conversion is loaded into the record and the new business team is notified of new conversion information. Each Teamworks activity will have embedded, detailed checklists to help the conversion team manage a conversion's service level and regulatory timeline requirements

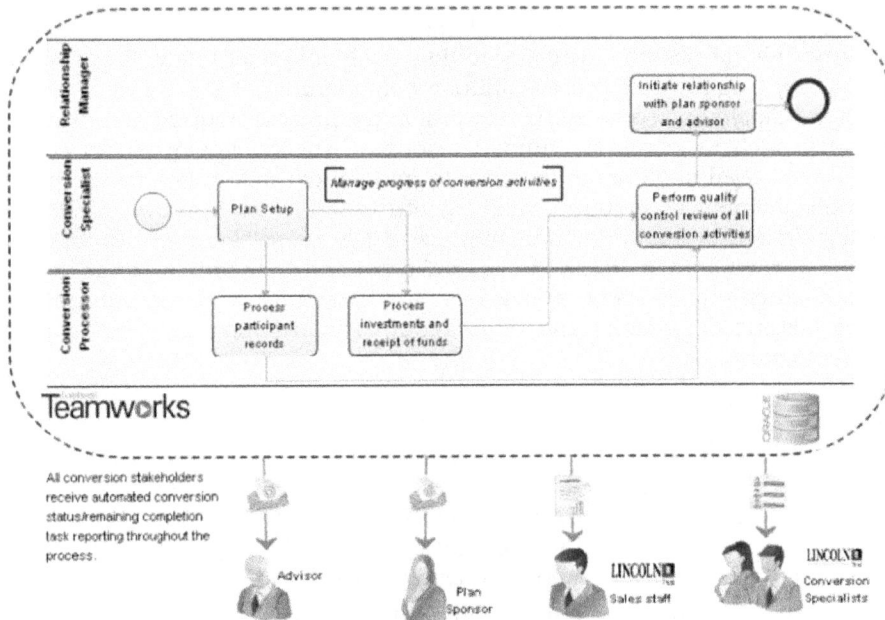

Relationship Manager — Initiate relationship with plan sponsor and advisor

Conversion Specialist — Plan Setup — Manage progress of conversion activities — Perform quality control review of all conversion activities

Conversion Processor — Process participant records — Process investments and receipt of funds

Teamworks

All conversion stakeholders receive automated conversion status/remaining completion task reporting throughout the process.

Advisor   Plan Sponsor   LINCOLN Sales staff   LINCOLN Conversion Specialists

Figure 1 Overview of new CRS New Business Process

This cloud-based integration legal document solution reduced multiple data quality issues and overall process delays due to legal documents not being received on time or filled out correctly.

Prior to the project, these legal documents and other files of plan information had to be manually uploaded and keyed into the line of business system. With the implementation of the "straight through processing" features of the project, upon receipt of the files, the data is 'scraped' from the documents and directly uploaded into the line of business system, eliminating significant data entry time, and reducing financial risks associated with data entry errors.

The "case management" process solution pattern introduced a new and successful BPMS process pattern to Lincoln Trust Company's process solutions. Instead of a typical business process diagram implementation in our BPMS requiring a user to complete low level tasks for each step in the real world business process, the user is presented with a centralized dashboard of all new business processes in flight, the current status, activities completed and those outstanding. This same visibility and process context information is available to indirect process participants like the relationship manager, department manager and supervisor and the sales staff. Various reports allow other views of the same information to others who prefer to consume the information outside of SharePoint and our BPMS (Teamworks).

In short, all of the features delivered in the project have eliminated time in the process to continually follow up on missing or incorrect documentation and key in data we've already received electronically. The impact to the business team is that they have freed up capacity for the CRS New Business Process and significantly reduced the need for any future hiring of additional staff. They've met a significant challenge and delivered in multiple iterations completed within five months time.

4.3 Process

The corporate retirement plan new business on-boarding process is notorious industry-wide for being challenging to do quickly and accurately. It is almost always a very long running process (industry standard is 90-120 days). Several key milestones, including some of the very first in the process, require non-expert participants, such as corporate human resource benefits employees, to complete complicated legal documents in order to initiate key milestones in the process. Legal documents also require a valid signature – either an approved electronic or original signature. A major source of process delay is getting these various documents returned from stakeholders in good order and in time to avoid delaying the process. Much time is spent by new business knowledge workers calling to follow up on missing documents and other required information in order to get the process to move.

The corporate retirement plan industry is also heavily regulated by the United States Department of Labour (DOL). The DOL has published intense regulations that sometimes declare how long certain process milestones can take. Consequences of delaying process can be as severe as plan "disqualification" where the employer sponsoring the plan will no longer be afforded the tax benefits of the plan and all money invested in the plan by the employer and its employees becomes taxable retroactively, among other penalties.

One example of regulations built into the business process requirements is what is called a "blackout period", where the retirement plan has already been established and is transferring assets from one custodian to another. During this time period, employees aren't allowed to perform certain transactions such as withdrawals, retirement plan loans and investment changes. The begin date and duration of this milestone is very clearly prescribed by law, with very specific participant notification requirements.

In general, the character of the new business process is unstructured and asynchronous, with over 150 tasks and milestones. The CRS New Business Process can require up to 14 different documents and various data files to initiate certain process activities. Prior to the start of the project, the CRS New Business Process was managed in Excel spreadsheets and all key data and documents were manually gathered and input into the line of business record-keeping system, Relius. Running this business process required an employee who was very familiar with regulations to closely monitor the process to make sure the employer and the client are not harmed. Because of the limitations of Excel, and manual processing, prior to the start of the project the team did not feel that they could manage more than a few plan conversion at any given time.

In the new process implemented as part of the CRS New Business Process Project, the process architecture is a design that integrates third-party systems, internal web applications, custom web services, the company's BPMS, imaging system and business intelligence application jobs.

During the lifecycle of plan establishment there are various participants involved – Sales Team, Plan Sponsor (or customer), and a new business specialist. When a plan sponsor has signed on as a new customer, the new business specialist initiates a BPMS process instance in Teamworks using in-house developed .NET application called "CRS PENS", which also generates the new Lincoln Trust Company account number, and sends e-forms for all required documents to the plan sponsor using DocuSign.

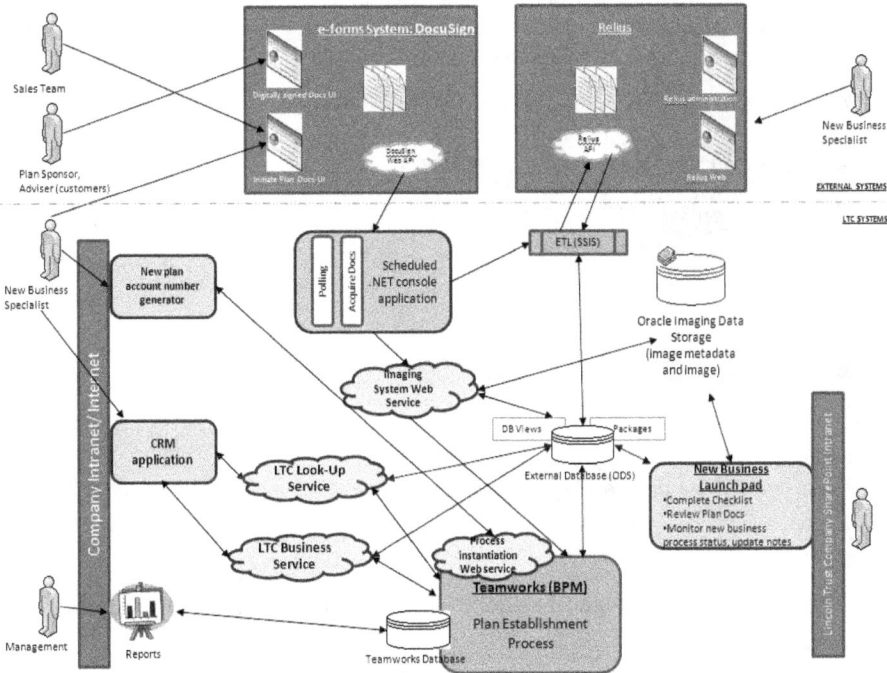

Figure 2 - Overview of CRS New Business Process technology/architecture

The plan sponsor then accesses, fills in and electronically signs information in the DocuSign e-forms. The completed documents are retrieved from the DocuSign system through a scheduled .NET console application. This application polls documents from DocuSign and stores them into our Oracle imaging repository via a web service wrapper created over the Oracle imaging system's web APIs and includes data massaging and exchange with our central company database called Operational Data Storage (ODS). Thus every time a new document arrives metadata is stored in Oracle's imaging database and a relationship between the document and corresponding active process instance is established. This feature, along with the DocuSign integration, eliminates paper legal documents from the process and also ensures that we keep the electronic documents in the same Oracle imaging repository as all other plan documents that will be received as the plan transitions from the new business process to normal daily business operations. This was previously a very manual process and was highly subject to the risk of missing or incorrectly classified documents.

For the line of business system STP features, the scheduled .NET console application invokes an "extract transform load" (ETL) job using SQL Server Integration Services (SSIS) to electronically submit new plan data to the Relius "Admin Module". This feature eliminates the need for manually keying in data (that we've already received electronically through the integration described above) into the record-keeping system.

Following SOA principles, Lincoln Trust Company developed various lookup services, such as plan lookup services, document lookup service and account lookup business web services. All these web services are widely consumed by diverse systems. Information about a plan can be retrieved and accessed by all authenticated users through an internal web-based CRM application, called "Plan Pop-Up". The Plan Pop-Up is accessed by different user groups including phone representatives and CRS management. This application also displays all DocuSign and any other imaged documents related to the plan.

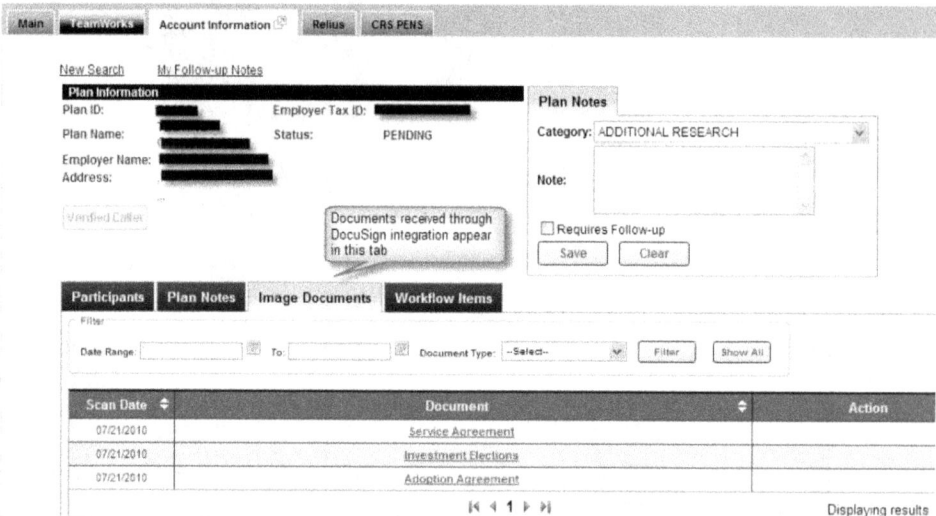

Figure 3 "Plan Pop-Up" application showing DocuSign documents

To track and monitor conversion process, instead of using an Excel spreadsheet, the new business specialist now uses a .NET user interface called the "Conversion Launch Pad". This application allows users to fill in a process checklist and initiate process events. Many of the 150+ process tasks that were not good candidates for automation became checklist task items rather than BPMS activities. However, certain checklist items *are automatically updated* as electronic documents and other information is received through the integration with DocuSign and our external portal.

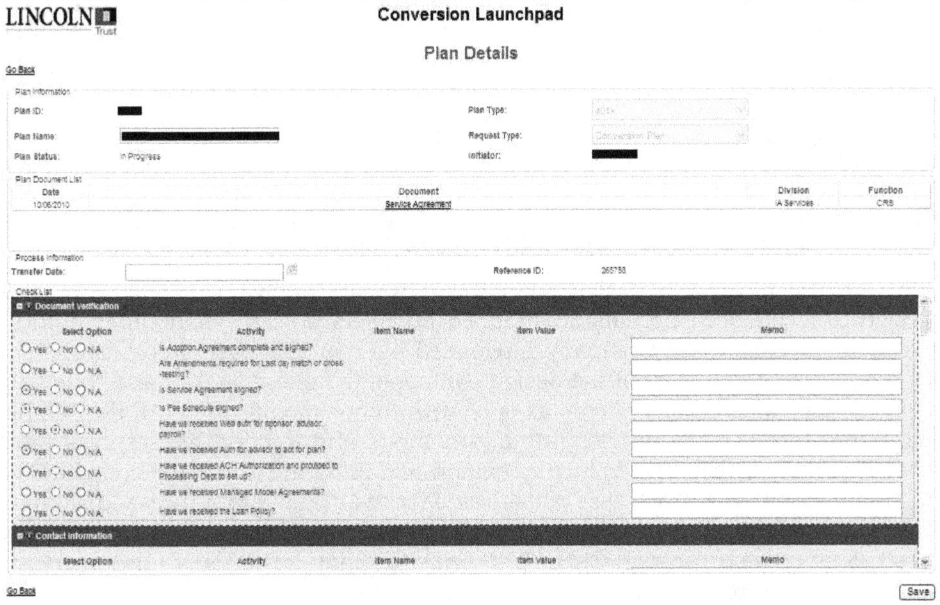

Figure 4 Conversion Launch Pad

Relevant process instance information is sent to an underlying Teamworks process from Conversion Launch Pad through Java Messaging Services (JMS) and web services. Architecturally the goal is to use this portal application as friendly user interface and eliminate any user need to look up process state through Teamworks Portal. This approach was chosen specifically because of our lessons learned from our prior project discussed later in the case study (Section 5, Hurdles Overcome). We knew it would be imperative that there be one centralized UI from which the user could conduct all relevant tasks. Using a .NET UI gave us the flexibility to make this interface as smart and visually appealing as possible, but we would still be using out BPMS as the "process backbone" and taking advantage of the infrastructure connected to it (imaging integration, portal integration, business data storage, SSRS reporting, etc.). Also, the process portal of our BPMS has a limitation where only one user can own a process instance at a time. Using .NET UI approach allows multiple users to access and update same process instance simultaneously. Many concurrency handling procedures have been incorporated into the design.

Lincoln Trust Company uses SQL Server Reporting Services (SSRS) as a reporting solution to design enterprise and ad hoc reports displaying CRS New Business Process data. A variety of SSRS reports have been created allowing the CRS Management team to monitor progress on a single new business process instance or cumulative new business process instances.

Plan Establishment Dashboard

Plan Number	Plan Name	Request Type	Reference No.	Plan Create Date	Days Pending	Document Type	Days Asset Transfer	Asset Transfer Date	Days into Post Asset Transfer	Hyperlink to Checklist App for the Process
	401k Plan	Conversion Plan	198626	6/7/2010						View
		Conversion Plan	231051	7/30/2010		Service Agreement,	3	10/15/2010		View
	401K PLAN	Conversion Plan	246975	8/24/2010	Highlights records needing urgent attention			Provides link to exact process		View
	401K PLAN	Conversion Plan	246976	8/24/2010		Service Agreement,				View
	RETIREMENT TRUST	Conversion Plan	265758	9/27/2010		Service Agreement,				View

Report Date:
10/11/2010 5:15:52 PM | Confidential- For Internal Use Only | 1 of 1
http://davpmosrep01:8080/ReportServer/http://thekey/reports/teamworks/teamworks/teamworks plan establishment dashboard.rdl

Figure 5 SSRS report with link to Conversion Launch Pad

With respect to process design adaptability, we are applying this same process design to a different, partially abandoned business process for another product group at Lincoln Trust Company referenced later in this case study (Section 5, Hurdles Overcome). Most of the design components adhere to SOA and thus they may interact with other systems as is or with minor modification. All the components have explicit boundaries, are autonomous and support generic type payload. This design allows us to further extend and integrate any of the components. In Teamworks, the CRS New Business Process "business process definition" (BPD) is metadata-driven and thus it is not necessary that a process instance need to be created through CRS PENS only. We may have many other mechanisms to initiate process instances that can be utilized in combination with this approach.

4.4 Organization

Before the CRS New Business Process, employees spent a significant amount of time dealing with missing or incomplete plan documents and trying to determine where in the new business process lifecycle a given instance was. Now employees spend less time asking the question "Where am I? What's left to complete? What deadlines are at risk?" and more time to provide "white glove" service. The knowledge worker (new business specialist) has been freed up to spread their time out across more incoming new business volume, which is a major step in the challenge to scale the business quickly.

5. HURDLES OVERCOME

5.1 Management

A major hurdle we faced was that for several years the CRS business unit had not been the primary focus for technology investment within the company. The vast majority of IT's focus had been on our IRA business and that resulted in a lack of trust on the part of the CRS business unit that IT would be committed to delivery. This was overcome by strong executive leadership over the BPM program and across organizational operating units. From the projects outset it was made clear that a business manager within CRS was responsible for the project along with IT leadership – success or failure was a shared responsibility and both CRS and IT staff embraced the challenge and formed a very strong partnership in the process.

5.2 Business

Lincoln Trust Company continues to be fortunate that our executive leadership has emphasized that nothing short of a dramatic transformation is required, especially related to business processes, across all levels of the organization. Because of this leadership we do not experience the level of resistance to change that was once much more pervasive in our company. One challenge the team faced early on, though, was the need to move quickly in our analysis phase and at the same time ensure that all process participants and stakeholders had a voice in the future state process. This was accomplished through a series of group meetings, facilitated utilizing Lombardi's Blueprint process mapping product that involved all process participants including the sales team, processors, relationship managers, department management, IT, and executive management. The current state process was mapped with all problems, problem severity and frequency, documented in Blueprint. Solutions and future state design were completed with a smaller working group and then presented to all process participants and executive management for review and input. The outcome of these exercises also included joint preparation between the CRS business unit and IT of a final business case that was presented to executive leadership for approval of the implementation phase.

5.3 Organization Adoption

We have not let up in the hard work it takes to create confidence and passion around the overall BPM program. The BPM program is regularly managing multiple project initiatives at any given time and the success of these initiatives has been widely communicated across all levels of the organization. Senior leadership continues to drive the BPM program roadmap, resource BPM projects, make key process architectural decisions and resolve conflicts needing resolution at their level. The executives also ensure that all BPM initiatives are managed with a project owner from both IT and business units that are equally responsible for success or failure of any particular initiative. This creates a great deal of ownership and accountability at an enterprise level that has enabled success at Lincoln Trust Company.

A specific design challenge for the CRS New Business Process Project that we felt at an organizational level, was that when we started the CRS New Business Process Project we were still dusting ourselves off from a fall "into a ditch" with a prior BPMS process implementation that had similar attributes. It was our first major setback in our BPM program related to the implementation of another very complex process in a different product group that is supported by several types of inputs and run in our BPMS. Like the new business process, this process had activity inputs of imaged forms, other documents from external firms, data submission via web, email and client phone conversations, internal email and phone conversations. During that project, we had worked side by side with the process owners and even hired external professional consultants to help us with the design and implementation of the process in the BPMS. We attempted to model the future state business process as best as we could, but there were several hundred use cases possible and we found ourselves having to make the process fit into the sequential constraints a BPMS.

In the end, we believe it was our attempt to model the process for the BPMS implementation so explicitly that created a proliferation of BPMS tasks and UI implementations (most of which were run by the same real world business participant) and we learned not too long after deploying the process to the production environment that it was just "too much BPMS" – too many clicks, too many activities, too much overhead for the wider team to use – without much payoff to them for using it. That business unit ultimately abandoned the new process for all but a few use cases and instead reverted back to using a basic workflow process pattern (with a single activity/UI where they can manage all documents and "case" details, mostly through accumulating required document attachments and updating notes) that we had implemented for them in the BPMS previously using a simple process model. This "solution abandonment" was a very clear indicator that we had failed in the design of this BPMS process solution and, as a result, we were very reflective about how we went wrong.

While there are several things we learned we could have done better in that prior project, the consensus was that our biggest miss was that we didn't recognize at design time that, for the more complex use cases, a case management pattern for the solution approach would have worked best. We also found that the key in what we need to do to correct the abandoned process, applied to the CRS New Business Process. We felt passionately about the need to apply the elements of case management process and UI design from research by Craig Le Clair and Connie Moore at Forrester Research (Forrester Research, "Dynamic Case Management – An Old Idea Catches New Fire", December 28, 2009), which is: 1) "design for people-build for change" and 2) follow "the seven tenets of the information workplace: role-based, contextual, seamless, visual, multimodal, social and quick." These became the guiding principles of our process design for the CRS New Business Process. In summary, we knew we needed to take an approach that was incremental to automate what was known, but leave many complex processes unstructured to avoid encumbering the knowledge worker.

6. BENEFITS

To date, our overall BPM Program costs savings as outlined in "BPM Excellence in Practice 2010" by Layna Fischer has now increased to between $3M and $4M. The BPM program at Lincoln Trust Company is a journey and we continue to build on our competencies and learnings.

Specific benefits for the CRS New Business process include:

6.1 Cost Savings

The same size business team can now handle many times more plan conversions concurrently, eliminating the need to hire employees as sales increase. The business case anticipates ongoing annual savings of $325,000, and the savings will increase as our business increases.

6.2 Time Reductions

Electronic signing of multiple conversion documents has reduced from a period of weeks to days, our ability to collect and review establishment forms. Straight through processing of plans to the host system has resulted in a reduction of hours to minutes for some plan documents.

6.3 Increased Revenues

We will be measure revenue increases over time, but we do anticipate additional referral business by our partner network because of our "white glove" customer process and overall plan conversion efficiency.

6.4 Productivity Improvements

Management and customer relationship managers can quickly view the detailed status of every step in a long running process, across plans, in real time. (The process was previously managed in excel with a separate document for each plan conversion. It was extremely difficult to determine the status of all plans or determine if any process steps had fallen through the cracks.) Conversion checklists integrated with the BPMS allow all team members to interact with a running process and collaborate on completion. Straight through processing, and data validation, with the core host system not only saves a tremendous amount of time, it also greatly reduces financial risk as a fund setup cannot be done incorrectly.

7. BEST PRACTICES, LEARNING POINTS AND PITFALLS

7.1 Best Practices and Learning Points

If you are dealing with a process that is complex, chaotic, asynchronous, ad hoc or collaborative (or has those elements): Consider researching and understanding the difference between traditional BPM implementations and "adaptive case management" (ACM) implementations. Application of the ACM implementation style and approach was a tremendous success in this project. A great book that we reference often is "Mastering the Unpredictable: How Adaptive Case Management Will Revolutionize the Way That Knowledge Workers Get Things Done" by Keith Swenson. We also reference research from Craig Le Clair and Connie Moore at Forrester Research, "Dynamic Case Management – An Old Idea Catches New Fire", December 28, 2009.

✓ Use professional services consultants or other partners that understand, and are open to, the difference between traditional BPM and ACM implementations

✓ Make sure the business is running the BPM project. We are fortunate to have many visionary business leaders at Lincoln Trust Company, one of whom ran this entire project and the various iterations from process discovery to solution implementation. This manager's command of his team's business processes, his management perspective and his grasp of technology were integral to the success of the project, far more so than any third-party expert (whether inside or outside of IT).

✓ We see this as an example of what Phil Gilbert of IBM has called the "democratization of BPM", where the business, meaning the actual business unit running the processes, runs the BPM projects. This "distributed model of COE" has proved so effective on so many levels for Lincoln Trust Company that the BPM program's entire non-technology focus is solely targeted on enabling these employees as much as possible.

7.2 Pitfalls

✗ Avoid lengthy development cycles. While some up front planning is required, especially from an enterprise architecture perspective, run the project and define solutions iteratively.

✗ Be careful not to model a process for the BPMS implementation so explicitly that it creates a proliferation of BPMS tasks and UI implementations. This can create too many activities, too many clicks, too much overhead for wider team use, potentially with limited benefit- especially if the participants are knowledge workers.

8. COMPETITIVE ADVANTAGES

In order for Lincoln Trust Company to continue to win business from its channel partners, it must provide new business with "white glove" service. If Lincoln Trust Company flounders in this endeavor, its channel partners will simply direct new business to Lincoln's competitors.

The CRS New Business Process solution delivered on the promise of "white glove" service for our new clients. While many competitors are following Lincoln's lead in automating the new business setup process, we believe Lincoln Trust Company has a superior offering. The foundation on which the CRS New Business Process solution was built enables Lincoln Trust Company to more quickly and effectively establish new business allowing us to be extremely competitive in our industry.

To sustain its competitive advantage, Lincoln Trust Company has plans to continue to automate additional processes, provide process analytics and additional Straight Through Processing (STP) through its entire value chain by leveraging our BPM competency and solution infrastructure. While Lincoln Trust Company has outsourced some of its business processes, our executive leadership has provided direction to fully automate these processes for further cost reduction, scalability, and competitive advantage.

9. TECHNOLOGY

The BPM solution architecture has been implemented leveraging the following core vendor technologies:

- **IBM Websphere Lombardi Edition (version 7.6 SP2) BPMS**- used for simulation, optimization, process orchestration and integration, process automation, team performance and SLA tracking.
- **Lombardi Blueprint**- used for process discovery, mapping, and inventory
- **DocuSign** - used for electronic document and electronic signature services.
- **Microsoft SharePoint**- used for internal and external portals including dashboard and scorecard capabilities
- **Microsoft SQL Server**- used for BI capabilities including Reporting Services, Analysis Services, and Integration Services
- **Cisco VOIP** – used for integrated with portal screen pop of customer information including process details when a call is received from a customer
- **Kofax Capture** – used for document capture and indexing
- **Oracle 10g RDBMS**- used for operational data store and active data warehouse
- **Oracle IPM**- used for customer document imaging repository
- **Sungard- Relius** - Core recordkeeping and administrative platform

The CRS New Business Process leverages our existing and proven process architecture implemented to support all corporate processes, including those of classical definition: human centric, system centric, and document centric processes. Our architecture is SOA and WOA and now leverages cloud technology to obtain customer signatures as a process input. Lombardi Teamworks is being used to enable process integration activity between multiple systems leveraging web services. Our BPMS is an architectural standard to orchestrate customer processes initiated from our internal portal, external website, and the cloud.

Internal forms were developed using both Teamwork's coaches and .Net forms presented within SharePoint. The CRS New Business Process also leverages our Information Delivery standards utilizing a "My Workspace" concept through Microsoft SharePoint Portal, and SQL Server Reporting Services Reports (SSRS). Critical data regarding current staff workloads, overall processing volumes, and SLA management is obtained. In addition, through SSRS, all end users have the ability to run secure, Web-based, interactive reports, designed with multiple filtering and drill-down options to view all the imaging and process data needed to conduct their jobs and service clients.

10. THE TECHNOLOGY AND SERVICE PROVIDERS

The majority of the project was delivered using our in house team. We also leveraged Amdocs (www.amdocs.com) and Cognizant Technology Services (www.cognizant.com) to assist with .Net development, project management, and testing.

Section 5

Pacific Rim

'us' - Utility Services
An Alliance between South East Water Ltd, Thiess Services and Siemens, Australia

Gold Award: Pacific Rim
Nominated by Interfacing Technologies
Corporation, Canada

1. EXECUTIVE SUMMARY / ABSTRACT

The 2009 executive team's strategic review of the *'us'* – Utility Services IT projects identified an opportunity to increase the value that its projects were delivering by taking a more holistic approach. Many of our IT projects, as is likely the case in many companies, were very focused and delivered value to a single business group or function but not necessarily across the business. This reality was amplified in our case because we not only work across departments, but also across multiple companies within the Program Alliance. The review concluded that value would be significantly increased by integrating solutions across functions and business groups through a better understanding of our end-to-end processes.

In response to these findings, we established an innovative Business Process Management (BPM) Centre of Excellence[12] (CoE) to 1) gain that understanding, and 2) integrate it into IT projects where appropriate. The CoE has positively affected several projects since its creation but the farthest reaching of them, and the focus of this study, is the *Job Costing Improvement* project. Herein referred to as *Job Costing*, the project has delivered reductions in cost and increases in data quality for financial and operational reporting through improvements across our core operations and maintenance processes.

We expect cost reductions of 25 percent to 50 percent in some cases and our cost recovery for chargeable works has already increased by 36 percent. Furthermore, it has initiated a cultural shift within the organisation as process owners take responsibility for the continuous improvement of not only the outputs from their processes, but their processes contribution to the outcome of the entire value stream.

2. OVERVIEW

The 2009 *'us'* – Utility Services Strategic IT Plan identified several shortcomings that the introduction of our automated works management system, Montage, has not been able to address. Operational and financial reporting have remained manual and labour intensive and certain business groups continue to resist the use of the standard system.

'us' - Utility Services is a Program Alliance between South East Water, Thiess Services and Siemens. The Alliance operates, maintains and improves South East

---

[1] "... BPM CoE comprises a group of committed individuals who focus on how the processes of the firm drive bottom-line profitability and performance. Such a group is usually responsible for supporting a number of BPM projects across the business, and keeping momentum going across a broad front. They provide a group of resources that are well versed in the best practices of process improvement. (Miers, 2006) At *'us'* – Utility Services, this role is taken on by the Business Information Services group.

Water's water and sewer networks, pump stations and treatment plants which serve over 1.3 million people in the Melbourne's South East. Employees from the three companies operate within the **'us'** – Utility Services organisation structure, essentially functioning as an independent company except that Thiess Services and Siemens invoice South East Water monthly for their labour, plant and material contributions to the Alliance.

Three years ago, we implemented a custom built system called Montage, which provided electronic control for all works and asset management processes. Montage is used to track work, either from public or internal requests, through planning, dispatching, execution, verification and closing. Preliminary analysis indicated variations in the way the system was being used by different business groups. Operational reporting was unreliable and financial reporting was manual and time consuming.

From the start, we knew our biggest challenge would be to gain consensus around responsibilities within the end-to-end value streams. All companies face this challenge, however it is amplified in our case. Our processes are highly complex not only due to the hand-offs between office staff, field crews and plant workers, but also because they often span across the three companies and three management systems. In 2009, we created a BPM Centre of Excellence (CoE) (see footnote p.1) to add a human focus and better business understanding to our IT projects and, at the end of the year, we initiated the *Job Costing Improvement* project to address the reporting and business alignment challenges.

Job Costing provided an opportunity for **'us'** – Utility Services to improve the efficiency and quality of the end-to-end value streams of our core operations and maintenance processes. We could not have seized this opportunity without the big picture understanding and the skill set that the CoE contributed to the project.

A key component of the initiative, and a primary tool for the CoE and the business in general, was a powerful technology that allowed us to model in a collaborative environment and easily validate the work with process owners. Using the Interfacing Enterprise Process Center® (EPC), we modelled processes from both an enterprise-wide, value stream perspective and from the day-to-day task perspective. This was crucial not only to our analysis, but also for showing value, sustaining executive support and for validating our work with process actors and owners.

On top of the quantifiable benefits such as a reduction in the time and resources required for reporting, increased operational efficiency and increased data quality, **'us'** Utility Services is using the operational understanding and consensus from *Job Costing* to drive a cultural shift towards an environment of open communication and continuous improvement. Through the EPC web portal, process owners now take responsibility for the accuracy of the process documentation and end-users can easily reference their current processes and procedures. The explicit end-to-end value stream has also contributed to process standardization as process owners better understand similarities across business groups and, in our case, across companies.

3. BUSINESS CONTEXT

The **'us'** Utility Services alliance delivers a range of design, engineering, construction, operations and maintenance services to South East Water's infrastructure. The water and sewer networks, pump stations and treatment plants serve over 1.3 million people or 600,000 residential, business and industrial customers.

Our core operations and maintenance processes span across several business groups and, also across company lines between the Alliance partners. These processes were not well understood and reporting on them was manual and very time consuming. In order to create reports, members of the finance team had to collect financial data that was spread across the three companies financial systems and work through the data with the works coordinators.

The data issues were further affected because the mechanical and electrical groups resisted the use of Montage and were only using parts of the system. Therefore, the data captured in Montage for was unreliable and could not be merged with data from other business groups.

The goal of the *Job Costing* project was to introduce sustainable financial management for **'us'** - Utility Services that would satisfy business requirements and time and cost constraints by improving the quality of and capturing all field work related data and costs within the works management system. This would facilitate ad hoc reporting and simplify the end-of-month reconciliation reporting process. The processes that fell under the scope of *Job Costing* were documented and published to the business using Interfacing Enterprise Process Center ® - EPC BPM software. This is to ensure clarity and consensus of processes and responsibilities among all the process stakeholders and actors.

4. THE KEY INNOVATIONS

Our key innovation has undoubtedly been the governance structure put in place to manage our BPM program.

'us' Utility Services operates in a complex regulatory and business environment. As the Operations and Maintenance provider for South East Water, we are required to work under a strict set of regulatory conditions. These guidelines are licence requirements of South Eater Water that are set by the Victorian State Government. These conditions are actively monitored and can incur significant financial penalty through non-conformance.

In addition, there are governance constraints imposed by the alliance partner organisations. Due to the terms of the Alliance agreement, the individual finance systems of each partner organisation must be used to manage financial transaction for the Alliance. This has resulted in a number of process duplication issues, which has then resulted in duplicated reports. This creates a high level of confusion for users, increased costs and reduced profitability.

In response to this complex environment we created an innovative governance structure to strategically guide process improvement while ensuring effectiveness, agility and transparency. This structured approach will help any size company to improve the chances of success of a process improvement initiative.

The sponsor of this programme of works is the General Manager of **'us'** - Utility Services. The responsibility for the application of the initiative is the Information Technology Council which meets monthly and is composed of executive-level representatives from the three companies, as well as IT specialists. The Council established a working group to oversee implementation and provide direction which meets every three months, or more often if required. The working group includes representatives from the business and the CoE project manager. The working group makes all necessary decisions regarding project priorities and direction but can refer a decision to the IT Council if deemed necessary. Finally, the project group is made up of several subject matter experts (SME) from the business that are cop-opted depending on the project, as well as members of the **'us'** Utility

Services BPM CoE, including a consultant from Interfacing Technologies, the vendor of the BPM software used throughout the process improvement work. The project group executes the work within the business.

The structure may seem heavier than needed, but when the responsibilities are well-defined, the outcome of this structure is highly engaged management that drives the cultural change towards BPM.

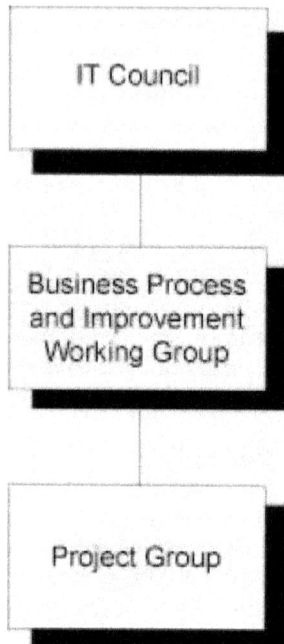

IT Council

Business Process and Improvement Working Group

Project Group

Figure 1: *'us'* – Utility Services BPM Governance Structure

4.2 Business

'us' - Utility Services is a customer-driven organisation. This is demonstrated by the positive results of our regular monthly customer satisfaction surveys. The improvements in data quality will increase the accuracy of the information we can provide our customers during interactions at any point during the works process, in turn increasing customer satisfaction.

'us' – Utility Services is now also able to be more pro-active with our suppliers. All works data and costs are now recorded within Montage, the works management system, and we can use the work order from Montage as the purchase order for sub contractors and suppliers. Previously, we were reliant on the sub contractor or supplier invoice as the record of work. The new pro-active approach will allow us to confirm the costs suppliers are claiming.

Finally, **'us'** - Utility Services is now in a better position to manage our labour costs. Previously, the systems of reference for labour were the Thiess Services and Siemens payroll systems which were, of course, managed by the owner organisations respectively. The fact that the works data and costs are now recorded within Montage is changing the dynamic of the relationship by moving the system of reference for labour under the management of **'us'** - Utility Services. We are now in a much better position to report on labour costs and to resolve any discrepancies.

4.3 Process

The process modelling approach we chose was strategic. We have two Process sets within the EPC, one that categorises processes in the cross-industry, APQC Process Classification Framework (PCF), which is available pre-built in EPC, and a second that displays the processes as value streams based on our products and services.

The processes were first defined within the PCF which is divided along functional lines, with a category for sales and marketing, a category for finance, a category for customer support, production, etc. These process definitions are quite low-level and include tasks and decisions to complete the processes but do not include the actors. The PCF process set is used by business analysts to store the process definitions to ensure no duplication of processes.

Extensive consultation was done with the business groups to determine the structure of the value streams process set. The goals were firstly to have a structure that the business users can easily navigate and secondly to display the processes within the end-to-end value stream of the business. The end result is a process set broken down by type of work, or service, e.g. Water Reactive Work, Electrical Planned Maintenance and more. Within each of these work types, we used a standard, very structured approach to the process modelling, analysing three distinct levels of detail, L0, L1 and L2. The L0 is the same for each work type and based on a standard work process of identify, plan, schedule, execute, finalise. This was done deliberately to encourage standardisation across the business groups and to highlight the similarities between the work that the different partners contribute to the alliance.

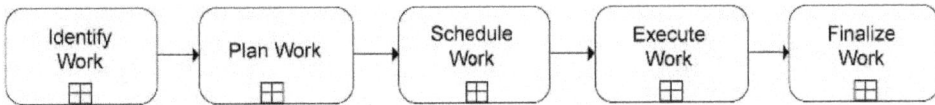

| Identify Work | Plan Work | Schedule Work | Execute Work | Finalize Work |

Figure 2: **'us'** – Utility Services Standard End-to-End Value Stream Work Process (9/23/10)

There is variation in the processes starting at the L1 level. This is because the processes which identify Water Reactive work, for example, are different to the processes used to identify Sewer Planned Maintenance. The L2, which is the lowest level of detail, are references to the definitions in the APQC PCF process set. This way, the same process definition, for example creating a Montage work order, appears in several of the value streams with all the same activities. The only variation is the actor performing the tasks and any specialized document such as guidelines for defining priorities. This approach facilitates the modelling exercise and ensures that standard processes are being used across the business which, in turn increase quality of service and data quality.

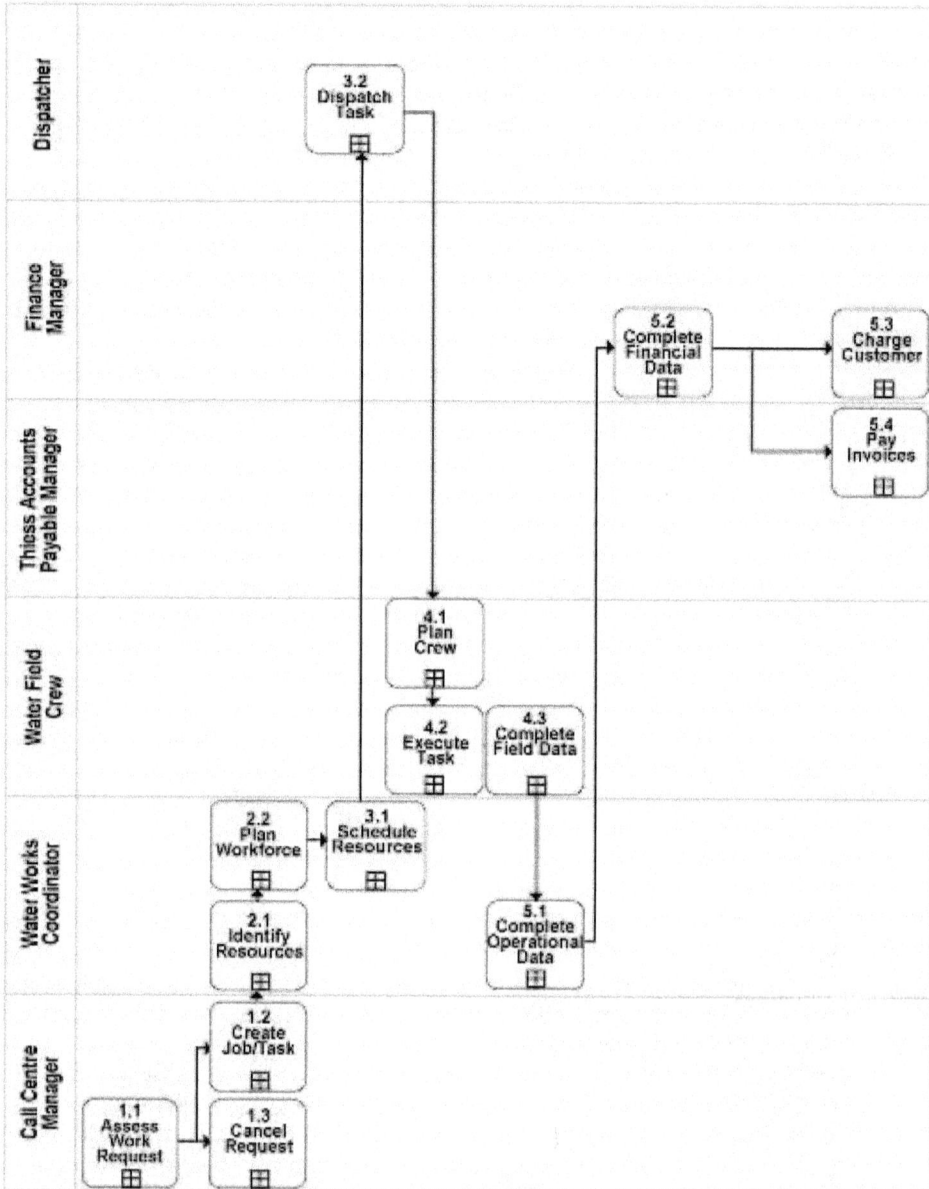

Figure 3: *'us' – Utility Services L1 Water Reactive End-to-End Value Stream Work Process (9/23/10)*

Our approach of re-using process definitions across multiple value streams has enabled us to standardise core processes such as:

- • work order creation
- • work order assigning
- • work order finalising/closing
- • invoice handling
- • recording materials used

- • chargeable works

Furthermore, through field staff training and site visits, we identified crews and even whole sections of business groups who were not using field terminals. There were different reasons for this, including lack of proper training, technical difficulties and others. The Job Costing project has enabled us to standardise on the use of field terminals across all field staff which further increases the accuracy and completeness of our works data.

Through *Job Costing*, we have also introduced the RACI responsibility matrix to our processes, clearly identifying the roles that are involved in each process, whether Responsible, Accountable, Consulted or Informed. The key point in our RACI matrix is that a single person is accountable for the outcome of each process. This person is the process owner and is responsible for ensuring process documentation is up-to-date and for initiating further process improvements. We have exposed the processes and all supporting documents through the EPC web portal, which provides a personalised view of relevant processes and documents for each user. This interactive portal has brought the processes to life by creating consensus around the inner workings, requirements and responsibilities of the business and by making them transparent to all involved.

4.4 Organisation

There is now much more importance put on data quality at all levels of the organisation. This is most evident through the core work processes which were the focus of the *Job Costing* project and this has significantly changed day-to-day operations for much of the workforce. The five main areas affected by this change are:

- • Work order creation
- • Field crew operational data
- • Closing the work order
- • Financial reporting
- • Timesheet processing

Work Requests are received from several sources; namely councils, the general public, planned bodies of work, scheduled works, observations from our field crews, and follow up to prior work. Depending on the origin of the request and on the group that will perform the work, work orders within Montage are created by different people. The creator can be a call centre operator, a sewer works coordinator, a water reactive supervisor. By using the EPC web portal to distribute and gather feedback on the work order creation sub process of the end-to-end works management process, we have been able to increase standardisation of the work orders.

As with all works management systems, the data recorded within Montage about a work order is very extensive. It includes the location (property or GIS coordinates) of the problem, origin of the request, any related work orders, priority, the asset to be investigated etc. Before *Job Costing*, the work order was seen simply as a reference number for communicating the work that had to be done but it was understood that not all data was correct. For example, if a crew working on a blocked sewer discovered a faulty manhole cover nearby that should be replaced; an extra task would often be created under the same work order using the logic that the work is at the same location. The downside to this is that when reporting on the cost of repairing blocked sewers, the labour and materials from the manhole replacement would be included, obviously corrupting the figures. Exposing the end-to-end process, including reporting, to the call centre operators and the works coordinators, has increased the understanding of how the data is used and, therefore, why it is important for it to be accurate. It is now well understood that in the previous example, when opportunistic maintenance is discovered, it should have its own work order so that cost will relate to the correct cost centre.

Field Crews have field terminals (tough laptops) that are kept in the trucks and the Dispatchers transmit work orders to them, whilst the field crews record works data and actions in real-time. The data capture potential of the field terminals had never been used to its full potential. It was almost accepted that the data relating to labour times, plant usage and materials used was unsuitable for reporting purposes because there was too much variation in how the system was being used. For some crews, the data was entirely accurate but for others it was not. *Job Costing* has significantly changed the expectation that the data surrounding their work should be accurate. This includes, travel times, work times, materials used, plant items used and description of the work done. The facility to record almost all this data was already built into the works management system but, because the info was not used consistently, there was no requirement on field crews to ensure it was accurate. As part of *Job Costing*, field crews were provided with refresher training in using the features on Montage to capture data, combined with a change management session on the new importance of data quality and subsequent field visits to reinforce behaviour. The field crews are now capturing data to a quality standard of above 95 percent as compared with the end-of-month reconciled data in all business groups.

For the same reasons that data quality had not been a priority for field crews, it had not been a priority for works coordinators and business group supervisors. By standardising the work order closing process, with the works coordinators as process owners, they are now responsible for the accuracy and completeness of the data within a work order once it is closed. As part of the changes to their roles, the works coordinators now collaborate with the data quality officer to identify data capture issues and propose remedial training with field crews.

Finally, through documenting and analysing processes, we uncovered a stand-alone system being used to capture labour times for part of the business. This functionality was clearly overlapping with the works management system but, for historical reasons, had been in use for several years. Furthermore, almost a complete full time equivalent was dedicated to data entry and validation from timesheets into this system when the labour data should be being captured directly via the field terminals by the field crews. Through training and redesign of the process, the stand alone system has been eliminated, and with it, the data entry role. This has also seen an increase in data quality and accuracy as there is less dependence on manual data capture and entry.

As the organisation shifts to a more process-centric view, the role of the BIS team has become that of a BPM Centre of Excellence. Responsibilities also include system support (Montage, GT Viewer, Field Terminals, etc.)

The team is made up of a project manager, two business analysts both with extensive experience in BPM and EPC and a system support officer. As required, consulting services are used for business intelligence and reporting tasks.

The challenge for us moving forward is to balance the team's workload as the backlog of process improvement projects that were uncovered throughout *Job Costing* is daunting. The approach, as it has been to date, will be for priorities to be driven by the IT Council and the BPM working group in order to deliver maximum business value.

5. HURDLES OVERCOME

Though the innovative governance structure that *'us'* - Utility Services put in place for the process improvement program has helped gather tremendous executive support and momentum, we have clearly had our share of hurdles to overcome.

Management

Front-line managers were very concerned that middle and upper management would not accept the results from the improved data quality. Because management's focus had not been based on an end-to-end processes view of the business, the business groups' performance metrics were compartmentalised, focused on small tasks within the end-to-end process. Pressure from upper management to meet and exceed these compartmentalised metrics encouraged front line managers to narrow the definition of the costs that should be attributed to these small tasks. The rest of the costs would be attributed to the operating budget. The result was continuously lowering costs for certain tasks at the expense of an ever growing operating budget which made planning and budgeting very difficult.

It was identified that front line managers' resistance, the existing performance metrics and upper management's potential reaction to improved data quality as big risks for the *Job Costing* project. We mitigated these risks by continuously communicating the progress of the project and, through the governance structure, having mid-level and upper managers re-affirming their commitment to the project as these issues were arising. Instead of front line managers being scrutinized, as they had feared, this actually led to a review and redefinition of the performance metrics to better align with the end-to-end process paradigm.

Business

As has been discussed throughout this report, *'us'* - Utility Services is an alliance between three independent companies which leads to a range of challenges. Each company manages its own general ledger, financial system, end of month reporting and, possibly the most challenging reality is that each company has its own corporate culture and identity.

It was a challenge to satisfy the requirements of the three financial systems and processes, however, from a technical standpoint, it simply required more thorough analysis and rigorous implementation. The real challenge was that the different corporate cultures and identities were obstacles to process standardisation. This was evident through the comment from many workshops, "yes but what we do is completely different from what they do."

The approach in tackling this challenge was to use a standardised high level work order management process as the basis for the end-to-end processes for all the business groups. The process (identify work, plan work, schedule work, execute work, finalise work) provides a view of the work we do that is irrespective of the type of work, e.g. water maintenance, treatment plant shutdown, etc. Through the EPC process hierarchy, the different business groups are continuously viewing their processes in a context that highlights the similarities and their resistance to standardising processes has been entirely overcome.

Organisation Adoption

We have integrated change management principals and strategy into every phase of our process improvement work. From defining and sticking to a high-level change management strategy, to the structure governing the work, the process frameworks, the training and extensive communications, each step has helped encourage organisational adoption.

Two specific hurdles stand out and both are inherent to the core business of asset operations and maintenance because the majority of our work force is made up of technicians.

The first hurdle is a huge variation in computer literacy throughout the work force. The field crews and works coordinators range from tradesmen who have completed a technical course thirty years ago to electrical engineers with Ph.D.s. The EPC presents processes and supporting documentation in a very visual and easy to use format. This was crucial in facilitating the rollout because, even staff members with very little knowledge of computers have been able to actively use the EPC web portal to consult, review and contribute to the process improvements.

The second hurdle was the phrase "My job is to fix the burst water main! Now, I'll be spending half my day doing data entry!" The resistance from field crews and works coordinators was completely understandable and expected. The administrative work is a part of their job that most do not enjoy and they perceive it to be secondary responsibility for them. The reaction was clearly an exaggeration but the resistance was real.

The change management strategy was critical in overcoming this challenge. The strategy, which, as previously mentioned, was integrated to all aspects of the *Job Costing* project, focused on empowering the organisation to understand the need for change and to contribute to the improved processes. Through workshops, training sessions and site visits with the field crews and works coordinators, we worked through examples of day-to-day applications of the new processes. Throughout these sessions, commentary was gathered and used, where appropriate, to improve the change in business processes. This was facilitated by the EPC interactive web portal. Finally, when the to-be process was deployed into production, field crews and works coordinators had experienced working with it enough to understood the processes and what is now required of them.

6. BENEFITS

Internally, the project has made a huge contribution to unifying the '*us*' - Utility Services staff by standardising the business processes. Because the business groups within the Alliance are loosely divided along the three parent company lines, there has always been a disconnect between the business groups. For example, between Water Operations and Maintenance and the Mechanical and Electrical Operations and Maintenance. The standardising of work processes has helped solidify the '*us*' – Utility Services identity, which in turn contributes to better cooperation and communication across the business groups.

Because all works data and costs are now recorded within Montage, the works management system, we are now in a position to use the work orders from Montage as the purchase order for sub contractors and suppliers. Previously, we have been reliant on the sub contractor's or supplier's invoices as the record of work. The new pro-active position is clearly better and, though the full benefits of this improvement have yet to be measured, the expectation is a reduction of 25 percent to 50 percent in labour costs due to increased traceability.

6.1 Cost Savings

One Timesheet officer role no longer exists which means an immediate cost saving of $60,000/year. Furthermore, the abolishment of the redundant labour-capturing system that this role was using means a savings of \$15,000/year in support costs. This cost reduction is in addition to the potential savings of mitigating the risks associated with a stand-alone system that only one user understands and has access to.

The month end reconciliation process before *Job Costing* involved 17 people and spread over 25.5 days (1.5 days per person), or, 204 person-hours. The centralising of all works data, including supplier and sub contractor costs into Montage has reduced the process duration to 102 person hours. This means a savings of 102 person-hours every month.

The ramifications for financial reporting are great but the single most important factor is that 25 percent of monthly costs previously attributed to "Operating Costs" are now defined specfically. By assembling all works data and costs into the works management system and using this for reporting purposes, the portion of costs attributed to "Operating Costs" have diminished to 8 percent and is expected to drop to 5 percent as the processes become more engrained. These costs are, instead, being attributed to the actual activities and, in turn, to the original requests for work that are triggering them. This is providing management with the appropriate knowledge to lower costs through better strategic decisions. Specifically, managers are looking into when to engage sub contractors and how best to respond to specific types of work requests from customers.

6.2 Time Reductions

This report has discussed the amount of time required for end of month reconciliation reporting, but the same issues affect any requests for ad hoc reporting. Extensive time was previously spent assembling data from multiple systems to create ad hoc reports. The centralisation of the data into Montage means that managers can get accurate and up-to-date reports, many through self-service using the Montage built-in reporting facility. In cases where the query is more complex, it is still much faster for the Business Information Systems team to create the report only having to query the single system.

6.3 Increased Revenues

When a third party, whether an individual or a company, damages South East Water's infrastructure, the work to repair the asset is chargeable. Prior to *Job Costing*, many jobs that should have been chargeable would not be marked as such. A job could be deemed too small, the job may be deemed too large, the party responsible for the damage may not be known or they may not accept responsibility etc. There was no defined process for the decision of whether the work would be charged so, in some cases, the call centre operator taking the original request would decide that the work was not chargeable, other times, the field crew arriving on site would make the decision, it could also fall to the works coordinator reviewing completed works or even through to the finance team deciding not to charge a customer. By standardising the works process, all works that are suspected of being chargeable are now completed as such and it is up to the finance team to make the decision whether or not to charge the customer. The expectation is that this will increase the cost recovery for chargeable work by 36 percent.

6.4 Productivity Improvements

A second timesheet officer role has been transformed into a data quality officer. The role previously provided minimal value as a data entry position. The Data Quality officer provides much higher value by analysing data quality issues and working with field crews and supervisors to review and correct the issues and ensure they don't persist. It therefore represents a significant improvement in productivity.

The data that has been centralised into the works management system, Montage, includes working times for vehicles and plant items such as excavators, compressors and crane trucks which was not being systematically tracked until *Job Costing*. Specifically, managers are reviewing the use of plant items and vehicles to determine whether they should be purchased or hired.

Finally, having documented up-to-date processes with the process owners responsible for the execution and the outcome of the processes, we now have a baseline to work from. Process owners were involved through the analysis and process re-design phases and their recommendations are what have led to the improvements listed throughout this report. This empowerment will continue thanks to the availability and dynamic nature of the processes through the EPC Web Portal.

7. 7. BEST PRACTICES, LEARNING POINTS AND PITFALLS

7.1 Best Practices and Learning Points

- ✓ *Set up a governance structure to institutionalise business process improvement*
- ✓ *The governance structure must include executive sponsorship*
- ✓ *Get stakeholders to re-affirm commitment throughout the process – "this will be a hard road, are you sure you want to go down this road?"*
- ✓ *Start with a project charter with explicit goals and as issues are discovered, manage scope very pro-actively!*
- ✓ *Change management - You cannot focus too much on the human-side of process improvement*
- ✓ *For users to trust the solution, they have to trust the team so lots of face time!!*
- ✓ *It takes time for people to accept change, it is a process. Some people will want to vent frustration, others need every detail to be explained to them, and others need a big picture explanation of why this is happening. The change management must provide time and the facility for people to deal with the change in their own way.*
- ✓ *Start small, scale quickly*
- ✓ *Business ownership*
- ✓ *Use standards and industry frameworks, where possible and appropriate*

7.2 Pitfalls

- ✗ *Do not impose a solution. Though that may be the end result stakeholders must be involved and feel a part of the process.*
- ✗ *Avoid partial roll-outs. An interim solution can often end up becoming the long term solution whether you like it or not. If you are going to roll-out an interim solution, be sure you can live with it for a while.*
- ✗ *Avoid secrecy or elitist information sharing. People need to know what is going on throughout process improvement work. Communication is key!*
- ✗ *Avoid a light switch system or process change-over. Allow time to change. Over-lapping of systems or processes from as-is to to-be is good because it not only gives people comfort, provides a backup in case any important details were missed during the analysis.*
- ✗ *Do not become a solution looking for a problem – there must be a clearly established business need for change*

✗   *Do not invent or create new standards – there are plenty of good ones that can be adopted to suit the business*

8.   COMPETITIVE ADVANTAGES

The water industry in Australia is a very complex context. Due to environmental challenges, South East Water is one of the few organisations who asks and works with our customers to help them use less of our product whilst, at the same time, charging them more for using it. In this environment, two goals have helped *'us'* - Utility Services become leaders in the industry and maintain that position over the past four years:

- Being a customer driven organisation
- Being industry innovators

The strategic partnership between South East Water, Thiess Services and Siemens has allowed us to consistently deliver excellent innovative service at lower costs. This business process improvement initiative will further streamline the collaboration as partners and solidify the best in class culture of *'us'* - Utility Services.

9.   TECHNOLOGY

'us' - Utility Services has implemented the Interfacing Enterprise Process Center® business process management software in support of our innovative business process improvement program. Differing from conventional process repositories, EPC's 'smart' process repository allows users to manage all objects from one central location, create and reuse process definitions across multiple value streams, view all object uses and process touch points, reuse objects across processes, create user defined attributes on all objects, conduct impact analyses, and much more. EPC enables users to effectively take a step back from their business processes and view all related process components, providing a blueprint of their business operations. Using EPC, we have been able to visualise and analyse our end-to-end processes and establish a clear path towards process standardisation.

Enterprise Process Center® is easy to use, requiring little or no training for rollout therefore lowering resistance especially from our employees who are less computer literate. Furthermore, EPC functionality allowed us to:

- Map processes graphically in the easily understood Business Process Modelling Notation (BPMN).
- Comprehensively document end-to-end processes, capturing critical hand offs between business groups.
- View process related documents, resources, assets, and all process touch points.
- Assign responsibility, accountability and ownership at all levels (RACI).
- Easily manage the entire lifecycle of a process - from documentation, review and approval to communication of change and ongoing feedback.
- Maintain transparency for compliance and governance within a complex regulatory environment

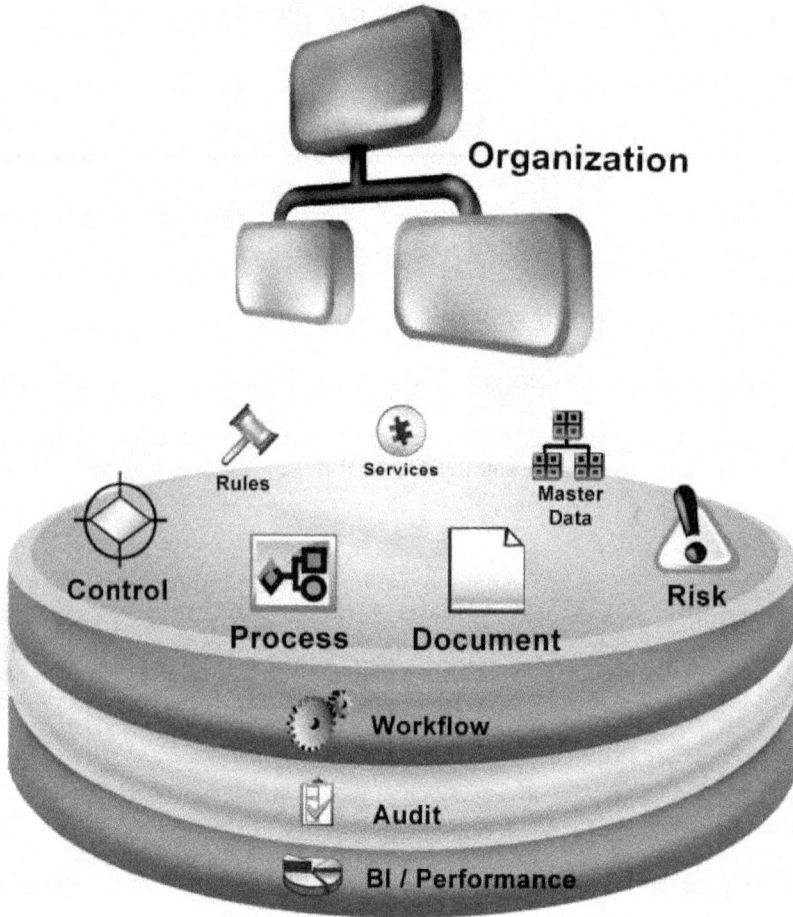

Figure 4: Interfacing Enterprise Process Center® Modules

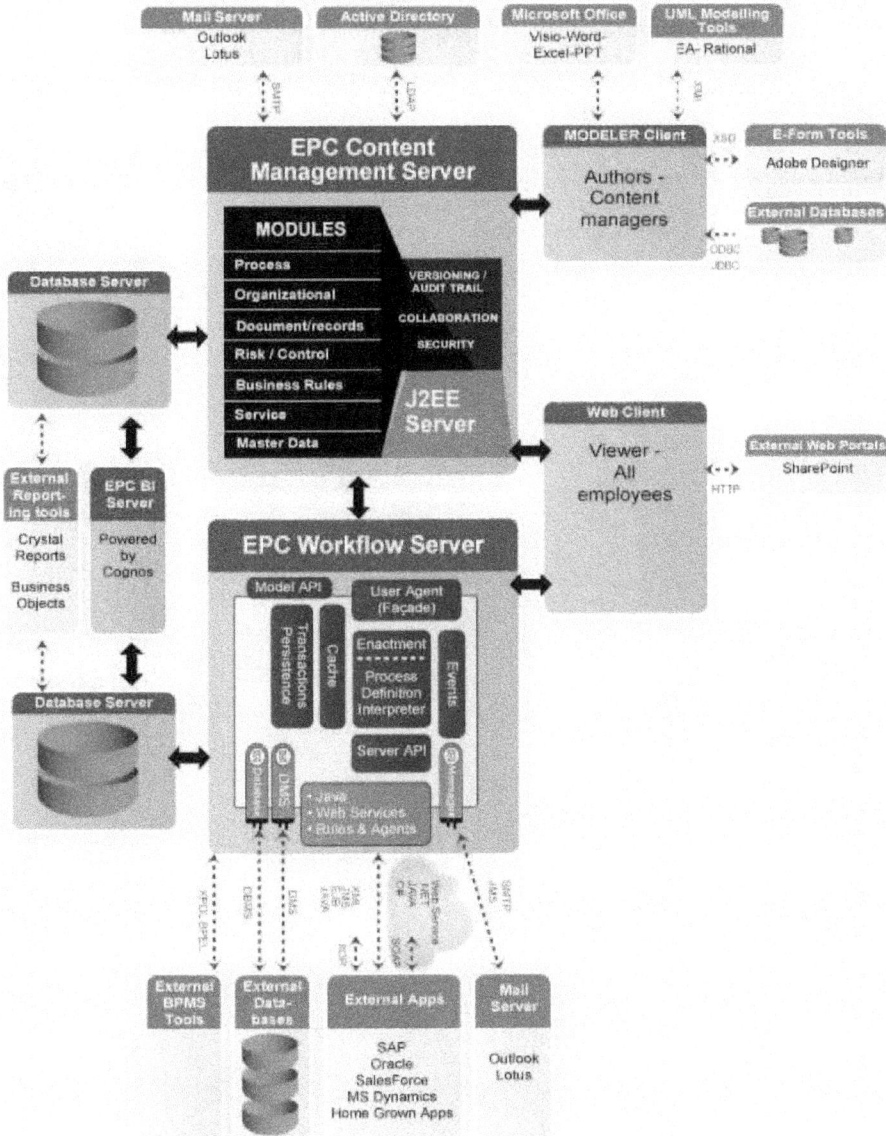

Figure 5: Interfacing Enterprise Process Center® Architecture

10. 10. THE TECHNOLOGY AND SERVICE PROVIDERS

Interfacing Technologies Corporation (founded in 1983) is a leading international provider of Business Process Management (BPM) software that allows organization to ensure compliance and governance by easily managing the entire lifecycle of processes, policies and controls. Interfacing's software and consulting services span the entire process maturity model: from static process modelling in their Free BPMN Modeller for MS Visio®, to their multidimensional collaborative BPM suite the Interfacing Enterprise Process Center® (EPC). Interfacing EPC is targeted at business users and supports a range of process management initiatives; alignment, analysis, governance, automation, monitoring and audit. Interfacing's solutions focus on tying the organization into the overall architecture in order to motivate users and create a sustainable process improvement culture. (www.interfacing.com).

11. 11. REFERENCES

MIERS, Derek. The Keys to BPM Project Success, BPTrends, Jan. 2006

http://www.bptrends.com/publicationfiles/01-06-ART-KeysToBPMProjSuccess-Miers.pdf

IndusInd Bank, India

Silver Award, Pacific Rim
Newgen Software Technologies Ltd., India

EXECUTIVE SUMMARY / ABSTRACT

Rapid Growth along with Social Responsibility:

IndusInd bank is among the first of the new-generation private-sector banks granted licenses in the mid-nineties, driven by the process of reform in the banking sector in India. The bank found out that there is a wide business growth potential for the various banking and security products along with other services it offered, provided they could become customer centric, scale up their operations and at the same time maintain cost efficiencies and targeted service levels.

Furthermore, in late 2008, the bank observed that the existing account-opening environment had grown more complicated, due to changing market environment and regulatory mandates.

The bank experienced that the manual movement of original physical documents resulted in a greater turn-around time (TAT) for the account opening, KYC and client on-boarding process. Moreover, for the documents transferred via courier, there was risk of physically losing them in transit.

The escalations and intimations were done manually via post / email. It was further observed that this manual process was prone to errors. The business process was subjected to high operational risks. The bank also needed to have a Business Activity Monitoring tool to monitor the operational and functional metrics.

The bank procured Newgen's BPM product suite-OmniFlow™, Document Management System- OmniDocs™ and Distributed Scanning solution- OmniScan™, to implement the project named IWorkS with the following objectives:
- Optimize manual work by changing how work is done rather than eliminating manual work itself and provide a systematic solution for implementation of processes.
- Improve cost efficiency by streamlining work handoffs and automating work routing.
- Raise employee performance by managing the available capacity required to complete a given amount of incoming work.
- Provide visibility into each individual piece of work allowing the bank to match service levels to the potential value of each customer.
- Decrease the transaction costs through elimination of paper based work routing and retrieval of paper records for post issue servicing and also through improvement in employee productivity.

The same platform was extended to many other processes and is currently being further expanded to accrue additional business benefits to the Bank.

The solution is environment friendly and enables gainful employment of differently abled members of the community employed to manage scanning hubs.

The bank reaped huge benefits by tapping the growth potential through Newgen's scalable solution which enabled improved turn-around-times (TATs), enhanced operational efficiencies and adherence to regulatory compliance.

OVERVIEW

Some of the key challenges were as below:

- High transaction volumes coupled with high annual growth rate being envisaged along with increasing geographical spread.
- Multiple products across CASA and Third Party Products being serviced across a wide geography through separate operating models as suited for each sourcing channel.
- Process implementation and monitoring not fool proof: Due to the spread and the multiplicity of processes, accentuated by the changes in the external environment like regulatory changes as well as competition, the changes to the operating processes were very frequent. Without a system tool, manual implementation of the processes was not foolproof. Variations could creep in at different centers, which were difficult to detect and impacted a uniform customer experience.
- Manual monitoring of operational metrics: The core banking system did not provide metrics for each work item for each stage of processing. Rather these systems only gave data for one of the stages in the process i.e. Account opening. Most of the customer issues occur pre and post account opening, for which there were no system metrics. These metrics were manually tracked and were costly to record due to it's duplicity of work and could at times be inaccurate.
- Process redundancies: All processes had significant redundancies around data capture, work forwarding since manual recording was done at each stage. The data captured at the previous stage remained in individual department PC files and was created afresh at the next stage.
- High cost of operations: The cost of operations was high due to manual work forwarding, movement of physical files through courier between branch and central operations, physical storage at field offices as well as costs and delays associated with the retrieval of physical records.
- High degree of operational risk: With all account / transaction documents existing only in physical form, without digital backup, the degree of operational risk was very high in case of a disaster which could impact the physical storage. Work rerouting and distribution across various geographical locations was also not possible due to dependence on the physical documents for processing.
- Non standard customer service: Due to variations in process implementation across locations and time taken to secure central operations approvals, the customer service and customer experience was not uniform across the various branches of the bank.

Process in brief

The bank procured Newgen's BPM suite- OmniFlow™, as a universal Workflow Solution with underlying document management system -OmniDocs™ and centralized scanning solution-OmniScan™.

Newgen automated the account opening process which is known as **IWorkS Account Opening Process** in the bank.

Along with automating the a/c opening process, the following additional processes were automated as well:

Deposit Acknowledgment Slip: IWorkS helps branches to generate Fixed Deposit acknowledgement slip which can be generated at the branches and handed-over to customers. This helps branches in achieving Customer Delight while the processing is centralized.

Additional Fixed Deposits: IWorkS enabled STP processing of customer requests for additional Fixed deposits

Renewal Instructions of Existing FD: IWorkS automates change in renewal instructions of existing Fixed Deposits. This helps branches reduce TAT and track status of instructions.

CPU Resource Management: IWorkS also provides CPU (Central Processing Unit) real-time dashboards of status of applications currently lying in various processing buckets that will hit various CPU in next few hours/days. This helps CPU to plan shifts and resources.

Regional Dashboards: BAM (Business Activity Monitor) a real-time dashboard helps regional teams and product team to track MTD activities at product, branch and sourcer level. BAM provides reports on New Account logins, Booking Status and FTR (First Time Right)

Mobile Short Text Messages: On introduction, IWorkS generates Mobile Text Messages which are sent to customers with a Reference Number and contact details of Contact Center which helps them to track status of applications.

BUSINESS CONTEXT

IndusInd Bank Demography

At that time IndusInd Bank had 250 branches across India and targeted at opening 100+ new branches in 2010 - 11. Branch Network of IndusInd Bank is across all categories of Cities including Metros, Semi Metros, Urban and Rural locations and two Representative Offices in Dubai and London to cater NR customer base and relationships from Middle East and Europe.

Initially, the bank had been undertaking manual processing of Account Opening which was distributed across branch locations. In early 2008, the processing was centralised in Mumbai to have better control and free branches from processing work. With growing volumes, centralisation led to increased TAT in both processing as well as exception resolution due to physical distance between branches and CPU. Moreover, compliance mandates were making the process even more complex to manage.

1. The bank needed a scalable process platform with capabilities of rapid expansion, visibility into operations and ability for continuous improvement.

2. As a leading bank of the new-age, focusing on technological initiatives for meeting its business objectives, IndusInd Bank had been constantly taking new steps to increase the focus on customer service, and increase its operational efficiencies. The Bank had computerized all its branches and Centralized Banking Solution (CBS) was already in place. The Bank also deployed several electronic delivery channels such as ATMs, Internet Banking, and SMS Banking etc.

Implementation of BPM solution for automating and streamlining the business processes was the next logical step in view of the above initiatives and to meet these requirements Newgen – a leading provider of BPM and DMS solutions was engaged by IndusInd Bank.

THE KEY INNOVATIONS

Although the financial services industry successfully automates many processes, manual work in Operations endures. Some manual processes and process steps are not easily eliminated, usually because they,

3. Correct the inevitable errors of automated processes

4. Require human judgment that is difficult to convert to automated decision logic

5. Involve handing over work from one step or process to another

Newgen provided the bank an innovative solution to overcome all the above problems.

Newgen's workflow management systems offered a new way to optimize manual work by changing how work is done rather than eliminating the manual work itself. Workflow systems improved cost efficiency by streamlining work handoffs and automating work routing. They raised employee performance by managing the available capacity required to complete a given amount of incoming work. Furthermore, the workflow technology provided visibility into each individual piece of work allowing the institution to match service levels to the potential value of each customer.

Project helped in fulfilling the mandate for Green Banking:

Bank is recognized as Green Bank with various initiatives such as Solar ATMs, Save Electricity Campaign, Plantation, Environmental awareness amongst employees and society. IndusInd Bank is also recognized by National Geographic Channel for its Green Banking initiative and Community Goals. The project helped in truncation of paper through digitization and thus promoted Minimal use of paper in the organization.

Project helped in fulfilling CSR initiatives of the Bank:

Since the solution was so user-friendly and easy to understand, the bank was able to further its social and civic responsibilities towards the physically challenged community.

In line with the CSR initiatives of the bank, all scanning HUBS in South Zone of India are managed by Differently abled people. Process of receiving inward documents, Scanning, Image QC and Physical Management is managed by resources having disabilities.

4.2 Business

The implementation of Newgen BAM solution (Business Activity Monitor) enabled business owners to take full control of their business operations by providing real time dynamic reports on the monitoring screen. Having real-time visibility over key business operations was a major concern for organization to make informed business decisions. Process or people oriented reports, generated upon dynamic data keep on refreshing on the monitoring screen. Key performance indicators, shown on those dynamic reports help business owners understand the real time business scenario.

IndusInd sends short messages to customers/prospects who apply for new accounts. The customer receives the information at key times in their engagement cycles. This is a part of a deliberate strategy to welcome customers, build loyalty, and provide periodic updates. These messages could be Welcome messages, informational updates, reminders and thank-you messages.

Based on the reference number sent to customer through short message, customer can then enquire about the status of application. Contact center provides accurate information from IWorkS about the status of application. This includes the status till welcome kit dispatch and acknowledgement status.

A key for any process is to track First Time Right instances of workitems processed on workflow. This is also an indicator for Quality Input and Speedy Processing. The solution has helped the bank to achieve significant improvement in FTR which is helping productivity and performance of operational resources.

4.3 Process

The Account Opening Process was implemented by IndusInd Bank on very fast track across all 230+ branch network at the time of implementation along with Representative Offices located abroad.

The Newgen solution benefitted the bank in the following ways:
- The solution encompasses a customer centric approach, thereby fulfilling the main objective of efficient Account Opening
- The solution has enabled the bank to reduce turn-around-time (TAT)
- The bank can now use the Newgen solution to achieve overall operational excellence
- Quick and easy retrieval of documents, resulting in better and faster decision making, as well as manifold increase in the efficiency of the entire process
- The system prompts the users regarding what to do and how to do, thus adhering to the "Best Practice" for processing the Account Opening form
- Cost cuttings resulting from documents being converted to digital scanned images as well as reduction in photocopying and courier costs
- Optimum use of the available resources with minimum investment in new resources
- Web based access to images from different locations
- Rights based access to the system for ensuring security

The implementation also involved setting up of independent scanning HUBs for high volume regions and branches. Entire process is compliant with norms of RBI (Central Bank of India) and Audit. Scanning HUB is not only responsible for Scanning but also responsible for Physical Form Management. **IndusInd has implemented process in record breaking time of 3 months which involves setting up scanning HUB at 30 key locations and training and initiation from all 230+ branch network.**

The solution provided by Newgen catered to the various sub-processes for the Account Opening process. The solution worked upon and enhanced the following sub-processes:

Branch Operations - The account opening applications were received and introduced in the workflow by creating work-items. An initial data entry is performed and the work-item is routed to the branch verification work-step. Cases can be routed to decision making authorities for Deviations from this workstep. After the approval of Branch Verifier the workitem goes to Branch Ops workstep and documents are now set for dispatch to scanning HUB. The classic example of this process is like passenger boarding on air-craft which involves Airport Entry, Security Check and Flight Boarding after all due diligence. Similarly Branch Operation processes an account by introducing the account to the Workflow by capturing key details to provide workitem visibility in the organization. Post this, using dynamic KYC checklist complying with RBI (Central Bank of India) guidelines, the form is verified and sent to the scanning HUB for Scanning and Account Boarding.

Scanning at HUB - The documents for all the introduced work-items against each application number are scanned at the Branch/HUB. The image QC is carried out at the Branch/HUB scanning station.

Quick Account Opening - It involves Document Verification at the CPU along with the data entry make and check feature. This is accomplished by viewing the scanned images available in OmniFlow™.

Welcome Kit & Audit – Post account opening after due diligence most important is to deliver Welcome Kit to customer and track status of deliverables. Solution is also interfaced with Courier feed files which updates status of Welcome Kit to Account to provide information such as Delivery Status, Delivery Date, Received By, Courier Reference Number. All opened accounts are audited by Bank's auditor from compliance and inspection point of view.

Signature Download - The OmniScan™ cropped signatures are available in OmniDocs™. The Newgen solution provides the feature of searching and downloading the signature along with the application form documents. This further leads to faster processing of documents.

Tatkal Process - The solution takes care of the Welcome Kit dispatch management system.

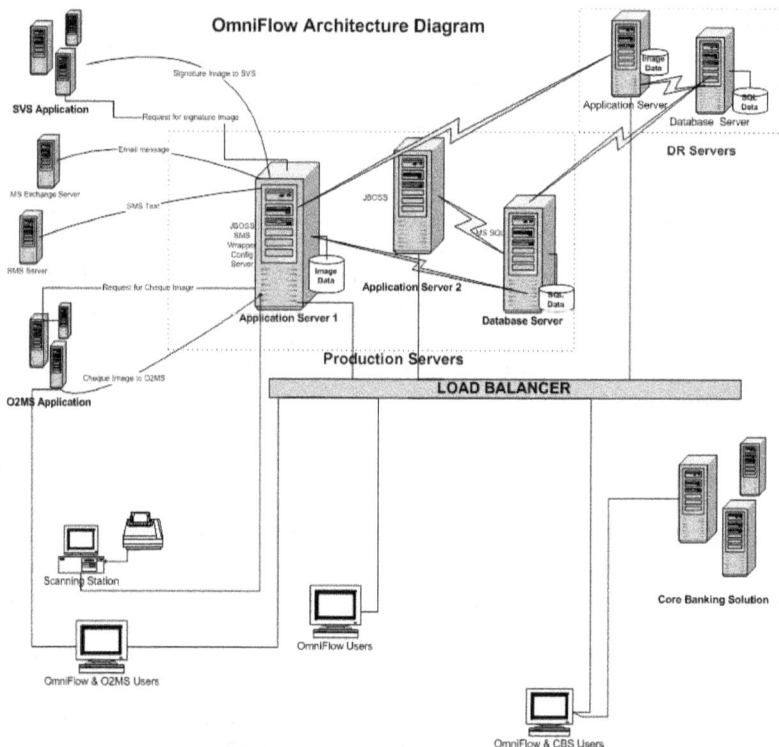

IndusInd Bank took an initiative to centralize a number of back office operations so as to improve operational controls, bring about standardization and reduce the operational work at the branches.

With Centralization, the bank experienced that the physical movement of documents resulted in a greater turn-around time (TAT) for the account opening process. In case of exceptions, the exception resolution added further to the a/c opening TAT since documents had already reached central operations and exception notification was not online.

A COE (Center of Excellence) was formulated and it works towards the continuous improvement of the processes.

The operational metrics were not real time, which lead to reactive managerial intervention.

Web services based Integration: For example, the integration with the signature management system has been done through Web Services.

The same platform was also used to automate the following processes, thus extending the business benefits of the BPM platform manifold:

- Accounts Payable – Processes vendors/service partners invoices and bills on fast track using DMS workflow
- Procurement Process – All procurements in IndusInd Bank are supported by DMS workflow and follow approval matrix along with budget for procurement in amounts and numbers
- Employee Certifications – All employees who opt for new certifications during the course of their employment can update their certificates to Human Resource department
- Life Insurance – Process to confirm LI business and incentive management
- Mutual Fund – Process to confirm MF business and incentive management
- General Insurance – Process to confirm GI business and incentive management
- Human Resource – Process to scan employee records and documents.
- Loan Processing System – Loan document processing workflow
- Inward Cheque Scanning – Cheque scanning initiative for Customer Responsiveness in Internet Banking and eStatements
- CAD Processes – Disbursement process flow for Credit department
- Cheque Return Escalations – Process flow for managing returned cheque to respective branches

Journey of this implementation is still on in IndusInd Bank and we have pool of demand of various BPM with DMS such as Employee Claims, Legal Documentation, Records Maintenance etc.

4.4 Organization

Center of Excellence

A COE was established with the cross-functional team from IndusInd and supported by the Newgen consultants works on continuous improvement of the processes.

- Installed an automation system that was automatically moving single piece of work across various disjointed base systems so as to improve efficiency and provide a way to match operating capacity with employees.
- It provided visibility to employees for all work items pertaining to them. It helped in streamlining their activities in an efficient way.

- It provided easy access from desktops to all documents and processing status of the case. The previous actions taken are easily traceable from the extensive audit trails.
- The best in class operations and productivity standards were established through analysis of the time and motion data coming out of the workflow databases rather than using traditional averages that could be skewed by idle time, low skilled staff and poor practices

HURDLES OVERCOME

Management was looking to set best-in-class operations and productivity standards. However shifting people from paper to images was a major hurdle. Also it was taking more time and users were not completing the tasks as defined in the process. This resulted in low FTR and more processing time. Newgen's BPM solution enabled analysis of the time and motion data coming out of the workflow. The data helped bank to address key areas for improvement. The benefits of workflow solution encouraged employees to process the cases efficiently.

BENEFITS

Due to the availability of all the data, shifts can be managed for agents based on the incoming load. Also expertise has been identified for specific type of activity. The same helps in faster processing of cases. The event-based data is available in the system and SMS messages to customers on event updates become possible.

Benefits accrued to the bank were both direct and indirect. Reduction in operating costs, travel and communication expenses, office stationary and infrastructure usage were some of the benefits achieved by centralization and implementation of the BPM solution. The bank also achieved other benefits like increase in productivity and reduction in IT infrastructure costs through better utilization of the resources.

6.1 Cost Savings

With each agent handling more number of transactions there were cost savings on agents. Previously, the bank used to maintain a photocopy for each application set, but with the new system no photocopies are required, and this has led to drastic savings. Apart from this, savings were realized on courier costs, as applications need not be sent back.

6.2 Paper Saving

IWorkS is helping in saving paper which earlier was being printed and used for AOF Checklist and KYC Checklist. 8 pages were printed per application and so far approximately 5,00,000 applications have been processed on IWorkS (Total papers saved by workflow and DMS is 5,00,000 * 8 pages, which is 40,00,000 paper sheets). For 5,00,000 applications branches now don't need to maintain photocopies, which is approximately 15 pages per application and comes to 75,00,000 pages. Thus, IndusInd has saved Photocopy (Toner, Electricity and Photocopier Life), Paper, and Storage costs.

6.2 Time Reductions

The process TAT was improved by 60%. Reduced TAT for Account Opening processes enabled the bank to add more customers into its portfolio with more than 3,00,000 New Accounts Opened, more than 250,000 of which have been opened in the last six months. These Account Opening requests (Current Account, Savings Account and Fixed Deposit Account) have been processed on IWorkS, built on the Newgen BPM Platform.

6.4 Productivity Improvements

- Processing capacity increased by over 41%
- Completing the process first time right (FRT), improved by 29%.
- Adherence to SLAs improved by 36%

BEST PRACTICES, LEARNING POINTS AND PITFALLS

7.1 Best Practices and Learning Points

✓ Consistently tracking prospects, opens new opportunities for cross-selling and up-selling

✓ Greater customer satisfaction, which demands immediate and informed response to their queries, is effectively implemented using Newgen's BPM solution

✓ The BPM solution establishes explicit and specific responsibilities with the stakeholders, thereby ensuring greater drive to accomplish work at their end.

COMPETITIVE ADVANTAGES

- Scaling up of operational activities enables the bank to keep pace with business growth and demands
- Compliance and Audit enable easy KYC Process
- Incorporation of banking norms in a very short duration due to flexibility and improvisation of processes

TECHNOLOGY

The bank procured Newgen's BPM product suite, called OmniFlow™, as a Universal Workflow Solution. It is a scalable, multi-tiered, platform independent Workflow Management solution built using the robust server-side Java technologies. It has a scalable architecture to cater to not only the small-to-medium workgroup usage but also the enterprise-wide workflow management requirements.

The Newgen Solution:

Newgen's OmniDocs™ solution tightly integrated with the OmniFlow™ solution enables document scanning, indexing, archival and retrieval processes once the documents/forms get transferred in the workflow. Thus, Newgen provides the BPM enabled workflow platform for implementing an automated Account Opening process.

Newgen's OmniScan™ enables the document scanning for the customer(s) at the Regional Processing office followed by transferring the documents to the BPM enabled workflow. Newgen developed a workflow automation solution for the Account Opening Process. With the help of this process, the bank is able to scan and process the various documents thereby promoting paperless processes across the bank. This has led to a drastic reduction in the turn-around-time.

THE TECHNOLOGY AND SERVICE PROVIDERS

The solution was implemented by the Newgen Implementation team and no third party team was involved in it.

Newgen consultants proposed a solution to the bank as per the best practices followed. The system study, solution design and implementation were carried out by Newgen professionals.

Section 6

South America

Unimed Porto Alegre Medical Co-operative Ltd, Brazil

Gold Award, South America
Nominated by BPM Soluções, Brazil

1. EXECUTIVE SUMMARY / ABSTRACT

Proper monitoring of the contractual instruments which govern relations between clients and providers is a prerequisite for the efficient management of an organization. Unimed Porto Alegre, the leading medical co-operative in the south of Brazil, recognizes the importance of optimizing the management of its contracts both with corporate clients and providers. Our priorities are standardization, monitoring, speed of response and risk reduction. Through the use of the BPM approach and the automation of processes we have been able not only to revolutionize the way in which we monitor and manage our contracts but also to open the way for a wide number of automation and optimization initiatives in other departments.

2. OVERVIEW

Unimed Porto Alegre is a medical co-operative offering healthcare services to 496,000 users throughout 46 municipalities in the east of Rio Grande do Sul, the southernmost state of Brazil. The area we serve includes the state capital, Porto Alegre. Our main products are health plans for individuals, families and businesses. There are also several hospitals and private treatment centers belonging to the co-operative which offer diagnostic, laboratory, odontological, test authorization and emergency treatment services at over 40 outlets. At present the organization works with the support of approximately 1,000 employees and has annual revenue of US$ 502 million (2009).

Unimed Porto Alegre is sector leader in the state capital and its metropolitan area, as well as in the Centro-Sul (South Central) and Litoral Norte (North Coast) regions. In Porto Alegre, it controls 39 percent of the health plan market. Its target market is collective business health plans: 85 percent of its clients are businesses. The family market accounts for the remaining 15 percent, which make up 77 percent of the sector. In its area of operation, the co-operative possesses a 28 percent market share, equating to 53 percent of family plans and 25 percent of business plans.

The large range of services offered generates hundreds of sales contracts annually for corporate clients, each one with over 40 pages. These contracts are based on over 70 templates registered with the ANS—Agência Nacional de Saúde Suplementar (National Agency of Supplementary Healthcare)—a government office connected to the Health Ministry, the responsibility of which is to regulate the supplementary healthcare sector in Brazil. Under this arrangement, sales contract templates cannot be altered without prior authorization from the legal department and the registration of the updated template with the ANS.

On the other hand, the high volume of operations, the number of treatment outlets and the complexity of the services offered necessitate the support of a wide range of external businesses, service providers and sufficiently diversified services, from fundamental issues such as monitoring and hygiene to the importing of complex diagnostic equipment involving sums ranging up to thousands of dollars.

The vast majority of these acquisitions are regulated by supply contracts established between the suppliers and Unimed Porto Alegre. At present, the number of active contracts amounts to almost 400 and comprises a total value of almost US$12 million. Initially, each department requiring services and products was responsible for managing its own contracts. This decentralization made for a lack of standardization, an absence of monitoring in contract processes and the risk of unowed payments, missed deadlines and lost documents.

We introduced a process automation plan using the BPM approach to overcome the difficulties encountered in the two processes outlined above. The plan was undertaken with the support of an external consulting agency and was conducted by the legal department, being divided into two phases. In the first phase we introduced the process relating to Contracts for Sale of Legal Entity in the period December 2008 through March 2009. The second phase focused upon the processes for Supplier Contracts and was executed during the months of August 2009 through February 2010. In both phases the processes were analyzed, redesigned, modeled and automated using a 100 percent web-based BPMS (Business Process Management System) tool produced by a Brazilian company. From this point on, the departments involved began to carry out their routine activities according to the system as implemented, and no longer in the irregular manual fashion employed previously. This approach has paved the way for various other initiatives to adopt BPM in other sectors. Some of these initiatives have already been implemented and others are currently in the process of being introduced.

3. BUSINESS CONTEXT

The company operates in an extremely competitive market and has been the sector leader in its geographical region for some time, offering new products and services each year. However, the high level of competition and regulation in the sector forces the company to adopt a strategy of constant investment and innovation.

Our legal department is responsible for the management of sales contract templates and, in co-operation with the Assessoria Atuarial (Actuarial Advisory), registers such contracts with the ANS for use by the commercial department. The legal department also analyzes, develops and approves contracts agreed upon with its suppliers. Management has placed the main responsibility for organizing contract processes upon the legal department, and it has taken on this challenge capably. After investigating alternative solutions, we elected to adopt BPM as a technical and methodological strategy for process automation, rather than adapting existing systems or acquiring a specialized system for contract management, both of the latter approaches having been shown to be highly complex and costly.

Initially, we were faced with the following critical questions in the two phases of implementation:

Sales Contract Process:

The digital contract templates were backed up to a server in draft form in Microsoft Word format. These files were password-protected against editing, only certain fields being left open for the commercial department to complete. However, protection of this kind is vulnerable to being "broken" even by comparatively simple methods. For this reason, there was a considerable risk of the contracts being altered without proper authorization;

Any contract that had been altered without such authorization represented a considerable liability to the company, since clients could demand (even through legal action) that the company honor any clauses which went beyond the normal range of services offered by Unimed Porto Alegre. At the same time, the use of un-registered contracts leads to legal action on the part of the ANS. In both cases, the impact on the finances and image of the company could be highly significant.

Each of the more than 70 types of product made available for sale by the company is supported by a template contract. Because of the way the contracts were stored and updated, there was a high risk of outdated templates being used, leading to client dissatisfaction and inefficiency when releasing new products on the market;

The guidelines for the approval of exception conditions—when a contract needed to be altered as a result of negotiations with the client—were recorded in non-standardized form, in e-mails or physical documents. The process of recovering development history for a particular contract placed considerable strain on both the commercial and legal departments. As monitoring of the process was conducted manually, there was no guarantee that all the competent powers had been duly consulted and given the opportunity to present their opinions.

Supplier Contracts:

Each area of the company was responsible for its own supply and service contracts. As a result, there was a high risk of attached documents or of the contracts themselves being lost. It was not possible to identify the quantity, variety and location of all relevant contracts with sufficient speed and efficiency;

The terms of these contracts (expiry, guarantees and increases) were monitored manually by the departments using them. This form of monitoring was prone to failure and increased the risk of supplier providing service after the expiration of the contract. By the same token, inefficient monitoring of the terms of increases meant that there was not sufficient time available to negotiate with suppliers and alert the financial department;

The legal department was responsible for analyzing and preparing supply contracts for the departments requiring them. This process was non-standardized, conducted by e-mail and checked manually, which made it extremely slow and difficult to trace.

Receipts originating from these contracts were paid on the authorization of department Superintendents and there was a high risk of payment being made on contracts which had already expired. In some cases there was no connection between the payments and the contracts.

There was no clear definition of the responsibility of each party participating in the process (the department requiring the contract and the legal, financial and management departments);

There was no systematic filing of the documentation or of the contracts themselves, which made loss more likely.

4. THE KEY INNOVATIONS

We were faced with the challenge of issuing and managing our sales and purchase contracts while meeting the security and monitoring requirements inherent to the process. The use of the BPM approach in implementing automation allowed us to visualize better our processes and modify the way in which we managed them. The main result was the centralization of task management in a standardized system which maintains an archive of all documents and authorizations, opinions and other records.

4.1 Business

One of the fundamental conditions for the success of the project was the participation and co-operation of the relevant departments, considering that the contract processes involved a number of different levels in the organization. The design for the process was developed by a multidisciplinary team made up of the commercial, IT and legal advisory departments and acting with the support of the external consulting agency contracted by the company. Opinions offered by individual managers were also incorporated into the new process. Our project meetings gave us the opportunity to revisit the relevant areas of responsibility and the points of contact between different departments, as well as allowing us to become better acquainted with the process in which we were involved.

The fact that the project also involved our clients and suppliers placed a greater responsibility upon the team for creating a practical, agile and functional process. For our clients, speed and assertiveness were fundamental to the handling of sale contracts, a key stage in the commercial process. For our suppliers, the automated process enabled Unimed Porto Alegre to keep them precisely informed of what stage their contracts had reached. Now that the project has been put in place, the system allows department managers to track the process as it moves forward and issue authorizations electronically. Even in cases where their authorization is not required, they have a guarantee that the process is being carried out according to established standards.

4.2 Process

The Process for Legal Entity Client Contracts comprises the following steps:
- Development of Contract (standard)
- Approval of Co-ordination of Sales (in cases where alteration of the contract is required)
- Analysis and statement of opinion by technical departments (Financial, Complementary Services and Occupational Health—in cases where alteration of the contract is required)
- Analysis, statement of opinion and approval by legal department (in cases where alteration of the contract is required)
- Approval by Superintendent of Marketing and Sales (where required)
- Approval by Executive Director (where required)
- Collection of signatures and conversion of paper documents into images

Initially, these steps were carried out in a non-standardized, manual way, mainly employing e-mail and physical documents. Some authorizations, including verbal ones, were not being recorded in the process. Responsibility for the development of contracts fell to five individuals in the Sales Administration department. Two Sales Coordinators were responsible both for approving contracts which required alterations and also for forwarding them to the technical departments for validation, a process which involved several other people in its own right. Finally, the legal department relied upon two lawyers to validate and update the contract before issuing the final version in PDF (Adobe) format. (The legal department was also responsible for creating contract templates, which were stored on the archive server in Microsoft Word format and made available to the commercial department at the beginning of the process.) Upon completion, contracts were forwarded to the client to be signed, after which the Sales Administration department obtained the final signatures of the Superintendent of Marketing and the Sales and the Finance Superintendent.

With the process automation, the Sales Administration department is able to start tasks within the BPMS, selecting the type of contract it wishes to issue by selecting the appropriate fields in the form.

A mainstreaming process retrieves the required contract template from a website in Microsoft SharePoint and a system task generates the final version of the contract in PDF format, complete with client information and full details of products and amounts. The PDF document is protected and cannot be altered. Finally, the Contract Administration department alerts the system that it has gathered the necessary signatures, and backs up the signed contract electronically. Should alterations to the contract be necessary for business reasons, the BPMS generates approval requests for the affected departments and, once the required validations have been obtained, issues a completed draft of the contract in Microsoft Word format in order for the legal department to make the necessary alterations and pass on the final version to the commercial department to be signed by the relevant parties. The following pictures show how the process is initiated, as modeled by the BPMS tool using BPMN (Business Process Modeling Notation):

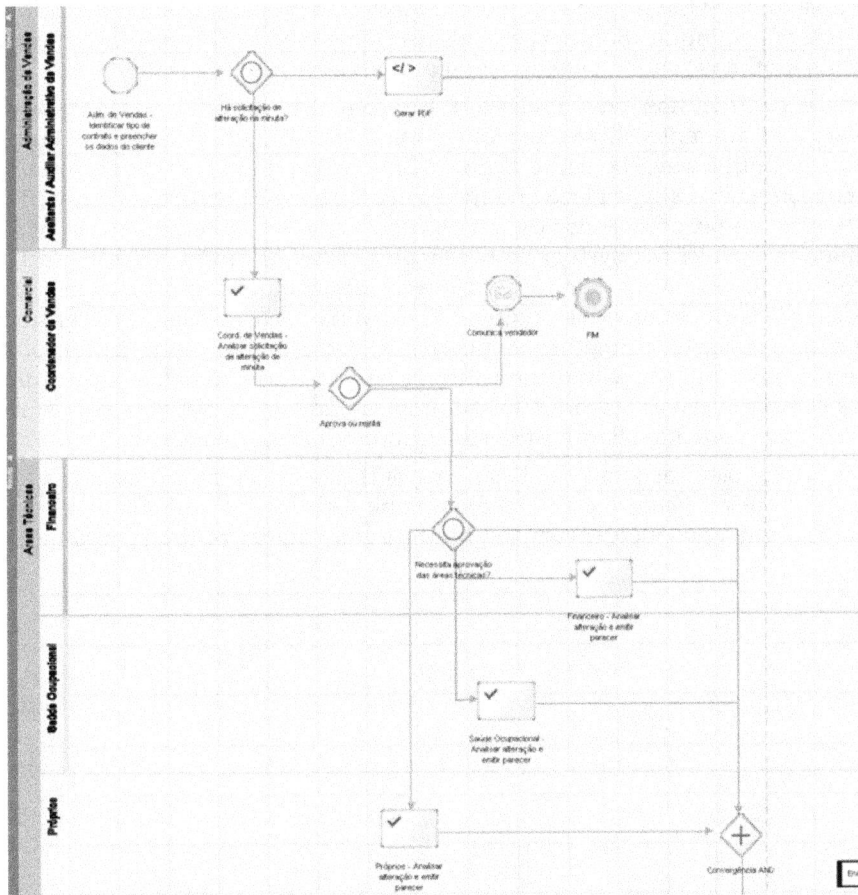

Picture—Initiation of Legal Entity Contracts Process, modeled in BPMS

With the automation of the process, the legal department is able to manage contract versions and templates directly using Microsoft SharePoint. It is the only department able to access contracts in this way. As a result, the risk of inappropriate alterations by unauthorized individuals, or of outdated versions of contracts being used inadvertently, has been eliminated.

In the past, the process of creating Supplier Contracts was initiated by means of an e-mail sent to the legal department by the department requiring the contract. Once the contract had been developed, the responsibility for its security and handling lay with the department requesting it. Each department had its own approach—whether based on system support or not—for the management of its contracts. If statements of opinion were required from managers, they were issued by e-mail. There was no systematic monitoring of the terms and electronic versions of the documents. Contractual alterations—both additions and deletions—were treated on a case by case basis in a non-standardized fashion. Fundamentally, it can be said that there was no real "process" at all prior to the implementation of the project. With the automation of the process, the departments requiring new contracts can request them—as well as any subsequent alterations—directly through BPMS by completing the electronic form with the information necessary for the legal department to create the instrument. Departments are now able to track the progress of their request step by step. BPMS also maintains a record of communication between all users involved in the process, as well as allowing for the validation of managerial authorities where necessary.

Once the contract has been finalized, the system organizes the terms (expiry, increases and guarantees), sending out e-mails beforehand to alert the legal department. In this way, the entire contract life cycle and the documents relating to it are recorded in a single place and monitored by a single department, specifically created for the purpose under the name Legal Contract Management. In order to facilitate the use of the system by all departments within the company, functionalities for the following four processes were designed and published on BPMS: creation of contracts, making additions to existing ones, concession (transferring control of contracts to another company), and dissolution and closure of contracts. In order to ensure that the contract database was updated with details of those contracts generated prior to the implementation of the project, a further process was created to allow for the registration of existing contracts.

The following pictures show the beginning of the New Contract Request/Addition process (modeled using the BPMS tool) along with the accompanying electronic form. The sequence also shows the background context of the process at each stage.

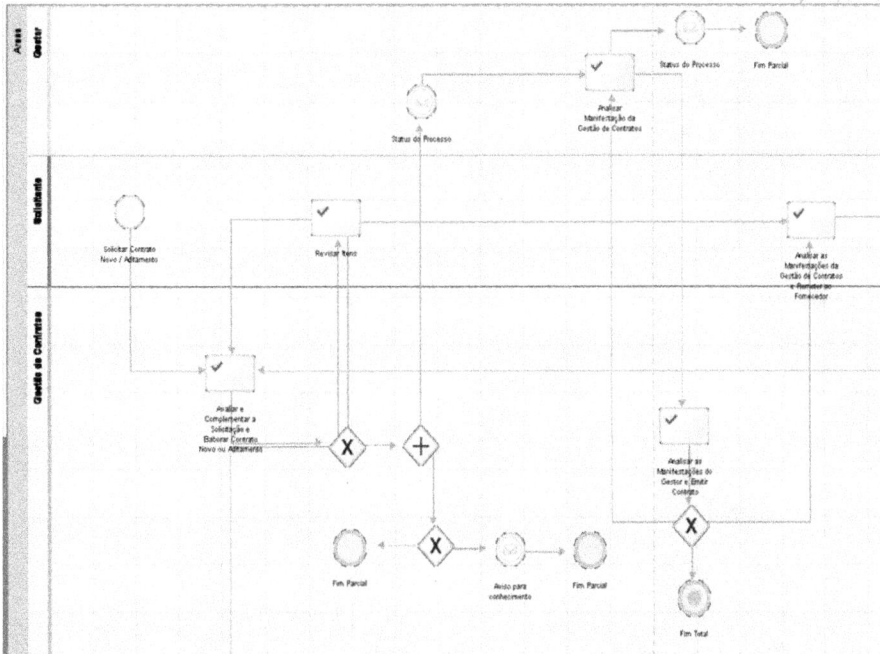

Picture—Initial Stage of New Contract Request/Addition Process modeled using BPMS tool

Picture—Electronic Form for New Contract Request/Addition Process (web) for submission of new processes

DETALHAMENTO DO PROCESSO

UNIMED - Gestão de Contratos de Fornecedores - Novo / Aditamento v.1 - Cód. 11970

Fornecedor: / Nº do Contrato: 632
Tipo de Operação: Contrato Novo

PASSO A PASSO DO FLUXO

Cód.	Tarefa	Início	Conclusão	Status	Concluído
28794	**Solicitar Contrato Novo / Aditamento** Atenção: Preencha os campos o mais detalhadamente possível e não esqueça de clicar na tecla "enviar". Em breve você receberá informações sobre o andamento de seu pedido. Caso você esteja solicitando um aditamento é necessário o número do contrato original. Se você não o tiver, entre em contato com a Assessoria Jurídica/Gestão de Contratos nos ramais 4814 ou 4897.	16/04/2010 - 16:19:22		enviar_gestao_de_contratos	✔
28795	**Avaliar e Complementar a Solicitação e Elaborar Contrato Novo ou Aditamento**	16/04/2010 - 16:19:23	27/04/2010 - 14:36:24	encaminhar_para_validador	✔
29999	**Analisar Manifestação da Gestão de Contratos (Gestor do Solicitante)** Prezado Gestor, necessitamos de sua avaliação sobre o pedido recebido cujas informações seguem abaixo. Após a análise, favor preencher com suas considerações no campo MENSAGENS. Não esqueça de clicar na tecla ADICIONAR para gravar sua mensagem. Após, clique no botão ENVIAR no final da tela.	23/04/2010 - 16:12:03	27/04/2010 - 14:34:01	Concluído	✔
30060	**Analisar Manifestação da Gestão de Contratos (Outro Responsável)** Prezado Gestor, necessitamos de sua avaliação sobre o pedido recebido cujas informações seguem abaixo. Após a análise, favor preencher com suas considerações no campo MENSAGENS. Não esqueça de clicar na tecla ADICIONAR para gravar sua mensagem. Após, clique no botão ENVIAR no final da tela.	27/04/2010 - 14:36:26	28/04/2010 - 14:36:26	Em andamento	

Picture—Department making the application monitor the process step by step

4.3 Organization

The existence of automated processes has allowed the company to create a new department specifically for the purpose of managing its contracts. Operating under the name Legal Contract Management, it is now responsible for centralizing and managing all processes related to sales and supplier contracts, providing assistance to the other departments involved in the process.

Immediate access to all information relating to processes has allowed the Legal Contract Management department to develop a broader vision of its role, incorporating contract management best practices into the company routine.

Those working with contracts can now be assured that the contracts belong to the company and not to individual departments or users, as they might have been considered to do under the previous system. Moreover, there is no longer any element of delay or uncertainty in meeting the demands of internal or external audits.

The commercial department can now issue its contracts automatically and maintain an adequate register of exception cases, while continuing to serve as a seal of approval to be used by those managers who require it.

Departments requesting supply contracts are now able to follow the process step by step, and no longer need to send e-mails or contact the legal department by telephone in order to request updates on the status of their request, an arrangement which frequently gave rise to communication breakdowns and even misunderstandings in some cases.

5. HURDLES OVERCOME

Management

The project relied from the outset upon the support of company management, as much in the first phase as in the second. However, the cultural shift being demanded often made it necessary to apply a great deal of "persuasion" where the second tier of the company was concerned. Emphasis was placed on ensuring that the project was viewed by all parties involved as a joint effort, and that participants felt able both to ask for help and information and to voice their own opinions about what was truly expected of the new processes. This approach was carried out with the constant support of upper management.

Business

Whenever an attempt is made to modify any of the processes which are deeply rooted in the culture of the company—and especially so when multiple departments and technical and financial questions are involved—it is inevitable that a number of difficulties will be encountered. We were faced with the challenge of putting our contract processes in place without interrupting the day-to-day operation of the company, at the same time as incorporating the ideas being generated by all parties involved and creating a computerized method of increasing the response time of these processes at low cost and within a reduced deployment time.

The support of an external consulting agency and the extra dedication shown by each member of the project team were vital to the success of the initiative.

Organization Adoption

Some initial resistance was encountered from users, mainly in the implementation of the Supplier Contracts processes. In order to discourage rejection, a manual was developed and a training program prepared for several groups containing key users designated by managers in each of the company departments. As well as including an explanation of workflow function, the training program provided an orientation on the strategic objectives of the project and the methodological approach which it employs, in order to make users aware that the change being implemented represented something more than simply the installation of a new system.

Moreover, it was constantly kept in mind from the outset that the work being undertaken was predicated, in accordance with the concepts of BPM, on the objective of continually improving processes. Attention was drawn to the fact that, while the first version of the project had not fully satisfied all parties, there would be opportunities in future for improvements and corrections to be made. The concept that "the perfect is the enemy of the good" was highly important in focusing individuals on a strategy of gradual and evolving implementation, moving forward step by step with a constant eye on our higher aims.

6. BENEFITS

6.1 Cost Savings

The project did not have cost reduction as its principal objective. However, there is a clear financial benefit in reducing time spent and the number of errors incurred in the execution of a process. At the same time, the reduction of risks related to contracts has an undoubted positive impact on company finances to the extent that it leads to a lower rate of legal actions due to contractual misunderstandings, as much in the case of sales as in that of product and service acquisition. Mitigating the risk of fines being applied by the ANS due to the issuing of unregistered contracts also has a cost-reducing effect.

6.2 Time Reductions

In the case of Sale of Legal Entity Contracts, the immediate applicability of the final versions of contracts—as a result of the adoption of BPMS integrated with a

SharePoint template database—has significantly reduced the time required to re-lease new products for the consumption of clients. In the case of Supplier Con-tracts, there has been an estimated 50 percent reduction in the time required for the development and analysis of contracts, provided that upon reaching the Legal Contract Management department the process has been properly implemented by the department requesting the contract.

6.3 Increased Revenues

The objectives of the project did not include profit increase, since it was a ques-tion of an initiative intended to improve operational efficiency and implement ef-fective process monitoring. Only one of the processes involved—the one dealing with Legal Entity Client Contracts—is directly connected to the core business of Unimed Porto Alegre. Be that as it may, it can be said that the increased efficiency in contract development, principally in the case of those contracts requiring the approval of several different departments, has contributed to reduction in the rate of client abandonment due to delay in this initial phase of concluding business deals.

6.4 Productivity Improvements

Improved productivity was the main objective of the project. First and foremost, the need for revision (barring alterations made for business reasons) when issuing standardized sales contracts has been drastically reduced, provided that the Sales Administration team completes the sale information in BPMS and that the latter immediately and automatically generates the contract in PDF form for printing. It is not possible to issue a contract if all fields have not been completed. Further-more, the system also automatically validates certain details, such as the CPNJ (Cadastro Nacional de Pessoas Jurídicas/National Registry of Legal Entities) numbers and the CPF (Cadastro de Pessoa Física/Social Security) numbers of le-gal representatives who are to sign the contract, thereby reducing still further the possibility of human error. Great benefits have also been achieved through the use of SharePoint, integrated with BPMS, for the management of contract tem-plates. There is no longer a risk that incorrect or outdated templates may be ap-plied.

Automated BPMS control has also brought great improvements in productivity, provided that the impact of each alteration requested is recorded and submitted for the approval of the responsible department.

The centralization of supplier contract management has made it possible to exert total control over all supply contracts used by Unimed Porto Alegre. With the in-troduction of automated processes, all relevant terms are now monitored by the system, allowing the Legal Contract Management department to take the neces-sary measures to guarantee that all departments using the system are served cor-rectly. All contracts stored in electronic format and the processes which have gen-erated them are centralized in a single location, eliminating the need to use e-mail and spreadsheets in conducting parallel monitoring.

7. BEST PRACTICES, LEARNING POINTS AND PITFALLS

7.1 Best Practices and Learning Points

✓ *The timely involvement of the right individuals and of the departments that play a role in the process was fundamental in guaranteeing the productivity of production and validation meetings. Making the right choice of executive team for the project is vital;*

✓ *The participation of the IT department was indispensable from the outset of the project, mainly because we were installing a new system and implementing a new approach in the development of software solutions;*

✓ *The support of upper management was frequently called upon in order to overcome certain internal barriers;*

✓ *The practice of correctly documenting the processes, their specifications and related technical questions paid dividends in the subsequent installation and training phases.*

✓ *The development of a process manual and of well-structured training programs for system users was useful in breaking resistance at the same time as making it possible for the project coordinators to remain informed of how the rest of the organization was viewing the initiative.*

✓ *It was highly important to understand the expectations of users at the same time as making it clear that the initial version of the process would not be the definitive one. BPM naturally implies the idea of continual improvement of processes. Everyone must keep in mind that "the perfect is the enemy of the good". When those involved realized that it was necessary to focus on the simpler initial aspects of the initiative and put in place a preliminary version of the process, the project began to move forward in a swifter and more assertive way.*

✓ *In the six processes which we put in place the only method of integration used was developed using Microsoft SharePoint, since it was vital for the installation of the first version of the process. More complex methods of integration were left for future implementation phases, so as not to render the initiative unviable by taking up project time and generating high costs at the outset.*

✓ *There were errors in the initial conception of the process (scope and functionalities) which were corrected as the project progressed. This led to an increase in both duration and cost. Subsequent initiatives will include a preliminary "pre-planning" phase in order to define clearly which functionalities will be implemented and which will be reserved for future phases.*

✓ *The professional support of an external consulting agency specialized in BPM and in the use of the BPMS tool was vital to the success of the project.*

✓ *In recent years the IT department of Unimed Porto Alegre has been implementing several improvement and governance measures with the aim of guaranteeing greater security for its information and the quality of service which it provides. This has an impact upon new rules and procedures for access to the infrastructure, use of servers and installation of new applications. In such a situation, even when conducting a process improvement initiative, close co-ordination and co-operation with the IT infrastructure department was essential for the implementation of the project.*

7.2 Pitfalls

✗ *The fixed-scope project management model, implemented according to the PMI (Project Management Institute) guidelines, has repeatedly been shown to be too rigid to provide the flexibility demanded by a BPM project. In projects conducted in a traditional way change is considered as an anomaly, whereas in BPM it is viewed as a learning experience. In the case of the first automated processes in particular, many alterations and changes of scope were necessary, leading to revised budgets. For future projects, the aim is to work with adaptable models and a more flexible scope.*

   ✗   *Integration with the Microsoft Office platform, notably for the generation of Word documents based on information produced by the processes, proved to be a technical challenge, since the software was not designed to be manipulated using programming code (despite possessing an API (Application Programming Interface).*

8. COMPETITIVE ADVANTAGES

The private healthcare and health plan sector in Brazil is highly competitive and regulated. There are over 2,000 healthcare operators in the country, with over 37 million beneficiaries, amounting to 18 percent of the population. The remainder, approximately 163 million people, are treated through the SUS (Sistema Único de Saúde/Unified Healthcare System), the Brazilian public health service. The regulation of health plans, introduced in 1998, has led to noticeable changes in the sector. The rigid legislation and monitoring imposed by the state have created norms which, among other things, create the need for certain operators to provide financial guarantees, mechanisms which prevent the unilateral abatement of contracts, and sharply defined rules governing the entry and exit of new companies in the sector.

The state exerts much of its control through normalization and inspection of the contracts used by healthcare operators. Through firm and controlled management of its contracts Unimed Porto Alegre is able, at present, to hold a position of prominence in its sector, respecting current norms and applying the highest levels of governance in its management. This is reflected in the best standards of quality, the greatest level of information security and the highest degree of monitoring of sensitive company information. By paying full attention to all of the legal requirements in its sector, Unimed Porto Alegre maintains itself as a prominent company and leader in its area of operation.

Moreover, its efficient management of contracts for the supply of products and services is directly reflected by savings in expenses, which continues to sustain a healthy growth rate from year to year. As we have seen from the figures presented above, the potential for expansion in the market is extremely high, since the vast majority of the Brazilian population still does not possess private health plans.

Long-term Plans for Sustaining Competitive Advantage

Since the implementation of this initial project, a number of other initiatives have already been put in motion at Unimed Porto Alegre. The introduction of BPM concepts and tools is an irreversible process which has been made possible thanks to the knowledge acquired and the rapid gains achieved in this undertaking.

Moreover, there already exist ongoing projects with the aim of implementing changes and improvements in suitable contract management processes, taking advantage of the opportunities observed during routine activities. The emergence and development of the culture of constant improvement and focus upon quality will serve as the basis for the further institutional development of the organization.

9. TECHNOLOGY

The technical implementation of the project was made possible by the following software platforms:

- **Orquestra BPM**: BPMS software produced by the Brazilian company Cryo Technologies. Orquestra BPM is exceptional for being a 100 percent web-based BPMS application, with a focus upon human-centric processes, speed of implementation and ease of change. Unimed Porto Alegre selected this platform because of its geographical proximity to the supplier and their adherence to the characteristics of the target processes. Orquestra BPM is responsible for the automation of all the contract management processes;

- **Microsoft SharePoint**: ECM (Enterprise Content Management) software produced by Microsoft, used to store, restrict access to and monitor successive versions of the drafts of all contracts managed by the project processes. Unimed Porto Alegre decided to use SharePoint because of the robust solutions it provides and in view of the fact that it was already in use with other units.
- **Microsoft Office**: backups of draft contracts are automatically generated in Word 2007 format, with the issue of the documents being under the control of the Legal Contract Management department;
- **Adobe PDF**: the PDF platform was employed in the generation of secure versions of contracts, which cannot be altered by unauthorized users;

The integration of Orquestra BPM and SharePoint proved to be essential to the project, since the former program is capable of managing process execution in a transparent way, while the latter is responsible for storing contract information. Future projects currently in development at Unimed Porto Alegre are also being coordinated according to this architecture.

Using PDF files as a standard ensured that the draft contracts, once generated, were not altered by unauthorized persons. The PDF format offers a number of different monitoring and security mechanisms. The PDF files only provide permission for the documents to be printed in cases where signatures need to be added.

The project made use of the following hardware:

Web server (shared)	
Processor	Xeon 3.0 GHz—1 Quad
RAM	8GB
HD	124GB Giga applications and 12GB systems
OS	Windows 2003 Server Enterprise Edition

Database Server	
Processor	4 Nodes: 02 Intel Dual Core Xeon 26 Hz
RAM	4 Nodes: 72 Gb
HD Storage	EMC$_2$ 2.5 Tb
OS Linux	Red Hat 5—64 Bits
DB Oracle	10g (10.2.04 Oracle Rac)

10. THE TECHNOLOGY AND SERVICE PROVIDERS

The consulting agency contracted for the implementation of the project was BPM Soluções (BPM Solutions), a Brazilian company specialized in BPM and possessing extensive knowledge of the BPMS software adopted by Unimed Porto Alegre, with projects being carried out by companies of various sizes in several sectors. BPM Solutions is an implementation partner of Cryo Technologies, a Brazilian company which owns the rights to Orquestra BPM Suite. Both companies have their headquarters in the same municipality as Unimed Porto Alegre and continue to cooperate on BPM projects for our company at the present time.

Web addresses: www.bpmsolucoes.com.br and www.cryo.com.br

ArcelorMittal Foundation, Brazil

Silver Award, South America
Nominated by AuraPortal, USA

1. EXECUTIVE SUMMARY / ABSTRACT

ArcelorMittal Foundation (AMF) is an organization created to carry out ArcelorMittal's private social investment actions, for the sake of those communities wherein the Company has industrial units. The Foundation develops its activities in 48 municipalities, through 14 social programs in the fields of education, health, environment and culture. As a result of its BPM initiative, within the cultural field, 100 percent of their project proposals can be submitted and evaluated via electronic forms. This represents an increase of 50 percent in the number of project responses. Also, a 50 percent reduction in the time to evaluate each proposal was achieved. As a result of this BPM initiative, which included a tightly integrated SOA environment, a new and improved AMF system was launched called the "CTRL Cultura" system.

2. OVERVIEW

The AMF has always had a strong background in managing cultural projects, but was becoming challenged with being able to adequately manage the increasing volume of project proposals sent by cultural agents. Along with the volume of transactions came a corresponding large amount of legal documentation and controls required each step in a cultural project evaluation process. During the period from 2004 to 2007, the foundation invested approximately $30 million in cultural initiatives (sponsorships, events, grants, etc.). The systems used in the past were not integrated and required the use of paper, combined with manual labor. In fact, the process of registering projects used to be done by the cultural agents in printed forms and then input into a database. All cultural project monitoring was done manually, looking for information on different systems and sources.

3. BUSINESS CONTEXT

A Process centric culture was a goal for the entire organization as a strategy to leverage its competencies in supporting cultural projects with an impact in the society. This was the primary "business" goal for the company and the Foundation. Practically speaking, AMF experiencing some low volume of projects evaluate due to excessive amount of manual work required reviewing each proposal. The previous processes had breaks in the flow work. For example, Project submissions needed an in person presentation by the social agent(s) and separate static databases were applied to manage the information. Basic issues existed with the number of people that were required to review projects and with the complexity in managing all project data internally, through a combination of independent databases and paper files. These constraints had limited the capacity to adequately select the most relevant cultural project proposals. The small team responsible for project proposal analysis were visibly a bottleneck in achieving the actual process goals, including responding to all requests to social agents in a timely fashion and selecting the best projects.

The company realized that the quality of the accepted projects could be increased if the company were able to select the best cultural project proposals in a faster, more agile manner by the standardization and automation of their processes. The company expected to continue to see a rise in the number of project proposals and knew it needed to optimize their processes in order to respond to requests in a timely fashion. Some of the other challenges identified:

- Need for a process-oriented collaborative platform for managing cultural projects within the Foundation.
- To promote project agents interaction through a common platform, thereby enhancing the flexibility in the procedures necessary to carry out a cultural project.
- To provide a 100 percent web based platform.
- To enable the orchestration of all foundation activities in a transparent and dynamic way for management.
- To reduce the processing time for projects.

4. THE KEY INNOVATIONS

4.2 Business

In 2007, AMF management decided to redesign its organization based on their Cultural Investment Policy with the aim of expanding access to goods and services, by training and qualifying leaders and artists of the communities served. It was established by the Culture Committee, composed of representatives from different areas of the company and by the Culture and Art department of the foundation. After the consolidation of the Cultural Investment Policy and the implementation of the Culture Committee, The AMF proposed the creation of a cultural management system, which represented all automated processes using BPMS technology.

4.3 Process

The combined system allowed the foundation to design and automate more than 18 processes, shown in the Figure 1, which controls all cultural management programs, and which resolved numerous problems: Sponsorship via tax incentives; development of artistic events that stimulate support of new values; developing programs in the different cultural areas, as well as expressing many of their cultural policies and their strategies; and using the independent Business Rules System offered by the system. Thus the organization would be creating the necessary workflows to integrate their employees and projects (Cultural Committees, Marketing and Communication Areas, Relationships with Institutions, etc.), by creating its collaboration environment using an Intranet portal, its website and also simplifying the user experience by providing process driven communication through the use of the email system. It would also provide some alternatives for their partners to receive tasks or check the status of their submitted projects. Within this collaborative environment, all information can be shared, including: Agendas, Documents, Tasks, Forums, Reports, Activity Monitoring, etc.

In Figure 1, a high level model is showing the combination of processes created to support all activities in an end-to-end mode, defined by the AMF team and the external BPM consultants. AMF has used the BPM platform to perform the ASIS analysis for each process in all levels of detail. The AS-IS models were then optimized by achieving all the TO-BE processes with the ability to document and retrieve different models version into the BPM platform.

As shown in Table 1, during the AS-IS and TO-BE analysis, many key areas for improvement were detected. The total automation of the process as a result of end-to-end detailed process definition was helping to highlight the primary activities within the different processes that could be optimized by avoiding manual work, paper, and the ability to directly involve the social agents into the process for cultural project management, from data submission to project conclusion.

The BPMS technology applied offered a flexible run-time environment, for immediate exception handling, and the use of declarative business rules that avoided the use of programming code. The entire process automation itself could be developed using zero programming code, resulting in a significant time reduction for delivering the process automation during the technology implementation phase, and also providing flexibility for changing the process "on the fly". Due to the fact that the BPM technology adopted did require coding, and the model could be put into direct execution mode with no human intervention; business people and process experts with no programming skills could be directly involved with automating the processes. Consequently, the IT people could focus on the SOA implementation and allow the business team to concentrate on the processes. AMF was able to achieve a high level of commitment throughout all organizational levels as a result of these BPM platform characteristics.

Mega Process – Operation- Partnership Management for Cultural Project	
Starts on	Proponent data received
Ends on	Cultural Project Closed
Case for Action	1. Lots of documentation required and being managed with paper. Too difficult to store, control and maintain all required documentation
	2. All work with expected response time being performed manually and not accurately.
	3. Lots of time demands for retrieving and joining all project data from different sources.
	4. Project Data missing.
	5. Project Data lost.
	6. Rework often required due to the need to resubmit a new project analysis for approval.
	7. Fewer projects evaluated per year.
	8. Lack of visibility of the project execution.
	9. Low rate of projects success.
Vision	1. Social Agents should be able to submit all data in a 100 percent web environment to reduce the time for processing the gathered data.
	2. Real time visibility could provide an ability to control the workload and to optimize the time for managing all phases of cultural projects.
	3. Reduce cycle time for gathering project data.
	4. Improve the data accuracy by eliminating missing data.
	5. All in a central database to facilitate control.
	6. Need for automatic documentation generation.
	7. Need to reduce the time for project approval.

	8. Eliminate in person presentations by presenting all project proposal data in a paperless manner.
Actors	- Social Agents
	- Cultural Project Analyst
Tools	- Isolated databases
	- Paper
	- Manual work
Metrics	- No. of project proposals received/year
	- Total time for new project data
	- Total time required for retrieving project data
	- No. of projects responded to per year
	- Total # of projects received/number of evaluators

Table 1. Process Summary: Partnership Management (Cultural Projects).

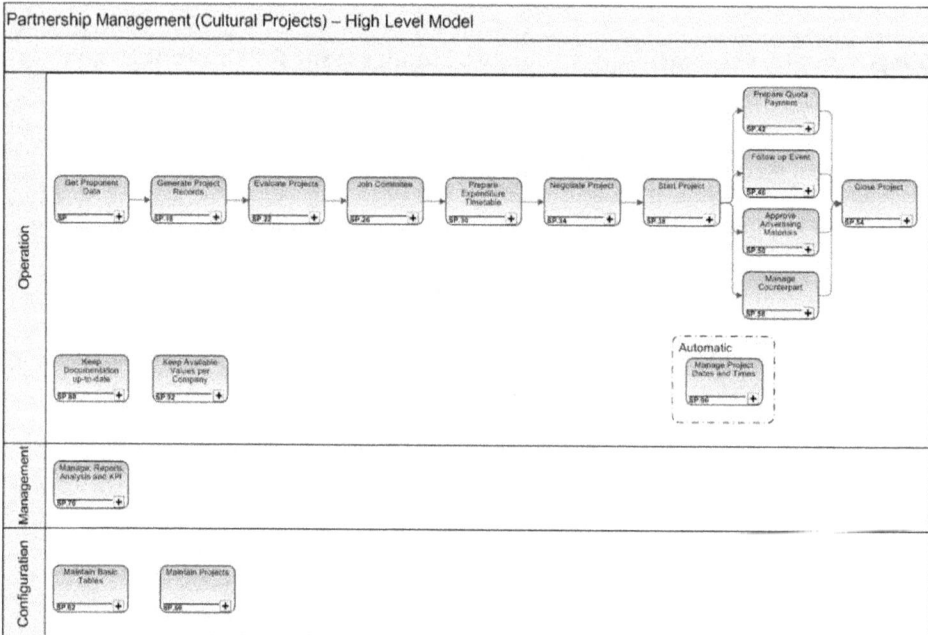

Figure 1: High Level Model of the processes automated in the AMF BPM Initiative. Source: AuraPortal/CSY.

Figure 2 shows the main challenges faced during the process mapping activities developed at AMF. The company realized that flexibility would be imperative in a day to day manner for adjusting the strategies and actions based on any compliance issue or need for reducing operational costs at the Foundation. The visibility in a real-time fashion was a promise of the BPM technology, and for this reason, AMF understood that process visibility combined with information generation for the decision making process could be the key for agile change eventually applied to the processes in a continual process improvement model. The unification of all data in a single, common database was critical also, due to the need for a more dynamic data management for retrieving data and managing all process indicators in real time.

Challenges, Implications and Alternatives

Challenges	Implications	Alternatives
Process integration between the Company, the Foundation and Partners.	End-to-end processes, from the request to the execution and presentation of the results for any cultural project.	Unified solution to support all stakeholders
	Flexibility to support the process changes based on company and compliance dynamics.	Ability to change or adapt the process dynamically.
Information for decision making.	Complete data colection about the project: preparation, execution and results.	Unified and integrated database for the company, its foundation and partners.
	Process data colection: volume, times, activities.	Database with the information about the process execution and real time follow up.
	Data transformation in KPIs.	KPI analysis and incident reporting, causes and actions.

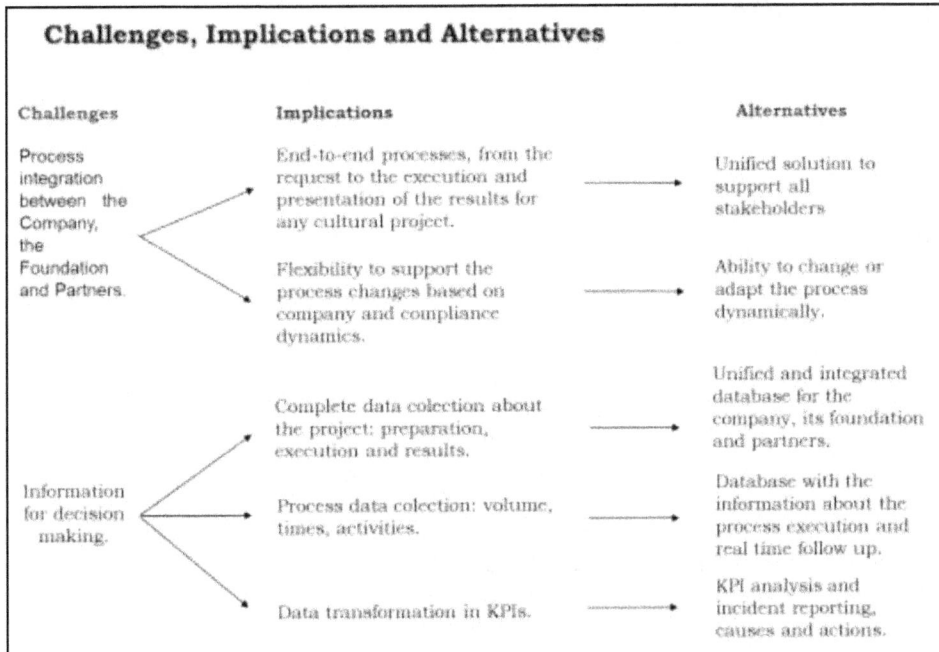

Figure 2. Process Challenges, Implications and Alternatives.

4.4 Organization

Once the BPM initiative started and after getting familiar with the methodology, the technology, and all people involved, the stakeholders decided to adopt a high level of commitment to BPM as a discipline. All people within all organizational levels understood that the process driven approach was the best way to achieve the defined goals of the AMF in supporting its initiatives. They improved visibility during the process mapping phase, and understood the need for cross functional processes which were critical success factors for achieving the goals of the BPM implementation. In addition, all the social agents from different types of social organizations were able to participate by providing feedback in how processes were modeled and how they could be executed. They were an integral part of the project.

The social agents and the AMF employees needed some training and education in the BPM technology implemented; something that was managed in a very positive environment because all stakeholders had participated in all phases of the BPM initiative. A major challenge could have been the assimilation of the changes from a chaotic way of doing things to a process driven approach for managing cultural projects with a real time visibility of all steps of the processes cycles. As a result, AMF prepared a "marketing campaign" to promote the new system which resulted in a very effective and efficient tool for convincing people to embrace the new process-oriented focus adopted for managing projects with BPMS technology. A training program coordinated by the process architects to the final users was critical in terms of making people understand how the new processes work and also for increasing their commitment in using the new system. The AMF has also created what they called "the process office", a team created by the BPM leaders, internal and external, for collaborating in process optimization and expanding the use of the BPM technology with all organizations involved.

5. HURDLES OVERCOME

During the different phases of the BPM initiative in AMF, all process leaders were concerned about achieving a good level of commitment and involvement from all people within all departments. The main challenge was to convince all levels of management of the necessity and value of the BPM implementation to the organization. Due to the high level of investment in cultural projects, the Foundation was not able to fully guarantee that such investments would provide the expected. In order to address this issue, the BPM leaders rolled out a series of workshops and meetings for "selling" the BPM initiative by justifying the initiative in terms of investment and time needed to complete the implementation. On the business side, typically, a Foundation is not the core center for budget allocation due to the need for doing more with less. This is something that put a strain on the discussions in terms of the budget needed for the project. The BPM leaders justified the project by assuring a low investment to short time return ratio. Also, AMF had to define some specific KPIs for evaluating the performance of their initiative which is typical for a normal business, but less so for an organization such as theirs. Therefore, they relied on external consultants to assist with this issue. From the beginning of the implementation it was difficult to explain to people in general, the need for a process definition that reflected all interactions across all levels of the organization. People normally know what they do in their own jobs, but they don't always notice what activities occur before or after they finish their task, or what the impact of their work is on others throughout the company. To assist with this issue, AMF and the consultancy firm organized some workshops to illustrate how each employee fits into the process, and how they impact others.

6. BENEFITS

Due to its systematic approach for the BPM initiative, AMF achieved a high level of integration of all information related to individual cultural projects, and was able to manage the projects efficiently and collaboratively across the organization. The ease of operation processing sponsorship requests, analysis, selection, monitoring and the evaluation of the results of projects, enabled the organization to operate more efficiently and select better quality projects.

As for some of quantifiable benefits achieved by AMF, there was a significant reduction in the execution time (50 percent) in the analysis of projects, and with 100 percent of the proposals generated in electronic format, the evaluation and response times were reduced significantly. The organization was also able to increase the number of proposals analyzed with no need to increase the number of employees.

Many indirect benefits were also achieved as a result of the BPM implementation at AMF. A process-centric culture in the day-to-day work in the Foundation was established and different resources were able to interact on the same platform, including internal agents of the Foundation and external constituents, using different channels like the use of email to interact with processes, public web and the common interaction platform. The newly automated system called "Ctrl-Cultura" offers accessibility in real time to all of the information required by any member of the team involved in the management of a project, which brings faster response to problems that may occur.

One interesting benefit was the ability of the new system to generate Key Performance Indicators using a specific process to orchestrate the process data in the system. At the same time, the system can retrieve and consolidate data from an external system within a separate platform for all automated processes related to the sponsorship requests, their analysis, selection, monitoring and evaluation of the results of the project, enabling better decision making when evaluating projects.

Full integration of all AMF applications involved in the processes, including the automation of the tasks performed by different systems and people, were orchestrated by the BPMS engine resulting in one Business Information System for handling Projects. (Their System Tasks - automatic - drive the communication with the rest of the Programs using the Web Services that can be invoked in real time for all information from the BPMS system).

Metrics	Description	Before BPM	After BPM	Cost Savings
No. of project proposals received/year	No. of project proposals correctly received and recorded.	714	1525	120 percent
Total time for new project data entering	Time required to create new project proposals records in the system	1 day	15 minutes	300 percent
Total time required for retrieving project data	Time required joining all documentation (legal, authorizations, etc.) for project analysis or checking.	30 minutes	1 minute	50
percent of projects responded per year	Total of projects responded/Total Project proposal received * 100	50 percent	100 percent	50 percent
Total No. of projects responded/number of evaluators	Productivity evaluation per month	12 (5 people)	42 (3 people)	40 percent

Table 2. Quantifiable results: Cost savings, Time reduction and Productivity increase. Source: AMF.

All quantifiable benefits are summarized in the Table 2 and AMF itself is subordinated to ArcelorMittal headquarters in Brazil and their mission continues to be striving to do more with less, as mentioned before. The AMF entity appears in the ArcelorMittal financial accounting system as an expenditure or cost, as it is difficult to show a tangible return on any investment due to its non-profit nature within the company structure. For this reason, AMF had always been driven to optimize their entire operation in order to make their initiatives totally supported within the tight parameters of the company budget. As a result, AMF decided to implement the BPM and its technologies to improve its efficiencies. By achieving these improved results, the Foundation is contributing more with the same budget, and all stakeholders can see all processes along with their real-time status, and grant financial approval for any project based on a pre-defined business rule, which directly contributed to the results presented in the Table 2. The ability to evaluate more projects in less time was responsible for reducing not only cycle times but also costs related to the paperless approach, and the reduced labor hours and manual activity. At the same time, with the goal to select cultural projects proposed by agents with the most interesting ideas, the Foundation could significantly improve the company's visibility in the social arena. This was something that was not possible in the past, but totally achievable now, since the company can involve more social agents, evaluate their performance, and have better control over selecting the best projects to support.

7. BEST PRACTICES, LEARNING POINTS AND PITFALLS

As a result of the AMG BPM initiative, the organization was able to generate best practices and learning points on:

- ✓ *The creation of a process committee to validate all BPM initiatives and new major optimization planned.*
- ✓ *The creation of a knowledge base for the entire company process architecture and cross-functional interactions starting with the use of Process Maps as shown in the Figure 1.*
- ✓ *Methodology applied for process automation and process improvement acquired as a result of the involvement of the consultancy company responsible for the implementation of the BPMS platform.*
- ✓ *Total and direct involvement of the social agents (including external constituents) into the process centric approach embedded in the daily AMF activities. Dynamic process change is critical for an agile process driven organization and BPM technology must provide that in an easy manner.*
- ✓ *The involvement of the business people and process owners in the process of automating processes, using the BPM technology was critical to reduce the time to deliver the expected results.*

Some of the Pitfalls identified were:

- ✗ *Avoiding modeling and automating isolated process in a clear lack of cross-functional view.*
- ✗ *Lack of commitment in all levels can jeopardize the success of such an initiative.*
- ✗ *It is imperative to set target numbers (metrics) before and after the process automation because at the beginning, it can be difficult to convince the stakeholders to develop ROI analysis or to extract some actual metrics for their processes.*
- ✗ *Expending lots of time design the technological solution. The BPMS tools must provide reduced time cycles for automating all organization processes.*

8. COMPETITIVE ADVANTAGES

Social responsibility is a key goal on the corporate business strategy at the ArcelorMittal.

The company is totally committed to develop all initiatives that represent the respect of to the environment protection social growth. On its region, all companies in the steel industry have a strong social and environment commitment with the society. ArcelorMittal and its Foundation in Brazil were pioneers in embedding BPM initiatives and technology for improving their social and cultural sponsored projects, recognized by local communities and government, and started to be used as an example of corporate social responsibility, which started to be followed by their competitors in the same way.

AMF achieved the lowest-cost operation compared to competitors, a benchmarking in this sector. The organization became a reference for all foundations in this marketplace. At the same time, the company plans more process optimization for cost reductions by diminishing time as a way to guarantee and to increase its budget in this area and to increase their market visibility.

9. TECHNOLOGY

AMF was looking for a BPM technology oriented to business people and process owners, some experiences and tests with other tools revealed that a more coding intensive tool could cause the costs and time to increase substantially. AuraPortal was the BPMS platform selected by AMF to support their BPM initiative by automating all required processes in all required areas. AuraPortal is a global BPMS (Business Process Management Suite) provider, delivering a solution that creates Business Process Workflow Execution Models without the need for IT programming. The platform is totally Web-based and for this reason the organization was able to create a multidisciplinary team from different areas: the people in the foundation, the IT support team located in other facilities and the consultancy company as well. It was integrated with existing systems using web services technology, Adapters Server Connectors, in SOA environment, importing tools and many types of systems tasks to perform automatic activities. Consequently, AMF could design processes that combined people and systems all reflected in the models. The Figure 3 shows the different tools used for performing the required integration between different systems.

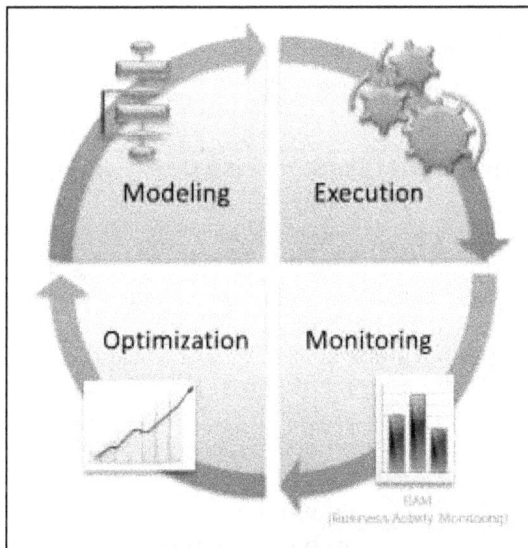

Figure 4. Process life cycle steps used in the BPMS solution.
Source: AuraPortal

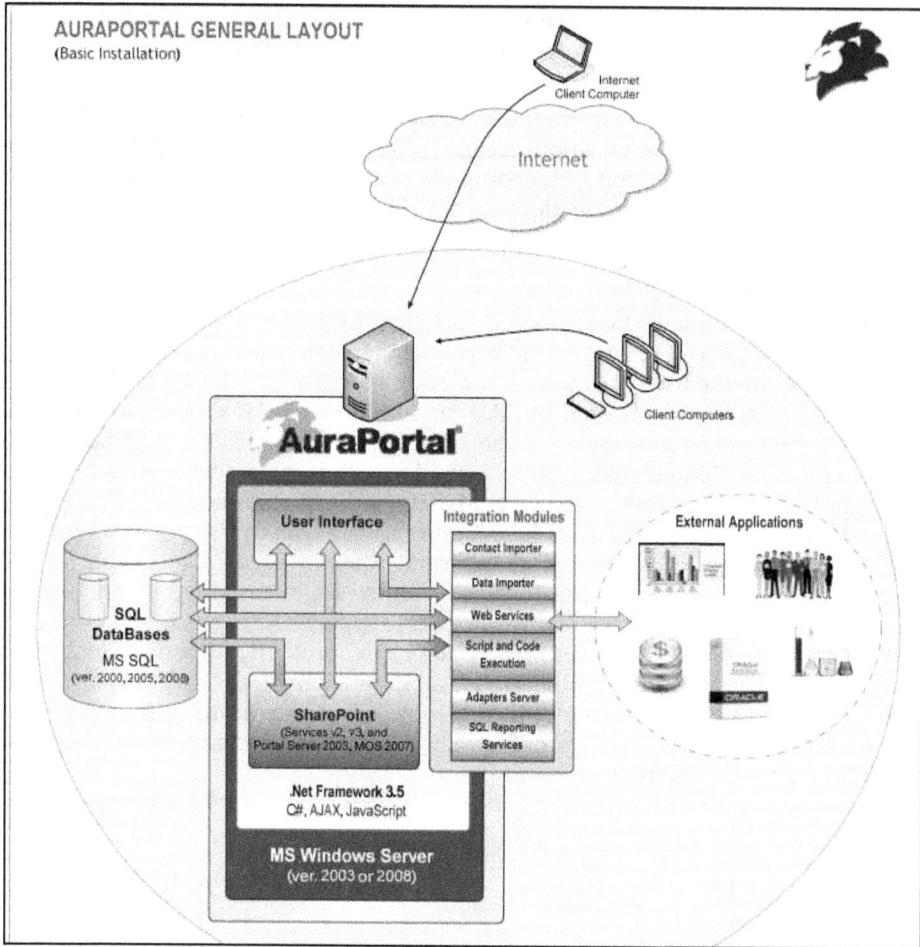

AURAPORTAL GENERAL LAYOUT
(Basic Installation)

Figure 3. AuraPortal BPMS Architecture. Source: AuraPortal.

The implementation of a BPMS system within the AMF and its proposed approach, orientated towards SOA and Process driven solutions, also included Business Rules, Document Handling, Intranet/Extranets, and the public website for internal and external users interacting in real time as shown in Figure 4, supporting communication and collaboration. As part of the requirements of the AMF, the project covered all steps spanning a cultural project; from the initiation of a request, through the management of a proposal to the conclusion and evaluation of the results and the impact of each cultural project on the Foundation. Also, a life cycle process management component was applied as part of the BPMS system approach for process automation as shown in the Figure 4.

The SOA approach was adopted to perform the required integration between different applications and platforms in both directions by leveraging the tools shown in Figure 3. Some specific Web Services components using SOAP protocol were created to provide different methods of invoking procedures directly within the processes modeled in the BPMS solution. As a result, there was "zero" point-to-point integration and the Web Services could be reused in all processes configured in the BPMS software. At the same time, additional ready-to-use Web Services were leveraged to automate some required transactions. The fact that a process start message could be transformed into a Web Services request with no need to develop code was critical in gaining improved time-to-delivery of the solution. One important requirement during the implementation of the BPMS system was the need for providing flexibility for users to interact with processes activities using flexible collaboration environment. In this sense, the selected technology offered multiple possibilities for creating Extranets, use of the public organization website and also the support for a process workflow by having the email system, where social agents could receive tasks on their email boxes with the information, prioritizing, link to the electronic forms in any mobile device. An example of these different environments is shown in Figure 5.

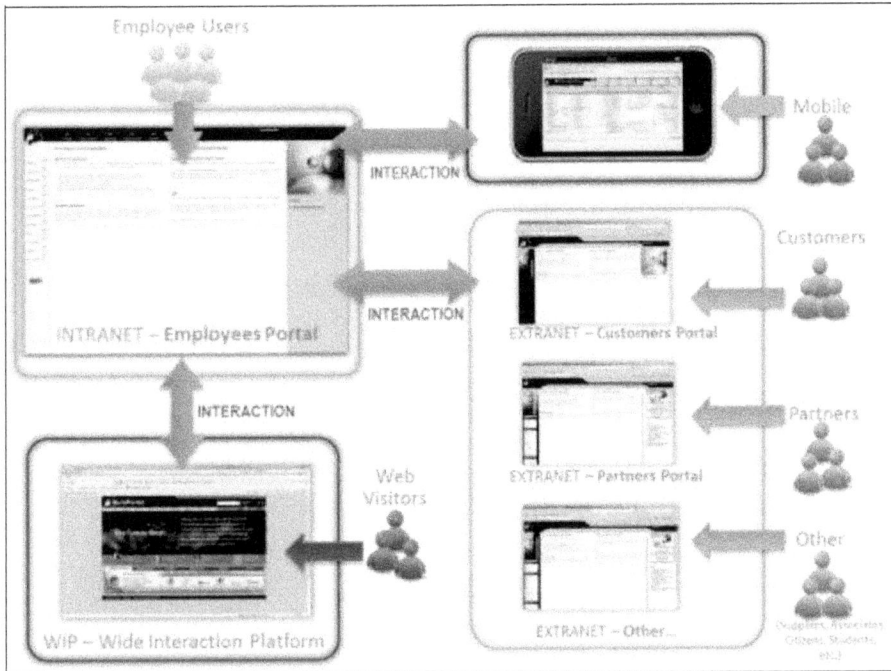

Figure 5. Collaboration Environments for Managing Processes.
Source: AuraPortal.

10. THE TECHNOLOGY AND SERVICE PROVIDERS

AuraPortal was the BPMS technology used the AMF BPM project. AuraPortal is a global BPMS (Business Process Management Suite) provider, delivering a solution that creates Business Process Workflow Execution Models without the need for IT programming. More info on: http://www.auraportal.com

Core Synesis was the consultancy company responsible for all services applied to the AMF BPM initiative. Core Synesis is an AuraPortal partner. More info on: http://www.coresynesis.com.br

AMS (ArcelorMittal Systems) was responsible for all infrastructures required for the implementation of the BPMS system. More info on: http://www.bms.com.br

Telecarrier, Panama

Silver Award: South & Central America
Nominated by PECTRA Technology Inc., USA

1. EXECUTIVE SUMMARY / ABSTRACT

Created in the year 2000 with the purpose of commercially developing the Central America region by rendering services of International Data Center, data and voice transmission, basic telephone and long distance, wholesale, and Internet, Telecarrier is a leading company in the telecommunications industry within the LATAM region.

It has a fiber optic network infrastructure with high capillarity levels, fully integrated with IP technology, capable of transmitting data, voice and video, assuring its customers a fast, reliable, redundant, and scalable service.

As a consequence of both the fast growth experienced by the industry and market consolidation, in November 2009 Telecarrier merged with the telecommunications group Medcom Holdings, INC, owners of Cable Onda, S.A.. This was an unprecedented merger in the market which made Telecarrier the company with the highest potential in the region.

It currently has thousands of domestic, multinational, corporate, and large customers among which is the National Government.

During the first half of 2008, the company identified the need to optimize core processes as part of an integral project that underpinned its market growth. Thus, commercial (pre and post sales) and backoffice (sales administration and finance) were earmarked as being the most significant processes in order to achieve competitive advantages.

At a technological level, proposals for customized development, and CRM (Customer Relationship Management) were analyzed as short–term solutions, or the adoption of a work philosophy based on process management, and the incorporation of BPM (Business Process Management) technology as a mid-term and long-term alternative; the latter having been chosen on account of its flexibility, scalability, and core-process traceability.

The implementation of the project took twelve months, and it involved the whole organization as well as the CEO's full commitment, as it was a corporate project designed on five pillars on which the work was initially carried out:
- Alignment of the project with the business strategy.
- Core process identification.
- Allocation of resources needed the setting of governance bases.
- And project document analysis).

Management metrics after the implementation are relevant, taking as a reference the original situation described. Among the most remarkable ones are the optimization of those processes linked to commercial presentations, sales closing rate, administrative processing, and productivity at the Human Resources level.

2. OVERVIEW

Due to the characteristics of the market in which Telecarrier operates, the adoption of a process management philosophy and the incorporation of a BPM technological tool implied a cultural challenge. Therefore, key aspects were spotted which were essential for the success of the Project: identifying the current situation, assessing the corporate culture and company style, understanding roles and skills, and choosing the best executive sponsor.

"The first of these aspects -"identifying the current situation"- was really key and forced all of us taking part in the project to find out which were the technical needs and opportunities to acquire new technologies; assess their use in the industry in which we were involved, the degree of technological maturity, define technology selection criteria in order to evaluate tools available in the market, and prepare the organization for a cultural change", explained Mr. Mariano Saibene, project leader.

"Prior to making a decision, we analyzed several options, and searched for success cases about similar problems in Panama. We ruled out acquiring a CRM because we considered that, information-wise, we were not mature enough to provide adequate input, and we explored, among other alternatives analyzed, an in-house development that contemplated specifically the problem to be solved", added Mariano.

"This first analysis-stage took us 6 months and allowed us to realize, from an organization point of view, how rigid our IT structure was when considering the needs of the business. This entailed the search for a technological tool that could bridge this shortcoming; thus, with the support of Universidad del Istmo (http://www2.unis.edu.gt/), which provided an objective view, BPM was chosen", concluded Mariano.

Qualitative results have shown a coherent alignment of the business dynamics in face of the technological requirements, and after over 12 months of use, final users appreciate a remarkable improvement in results, when compared to the previous situation: "the best feature of this project is its flexibility to adapt to change, its speed, and the simplicity with which business rules may be changed, providing superb response time both at the process and the implementation level" (applications), as its main final users mention.

3. BUSINESS CONTEXT

As an organization, Telecarrier had information scattered in various places, few processes (mostly informal ones), and a lack of traceability of the company's core-process –Sales. This was the outcome of an exponential growth, well over the original scheme of the business plan, which was chaotically administered, with tasks carried out manually and with high levels of inefficiency.

"When the project was started, we did not face any financial or context-related challenges. It was the time to find a solution to the problem. The task we had identified promised to be arduous, for the company did not have any documented and sustained processes. The few existing processes were completely informal", explained Mr. Mariano Saibene.

The team acknowledged that getting both, process owners and final users, involved in whichever project would be faced was essential. To this end, several internal activities were carried out to enable the joint selection of the technology the company needed in line with the problems spotted.

"During the stage prior to the commencement of the project, we really felt eager to attain improvements, but we did not know where the starting point was, which resulted in several mistakes, typical when trying to identify a technological solution beyond our reality as an organization", Mariano added.

This situation made Telecarrier aware of the need for a process map, for identifying improvement points, and for thinking which the technology that would adapt to the business requirements was. The requirements at an IT and business level, were clear: The organization called for a work philosophy that would allow the deployment of a continuous improvement process, sustained by a flexible and agile technology.

The process to assess suppliers of BPM technology was lead by an interdisciplinary team, which involved different levels in the organization, from the CEO to the sales staff, who planned to execute the process at an operational level. In order to achieve a better level of organization, bid specifications were prepared including –besides legal and administrative aspects- a number of technical requisites that would allow for consistent assessment. Among these, the following stood out: the requirement of a concept test (relatively simple with few activities), with the alternative of requiring integration tasks, the definition of indicators that would enable process performance measurement, delivery of a document with the written detail of the process, a short list of changes to evaluate the flexibility of BPM technology. And lastly, the requirement that the concept test should not stretch beyond three work days.

"These points provided a homogenous understanding of the different alternatives available in the marketplace, given that at the beginning of the Project we found technological alternatives that partially contained BPM functionalities", explained Mariano.

The Key Innovations

At a business level, Telecarrier identified value loss in three areas: the first "gap" was found in how to convey the company's strategy in business processes; then, in how to achieve process implementation through technology, and thirdly in the very structuring of processes which add value.

"At the senior management and department heads levels, we were convinced that if these gaps were not closed, an integrated concept would be hard to achieve. We knew that process management was not a simple concept, and that BPM technology would demand a significant effort from the organization. But there was something we were absolutely sure about: it created value for our customers and for our business", explained Mariano.

With this in mind, Telecarrier drew a cultural line identifying BPM technology as a management discipline that considers processes as assets that contribute directly to corporate performance, boosting operational excellence and business agility. With this definition, the company was able to acknowledge BPM's impact on the business, and how, by means of the incorporation of technology, it was possible to attain competitive advantages in a booming market.

4.3 Process

The initial situation entailed a problem with a high impact on commercial performance: Telecarrier recognized that it was losing sales opportunities due to the lack of a process that would enable measuring the time of each of the processes which added value to the company.

Among those aspects linked to the diagnosis, the following stood out:
- Lack of documented processes.
- High percentage of commercial proposals to prospective and actual customers containing both qualitative and quantitative errors.
- Too many rework tasks.

- Oversized areas involved in audit tasks prior and after sending commercial proposals.
- Activities carried out 100 percent manually, highly dependent on physical material.
- Lack of traceability of documentation from intervening areas.

"At the beginning of the project, our organization did not have processes documented. This was a drawback that we were able to turn into opportunity as it proved more effective and efficient to start process design from scratch", explained Mr. Mariano Saibene.

The consequences of this diagnosis were clearly reflected in:
- Lack of pipeline and forecast measurement.
- Sales cycles above the industry average.
- Lack of proposal analysis per business line.
- No measurement of commercial performance of commercial officers.
- Market share loss.

Those processes surveyed which were later automated involve 100+ people -who perform 20 activities simultaneously- belonging to Pre-sales, Sales, Sales Administration, and Finance.

There follows the process map:

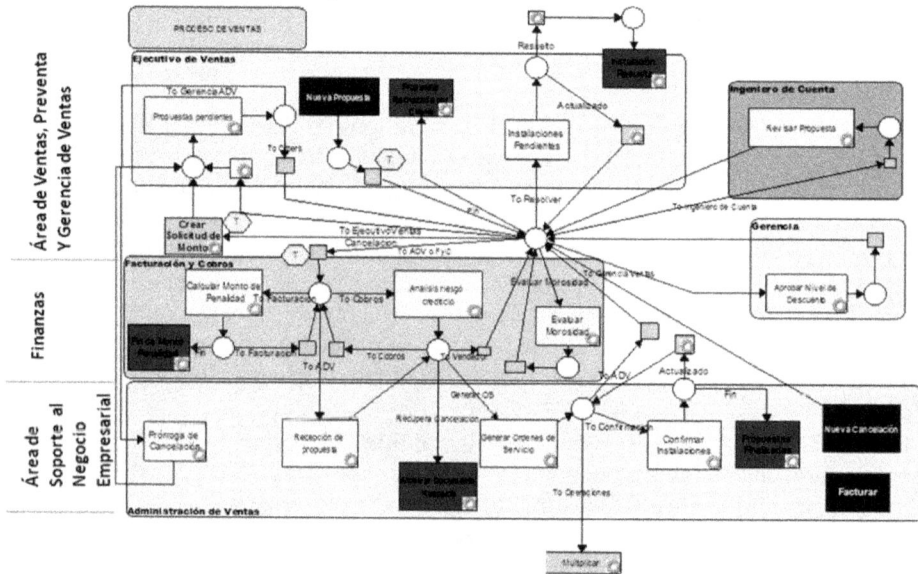

4.4 Organization

As mentioned in point 1 (Executive Summary/Abstract), the implementation of the Project took 12 months, and involved the entire organization, including the full support of the CEO, as it was a corporate Project. Such leadership was key to achieving the alignment of all resources taking part in the project, at every stage: prior, during and after launching. During the initial stage, Telecarrier organized several courses aimed, in essence, at getting familiarized with concepts and general principles of the business process management philosophy, of both macro processes and sub processes.

"We were convinced that, besides technology, we needed to wisely go through aspects associated with change management. For this purpose, it was essential that the entire organization acquire the corresponding training", explained Mariano.

During the project implementation, Telecarrier directed training resources at getting the organization to understand the fundamental role of change agents in business processes: people, structure, the organization's culture, and the use of information technologies for the business. This enabled the full understanding and appreciation of the development of a business process architecture, thus ensuring the simultaneous fulfillment of both business and market needs.

At an IT level, training was oriented to understanding BPM within the context of prevailing topics and practices in technology, management, organization, and relationships, including: Service Oriented Architecture (SOA), Customer Relationship Management (CRM), Supply Chain Management (SCM), Enterprise Content Management (ECM), and Business Intelligence (BI).

4. HURDLES OVERCOME

At a management level, adopting the process management philosophy, and incorporating BPM technology helped Telecarrier define, measure, and manage fulfillment of its strategic goals.

"Before the automation of our organization's core process, it was hard for us to clearly define commercial goals because we were always running into "bottlenecks" which diverted our center of attention from the main focus of the business", explained Mariano. "Nowadays, we have management metrics on top of which we can build a process of continuous improvement, our ratios measuring customer satisfaction, commercial closing, and tactical marketing investment have improved" states Mariano.

In business terms, the main contribution of process automation was the attainment of a competitive advantage. Today, Telecarrier is the company exhibiting the highest growth in the central region, and its strong commercial approach has allowed it to enter in new sectors of an industry more and more dynamic, where commercial agility is a key element.

Lastly, as mentioned in point 4.4, the main challenges arising from change management were successfully met on account of the CEO's strong involvement, coupled with the active participation of both the team which lead the project and final users at every stage of the project, even from its inception, when various technological options were still under analysis.

"Currently, key executives in the organization possess the ability to design, simulate, and monitor processes automatically, without the involvement of technical users: BPM has flexibility and capacity to adapt to the business that we needed something that no other technology offered", explains Mariano.

Additionally, from the organization's point of view, Telecarrier was able to direct efforts in a planned manner, aligned with its strategic goals, acquiring a road of continuous improvement and efficiency, as it turned inefficient activities into reduced costs by means of the use of process-oriented technology.

5. BENEFITS

Automating the sales process enabled Telecarrier to obtain the following results:

- 60 percent improvement in management metrics related to commercial presentations.

- 28 percent increase in commercial effectiveness (closing rate).
- 75 percent improvement in ratios measuring performance of administrative processing.
- 0 percent error in contract-making.
- 22 percent optimization at the Human Resources level as a result of an improvement in efficiency and productive task reallocation.

6. COMPETITIVE ADVANTAGES

By adopting the process management methodology and incorporating BPM technology, Telecarrier S.A. was able to optimize the industry's key process, which in turn paved the way to gaining competitive advantages, such as Go To Market and Time To Market, which support the company's strategic planning.

7. THE TECHNOLOGY AND SERVICE PROVIDERS

The project was developed by PECTRA Technology Inc.: a company specializing in Process Management, with over 12 years of experience in the market and 200 successful implementations in the USA, Argentina, Mexico, Colombia, Spain and Chile. We have an extensive network of partners in the entire Latin American region and we provide services to more than 50,000 end users who, in turn, serve 6,000,000+ users/customers.

For more information, please visit: www.pectra.com.

Telecarrier's IT Department along with PECTRA Technology's Marketing Department has planned the data searching and writing this important document. Different techniques were used to collect the information. Interviews to the people in charge of the solution's design and implementation were carried out (in an average of two hours each); and also a performance evaluation was carried out in the entire company to respond appropriately to the requirements demanded by the Global Excellence in Workflow Awards for innovation and excellence in workflow implementations.

Section 7

Appendix

Awards Contact Directory

Business Process as a Service: Enterprise Cloud Computing

Jon Pyke
CIMtrek, United Kingdom
www.cimtrek.com

The Difference Between BPM and Adaptive Case Management

Nathaniel Palmer
WfMC, USA
www.wfmc.org

Advantages of Agile BPM

Keith D. Swenson
Fujitsu America Inc., USA
us.fujitsu.com

Business Driven Architecture: Combining BPMN 2.0 and Semantic Technologies

Ralf Mueller, Linus Chow, Jean Prater
Oracle, USA
www.oracle.com

EUROPE

Finalist Award

epa connect GmbH, Germany
Markus Humberg, CEO
m.humberg@impuls-systems.de, 650-762-2983

Nominator:

Adobe Systems Inc., USA
Caroline Skinner,
caroline.skinner@edelman.com, 650-762-2983

EUROPE

Gold Award

Instituto de Crédito Oficial (ICO), Spain
Olga Garcia Frey,
olga.garcia@ico.es, 91 592 16 00

Nominator:

BizAgi, United Kingdom
Marcel Manser, BPM Managing Director
marcel.manser@bizagi.com

EUROPE

Silver Award

LSC Group, United Kingdom
Kimberley Werrett, Marketing Manager
kiw@lsc.co.uk, +44 (0) 1543 446870

Nominator:

TIBCO Software Inc., USA
Danielle Wood, Corporate Communications
dwood@tibco.com, +1 650-384-9704

MIDDLE-EAST AFRICA

Gold Award

Nokia Siemens Networks, UAE
Nick Deacon, Global Head of Business Process Management
nick.deacon@nsn.com, +971 505508729

Nominator:

Appian, USA
Ben Farrell, Director
ben.farrell@appian.com, +1 703-442-1067

NORTH AMERICA

Gold Award

Department of Energy, USA
Sonia Taylor, Media Relations, Loan Programs Office
Sonia.taylor@hq.doe.gov, +1 202 583 538

Nominator:

HandySoft, USA
Garth Knudson, Director, Sales
gknudson@handysoft.com, +1 703 645 4515

NORTH AMERICA

Gold Award

Farmers Insurance Group, USA
Shohreh Abedi, Vice President of Claims Applications
shohreh.abedi@farmersinsurance.com, +1 805-306-6974

Nominator:

Pegasystems Inc., USA
Gary W. Kirkham, Principal, Insurance Industry Solutions
Gary.Kirkham@pega.com, +1 617.866.6590

NORTH AMERICA

Silver Award

Lincoln Trust Company, USA
Helen Z Cousins, EVP / CIO
Helen.Cousins@lincolntrustco.com, +1 303-658-3333

Nominator:

Lincoln Trust Company, USA
Bob Beriault, Chairman and CEO
Bob.Beriault@lincolntrustco.com, +1 303-658-3007

PACIFIC RIM

Gold Award

'us' - Utility Services, Australia
John Csorgo, IT Senior Business Analyst
john.csorgo@sewl.com.au, +61 9552 3763

Nominator:

Interfacing Technologies Corporation, Canada
Scott Armstrong, Business Development Manager
scott.armstrong@interfacing.com, +1 514 737 7333 x 40

PACIFIC RIM

Silver Award

IndusInd Bank, India
Mridul Sharma, Senior Vice President, Head – Solution Delivery Group
Mridul.Sharma@IndusInd.com, +91-22-66412340

Nominator:

Newgen Software Technologies Limited, India
Rohit Thakur, Manager - Products and Solutions
rohit.thakur@newgen.co.in, +91 22-40773620

SOUTH AMERICA

Gold Award

Unimed Porto Alegre Medical Co-operative Ltd, Brazil
Ana Carolina Tavares Torres, Legal Adviser
ana.torres@unimedpoa.com.br, +55 5133164814

Nominator:

BPM Soluções (BPM Solutions), Brazil
Jeferson Rech Padilha, Project Manager
jeferson.padilha@bpmsolucoes.com.br, +55 5133953466

SOUTH AMERICA

Silver Award

ArcelorMittal Foundation, Brazil
Marcelo Santos, Manager
marcelo.santos@arcelormittal.com.br, +55 3130 486320

Nominator:

AuraPortal, USA
Scott Rich, General Manager of the Boston Headquarters
scott.rich@auraportal.com, +1 781 569 5940

SOUTH AMERICA

Silver Award

Telecarrier, Panama
Mariano Saibene, IT Director
mariano.saibene@telecarrier.com, +507 300-0088

Nominator:

Pectra Technolgy, USA
Juan Chacon, Marketing Manager
jchacon@pectra.com, Tel: (713) 335 5562

Additional BPM Resources

NEW E-BOOK SERIES ($9.97 EACH)

- Introduction to BPM and Workflow
  http://store.futstrat.com/servlet/Detail?no=75

- Financial Services
  http://store.futstrat.com/servlet/Detail?no=90

- Healthcare
  http://store.futstrat.com/servlet/Detail?no=81

- Utilities and Telecommunications
  http://store.futstrat.com/servlet/Detail?no=92

NON-PROFIT ASSOCIATIONS AND RELATED STANDARDS RESEARCH ONLINE

- AIIM (Association for Information and Image Management)
  http://www.aiim.org
- BPM and Workflow online news, research, forums
  http://bpm.com
- BPM Research at Stevens Institute of Technology
  http://www.bpm-research.com
- Business Process Management Initiative
  http://www.bpmi.org *see* Object Management Group
- IEEE (Electrical and Electronics Engineers, Inc.)
  http://www.ieee.org
- Institute for Information Management (IIM)
  http://www.iim.org
- ISO (International Organization for Standardization)
  http://www.iso.ch
- Object Management Group
  http://www.omg.org
- Open Document Management Association
  http://nfocentrale.net/dmware
- Organization for the Advancement of Structured Information Standards
  http://www.oasis-open.org
- Society for Human Resource Management
  http://www.shrm.org
- Society for Information Management
  http://www.simnet.org
- Wesley J. Howe School of Technology Management
  http://howe.stevens.edu/research/research-centers/business-process-innovation
- Workflow And Reengineering International Association (WARIA)
  http://www.waria.com
- Workflow Management Coalition (WfMC)
  http://www.wfmc.org
- Workflow Portal
  http://www.e-workflow.org

More Unique Books on BPM and Workflow from Future Strategies, Publishers (www.FutStrat.com)

2008 BPM & WORKFLOW HANDBOOK

http://www.futstrat.com/books/handbook08.php

Spotlight on Human-Centric BPM

Human-centric business process management (BPM) has become the product and service differentiator. The topic now captures substantial mindshare and market share in the human-centric BPM space as leading vendors have strengthened their human-centric business processes. Our spotlight this year examines challenges in human-driven workflow and its integration across the enterprise.
Retail $95.00 (see discount on website)

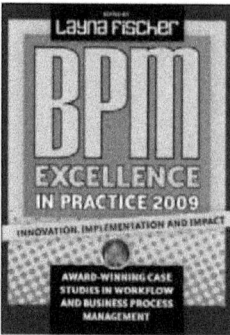

BPM EXCELLENCE IN PRACTICE 2009

http://www.futstrat.com/books/eip9.php

Innovation, Implementation and Impact

Award-winning Case Studies in Workflow and BPM

These companies focused on excelling in *innovation, implementation* and *impact* when installing BPM and workflow technologies. They recognized that implementing innovative technology is useless unless the organization has a successful approach that delivers—and even surpasses—the anticipated benefits.
$49.95 (see discount on website)

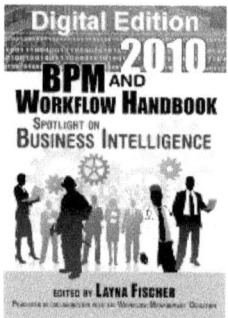

2010 BPM & Workflow Handbook

http://futstrat.com/books/handbook10.php

Business Intelligence

Linking business intelligence and business process management creates stronger operational business intelligence. Users seek more intelligent business process capabilities in order to remain competitive within their fields and industries. BPM vendors realize they need to improve their business processes, rules and event management offerings with greater intelligence or analytics capabilities. **Retail $75.00 (see offer on website)**

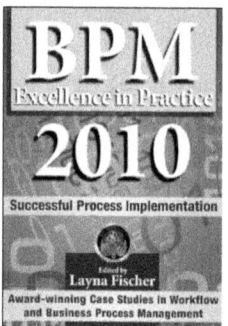

BPM Excellence in Practice 2010:

http://futstrat.com/books/eip10.php
Successful Process Implementation
Award-winning Case Studies in Workflow and Business Process Management

For over 19 years the Global Awards for Excellence in BPM and Workflow have covered virtually every economic environment, from bubble to bust and back again. The first modern process era emerged from the economic downturn of the early 1990s. Then, after years defined by relentless cost-cutting, the new charter for business shifted toward enhancing capacity to address the return of customer demand. **Retail $49.95**

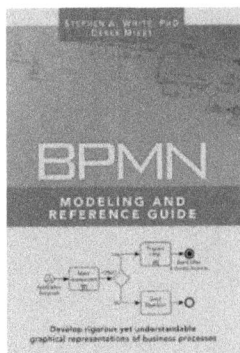

BPMN MODELING AND REFERENCE GUIDE

http://www.futstrat.com/books/BPMN-Guide.php

Stephen A. White, PhD, Derek Miers

Understanding and Using BPMN

Develop rigorous yet understandable graphical representations of business processes.

Business Process Modeling Notation (BPMN) is a standard, graphical modeling representation for business processes. It provides an easy to use, flow-charting notation that is independent of the implementation environment. **Retail $39.95**

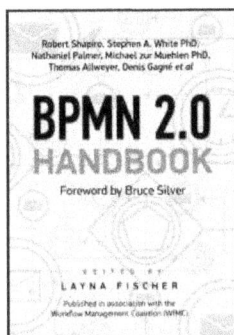

BPMN 2.0 Handbook (see two-book offer on website)

http://futstrat.com/books/bpmnhandbook.php

Robert Shapiro, Stephen A. White PhD., Nathaniel Palmer, Michael zur Muehlen PhD., Thomas Allweyer, Denis Gagné et al

Authored by members of WfMC, OMG and other key participants in the development of BPMN 2.0, the BPMN 2.0 Handbook brings together worldwide thought-leaders and experts in this space. Exclusive and unique contributions examine a variety of aspects that start with an introduction of what's new in BPMN 2.0, and look closely at interchange, analytics, conformance, optimization, simulation and more. **Retail $75.00**

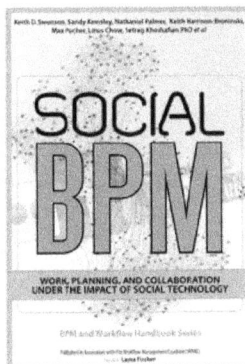

Social BPM

http://futstrat.com/books/handbook11.php

Work, Planning, and Collaboration Under the Impact of Social Technology

Keith D. Swenson, Nathaniel Palmer, Sandy Kemsley
Keith Harrison-Broninski, Max Pucher, Manoj Das, et al

Today we see the transformation of both the look and feel of BPM technologies along the lines of social media, as well as the increasing adoption of social tools and techniques democratizing process development and design. It is along these two trend lines; the evolution of system interfaces and the increased engagement of stakeholders in process improvement, that Social BPM has taken shape.
Retail $59.95

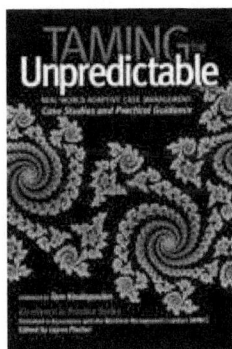

Taming the Unpredictable

Real World Adaptive Case Management: Case Studies and Practical Guidance

http://goo.gl/kiuWa buy at Amazon.com

Keith D Swenson, Nathaniel Palmer, Bruce Silver, et al with foreword by Thomas Koulopoulos

Adaptive Case Management (ACM) assists the knowledge worker to apply know-how and make decisions. One core adaptable quality of ACM is support for goal-seeking and goal-driven processes, where goals can be modified "in flight" by the knowledge worker. **Retail $49.95**

Get 25% Discount on ALL Books in our Store.

Please use the discount code **SPEC25** to get 25% discount on ALL books in our store; Print and Digital Editions. www.FutStrat.com.

www.ingramcontent.com/pod-product-compliance
Lightning Source LLC
Chambersburg PA
CBHW051410200326
41520CB00023B/7187